Praise for *Emotional Resilience*

In a world struggling to deal with toxic stress and burnout, Dr Harry Barry's book provides invaluable advice on how to tackle these modern scourges. Strengthening our emotional resilience is a key skill; the book's emphasis is on helping you to help yourself, no matter what are you are or how stress has affected you. Another masterpiece from a cutting-edge expert on our emotions, thoughts and behaviours.

Dr Muiris Houston, Medical Correspondent and Health Analyst, The Irish Times

Every reader will find this book extremely insightful and thought-provoking. It affords a valuable insight into the skills required to make us all truly resilient as human beings, opening a window into why, for example, we get anxious and what to do when we do! A must read!

Enda Murphy, CBT therapist and author

Simply but expertly, *Emotional Resilience* gives you the tools to heal yourself and deal with the slings and arrows of modern life.

Cathy ⋯ best-selling author and UNICEF ambassador

Emotional Resilience is an excel⋯ ⋯who seeks a better understanding of their emotion⋯ ⋯ represents a practical guide of how to a⋯ ⋯d to everyone; from younger to older⋯ ⋯problems.

⋯ of Psychiatry,
⋯elaide, Australia

Dr Harry Barry has captured the necessity for resilience in all our lives. His book is practical, encouraging and shows an incredible level of empathy and understanding of human suffering. I have no doubt that we will all have a need at some stage in our lives to follow the intelligent advice laid out in these chapters.

Senator Joan Freeman, founder of suicide-prevention charities
Pieta House and Solace House

Dr Barry has again skilfully crafted another book that will be immensely helpful to many. I highly recommend this to people of all ages, from teens to elders, who want the very best advice from a mental health clinician at the pinnacle of their craft.

Professor Raymond W. Lam, Professor and BC Leadership Chair in Depression Research, University of British Columbia, Canada

This is a wonderfully practical, insightful book on how to develop and practice emotional resilience. It offers strategies, powerful techniques and exercises that are suitable for the self-empowerment of the client and as a resource for the therapist.

Iggy Clarke, counselling psychotherapist, ProConsult Counselling Institute

Dr Harry Barry's impeccable timing in writing this book is prescient. This practical guide will enable those aiming to enhance their coping, interpersonal and problem-solving skills so that they can rebound in the face of life's emotional challenges.

Professor Patricia Casey, Professor of Psychiatry, University College Dublin, Ireland

This book complements other care individuals may partake in and provides strategies useful in the long-term for overcoming challenges and living life to its fullest. A manual for life!

Dr Larry Culpepper, Professor of Family Medicine, Boston University School of Medicine, USA

Like a classical compendium of practical philosophy only more, this book is full of well-researched information and guidance, seasoned by years of real-life experience. Forget all the SAS Commando-style handbooks, if you want just one 'whole of life' survival and troubleshooting guide, get this one.

Dr Justin Brophy, Foundation President, The College of Psychiatrists of Ireland

I found *Emotional Resilience* to be a riveting read and would highly recommend it.

Maria Molloy, former Chairperson, Mental Health Ireland

EMOTIONAL RESILIENCE

How to Safeguard
Your Mental Health

DR HARRY BARRY

I would like to dedicate this book to Sr Kieran Saunders MMM (1909 – 1997) who taught me the importance of unconditional self-acceptance and how to be truly emotionally resilient. I learnt at the feet of the master. May she continue to guide her 'adopted family'!

First published in Great Britain in 2018 by Orion Spring
an imprint of The Orion Publishing Group Ltd
Carmelite House, 50 Victoria Embankment
London EC4Y 0DZ

An Hachette UK Company

1 3 5 7 9 10 8 6 4 2

A CIP catalogue record for this book is
available from the British Library.

ISBN: 978 1 4091 7457 8

Typeset by Input Data Services Ltd, Somerset

Printed in Great Britain by CPI Group (UK) Ltd, Croydon, CR0 4YY

MIX
Paper from
responsible sources
FSC® C104740
FSC
www.fsc.org

www.orionbooks.co.uk

CONTENTS

PART THREE: SOCIAL RESILIENCE SKILLS

PART FOUR: LIFE RESILIENCE SKILLS

FOREWORD
The Resilient Reeds

One of my favourite childhood stories was that of the oak tree and the reeds, based on one of Aesop's Fables. The mighty oak tree grew near a stream. At its base lay some quiet, unadorned reeds. When the wind blew, the reeds would bend, while the mighty oak stood firm. The oak felt invincible and was not shy of letting the reeds know their place, ridiculing them for bending so low in the breeze.

But then along came a hurricane. In the storm-force winds that followed, the mighty oak tree, unable to bend or give way, was torn from its roots and upended. However, the resilient reeds, which could bend low, allowed the howling winds to roar above their heads. The story ends with the mighty, proud oak tree lying among the reeds, devastated, while the reeds had weathered the storm and survived. Their capacity to adapt to their environment had kept them safe from the hurricane.

I have always loved the mighty oak tree, with its majestic appearance, delicately shaped leaves and changing colours throughout the seasons. It has been in existence long before I was born and it is likely to be around long after I have departed. But as time has passed, I have developed an even deeper respect for the more adaptable reeds. While lacking the majesty and splendour of the mighty oak tree, they have instead learned how to duck, weave and dance their way through the seasons. They are the ultimate survivors, capable of adjusting effortlessly to the hostile nature of their environment.

Are the resilient reeds a metaphor for life . . .?

INTRODUCTION

There are many challenges facing our mental health. We are living amid an anxiety epidemic. Depression is one of the most significant mental health issues of our time. Self-harm is endemic among our school-going adolescents and the scourge of young male suicide continues to be of concern. Toxic stress is flourishing. Technology and social media are insidiously, pervasively invading our space.

Mental health is defined by the World Health Organisation (2013) as 'a state of well-being in which every individual realises his or her own potential, can cope with the normal stresses of life, can work productively and fruitfully, and is able to make a contribution to her or his community'. Life is a constant struggle – a roller-coaster emotional ride. But some of us seem to cope better with this emotional roller coaster. They seem calmer, effortlessly dealing with life's challenges, immune to mental health difficulties. These are the people we envy and want to emulate. What makes them different? Why do they seem wiser, a source of stability for those seeking assistance and support?

The answer lies in emotional resilience; that is, their emotional capacity to deal with the difficulties of life. Many assume emotional resilience is a gift handed down only to some lucky individuals, blessed in the lottery of life. They must have better genes, more secure upbringings, or maybe they are simply fortunate in how things work out for them. The rest of us struggle on. While genes and upbringing are relevant in some of those with emotional resilience, what makes this group special is their unique ability to pragmatically interpret and manage the stressors of life.

Would you like to develop and strengthen *your* emotional resilience? The answer is probably yes! But how do you develop this elusive ability? Why do so many of us struggle to achieve it? The explanation, I believe, lies in the presence or absence of key personal, social and life skills, which can be learned, practised and passed on to others. In *Emotional Resilience*, I enumerate the essential skills that can transform your life. Develop and practise them, and the mental health benefits that you reap will be incalculable.

Why Write a Book on Emotional Resilience?

Over decades of assisting those with mental health difficulties, especially depression and anxiety in its many forms, I have noticed how those who developed and practised emotional resilience skills recovered faster and stayed well. They grew in confidence and became more resilient to whatever stressors came their way. My initial objective is therefore to illustrate how we can best develop such skills. The emotional resilience skills contained in this book are the basic building blocks for life that we require to improve motivation, increase self-confidence and foster a sense of self-reliance, where 'I can do it' becomes our new motto. If we can build up a reserve of emotional resilience, then we will be able to take life in our stride and surf the waves.

We also live in a world where it is increasingly assumed that only the 'expert' can solve our problems. We sometimes fail to recognise the rich resources within ourselves that are available for us to draw on. To realise our own potential, we need to be able to tap into these resources. To do so, however, requires information and knowledge in an accessible form. Many of us also struggle to find the language to express what is going on in our emotional world. To know these skills, we need to name them. I have tried to address some of them in this book.

I strongly believe that many of these basic but essential resilience skills should be taught at all stages of the education system, from primary school level, in an age-appropriate manner, and throughout secondary and higher education. On discussion with many parents, teachers and lecturers, it has become increasingly obvious to me that our young people are often academically more advanced than their predecessors, but sometimes lack knowledge of the simplest resilience skills so necessary for life.

This is important as we know from research that up to 75 per cent of mental health problems will arise for the first time during the adolescent period. We also know that anxiety and depression are significant problems within this age group and that self-harm is extremely common. A recent school-based study of mental health and suicide prevention by the National Suicide Research Foundation (Young lives in Ireland, 2017) supports this view. This study of 13–16-year-old adolescents noted that 25 per cent of the young people taking part in the study suffered from significant anxiety, 14 per cent had significant depressive symptoms, 7 per cent had experienced suicidal thoughts and 4 per cent had attempted suicide at some stage in their short lives. These conditions are present, therefore, from early on in adolescence and represent a significant challenge to the mental health of those affected as they traverse this difficult phase of development. If students were better equipped with the necessary tools, many of these conditions could be avoided or greatly ameliorated. It is my hope that some of these ideas and concepts might be of assistance to parents and teachers, as well as to young people themselves.

Technology in the twenty-first century is also all-consuming and inescapable. It can both empower and disarm us. It generates within us all an expectation of instant responses and immediate results. There is no gap in-between. However, this can be an illusory world. There are many life difficulties it will be unable to assist us in dealing with. Technology is just a tool. The human being is more complex, and as such can choose to use this tool sensibly or not. If we can develop some essential emotional resilience skills to manage life, we can use these skills to manage technology more effectively. It is my hope that this book will be of use on that journey.

I wanted to highlight how often many of us, not suffering at this moment in time from any significant mental health difficulty, can also lack some of these simple, important skills. We are not as emotionally resilient as we could be. Life is a constant challenge and the more resilient we can become, the more we can adapt, staying mentally healthy as a result. Developing some extra skills can make all the difference.

Is this Book Written for a Specific Age Group?

The answer is unequivocally no. *Emotional Resilience* is written for all age groups. We will all require different skills at different stages of life. Many of our adolescents and young adults are especially vulnerable to an absence of such skills. I have noticed in my own work that secondary-level students and those in higher education often struggle due to a dearth or shortage of such skills. But there are many significant periods during our lives where the stressors of life inevitably intrude and may overwhelm us. It may be your first job, or when children enter your life, or parents or loved ones become ill or die, or we lose partners or other loved ones as we age. These are the times when the presence or absence of some key skills will reveal themselves. We can learn these skills at any stage in our lives, through neuroplasticity, our brain's ability to reshape connections and pathways. We deal with this concept in some detail in *Flagging the Therapy* and *Anxiety and Panic*.

What Makes this Book Different?

There are so many self-help books out there, on so many different aspects of mental health. Resilience has very much been associated with the workplace, and there has been a lot of interest in how best to improve the resilience of employees. What, therefore, makes this book any different? Why should you take the effort to read it or put into action any of the skills detailed in it?

The answer lies in my background and expertise. I have, over decades, assisted many people on a *personal* level to face the multiple and complex mental health issues, as well as other challenges, that life has thrown at them. This experience has shaped my views on the whole world of emotional resilience.

While others, much more skilled than I, have explored the world of occupational or workplace resilience, my own approaches have been honed by walking alongside those struggling with conditions like depression and all forms of anxiety. I have also worked with those struggling with painful and complex life situations, where the answers are equally challenging. This has allowed me the opportunity and privilege to identify the skills contained in this book. It has also shown me their power, on occasion, to completely transform people's lives for the better. I have been as much the student as the mentor!

I owe much to the people I have assisted and indeed to many other expert professional colleagues, in the form of psychiatrists, psychologists, family doctors and therapists, such as leading CBT tutor and therapist Enda Murphy, for educating and shaping my views on mental health. The clinical stories within the book demonstrating how others have learned to develop specific skills are also deeply rooted in my decades of experience as a family doctor specialising in mental health.

Many self-help books, while useful in their overview, lack practical advice as to how best to develop many of the necessary skills. What makes this book different is the down-to-earth, practical exploration and application of these tools.

At the heart of my approach is my belief that we do not always need experts to teach us how best to manage our mental health. We all have deeply rooted inner emotional reserves. We just need some knowledge and a desire to change ourselves. I strongly believe in the concept that we, in the long run, heal ourselves, irrespective of whatever therapy or approach is used.

So many of us are seeking El Dorado, some magical secret that will transform our mental health and well-being. However, the secret lies within us all, in the capacity to tap into our inner emotional potential. This book has the power to unlock that potential, helping you to develop your emotional resilience reserves and safeguard your mental health. All that is required is an open mind and perseverance.

How to Use this Book

If you would like to get a complete overview of the whole area of emotional resilience, then read this book as it has been laid out. You can then pick out which skills you would like to do some work on. Start with the ones most relevant to you and begin to put them into action one by one. Focus on the practical exercises laid out in the relevant chapters. I would suggest that you should never try to acquire more than two to three skills at any one time.

If you are interested in developing a specific skill or set of skills, then visit the relevant chapters and once again focus on the practical exercises as laid out. Once you have achieved this objective, you might then choose to read through the whole book to develop a more rounded understanding of emotional resilience.

If you are suffering from depression, it might be worth reading *Depression: A Practical Guide* first and then moving on to *Emotional Resilience*. This will allow you to develop a better understanding both of this illness and how the skills in this book can be of assistance in increasing your emotional resilience, which may in turn reduce the risks of further bouts.

If you are having difficulties with anxiety or panic, then it also be might worth exploring *Anxiety and Panic* first, to learn how to manage these conditions. You might then progress to reading *Emotional Resilience* to identify which resilience skills might be of value to you to further strengthen your mental health.

If you are feeling emotionally distressed but unsure of the cause, then I would also suggest reading the above two books first or having a chat with your family doctor or a therapist to track down the cause of your distress. Only then would I recommend reading *Emotional Resilience*, to identify the relevant skills that might be useful for you to acquire.

If you are a parent or teacher and interested in sharing some of these resilience techniques and skills, then my suggestion would be to read the book from the beginning and try to apply the specific techniques in your own life first. This will make it easier to share them with others.

PART ONE

Setting the Stage

1.

WHAT IS EMOTIONAL RESILIENCE?

Emotional resilience is our individual capacity to cope with adversity in life. The word resilience comes from the Latin *resilio*, which means 'to bounce back' or 'recoil'. The term resilience has been in use for decades to describe how individuals respond to stress. In *Toxic Stress*, we explored the genetic and environmental factors predisposing some of us to be more resilient to stress.

But it is the addition of the word 'emotional' that has changed our perspective. In the past, it was recognised that some children emerging from severely deprived backgrounds or the horrors of war seemed to 'survive' such experiences, without significant ongoing emotional or mental health difficulties. These children were classified as resilient. It was assumed initially that their individual ability to adapt and survive was secondary to their genes or personality. With time, it has become increasingly obvious that how well children, and indeed adults, manage their emotional responses to such adversity is what will determine their resilience.

As a family doctor who has witnessed pretty much everything that life can throw at children and adults, this has been apparent to me for decades. Those who cope best can recognise and manage their emotions. Their behaviour patterns are often healthier than those who succumb to such traumatic stressors. This is most obvious when one deals with large families where hardship, addiction and poverty combine to create extremely challenging upbringings for the growing child and adolescent.

This fresh insight into emotional resilience has opened up a world of new possibilities. Emotions, as we will explore later, are created by thoughts. They are also associated with specific behavioural patterns. Some emotions are also associated with physical symptoms.

This leads us naturally into the world of CBT. Underlying this therapy is an understanding that we can develop skills to change our thoughts and behaviour for the better, at any point in a person's life.

Emotional resilience is within reach of all of us. We just need to identify the skills required, then develop and put them into practice. So, join me on a journey of discovery to unveil the secrets that can transform your life. To begin this journey, let's firstly explore the world of emotions.

What Are Emotions?

Emotions relate to how we feel, lasting for relatively short durations, usually minutes to hours. If lasting for longer periods – hours or perhaps days – we call them moods. Some experts join emotions and moods together, calling them feelings, but I prefer to keep them separate as it reduces confusion. Emotions can be positive or negative and healthy or unhealthy.

Positive emotions include joy, happiness, pleasure, love, awe, trust, contentment and peacefulness. Negative emotions include anger, fear, guilt, shame, hurt, jealousy, emotional pain, sadness and loss. Healthy negative emotions include grief and loss, sadness, disappointment, annoyance, irritation, regret and remorse. Unhealthy negative emotions include anxiety, depression, anger/rage, emotional pain, shame, guilt, jealousy, envy and hurt.

Emotions are often associated with physical symptoms – such as fear with palpitations, dry mouth, and difficulty taking deep breaths, or frustration with clenching of muscles or tension headaches.

Just because emotions are negative or unhealthy does not mean the person experiencing them is distressed or unwell.

Later we will examine in more detail the link between our emotions, thoughts and behaviours.

Identifying Your Emotions

For decades, I have marvelled at how difficult it can sometimes be to identify our emotions. I frequently ask patients, 'How did this event make you feel?', to be met with an uncomfortable silence. We are often unsure as to how we feel. There are many reasons for this difficulty. Although emotions rule our lives, we often feel strangely uncomfortable reflecting on or discussing them. Men, especially, struggle to identify or accept their emotions.

What Is an Emotional Menu?

One of my first tasks when faced with a distressed person, unsure of how they feel emotionally, is to provide them with an 'emotional menu'. I ask them to write down the following list of typical unhealthy and healthy negative emotions.

Unhealthy negative emotions may include:

- Anxiety
- Depression
- Hurt
- Anger
- Shame
- Guilt
- Frustration

Healthy negative emotions may include:

- Concern
- Sadness
- Remorse
- Regret

- Disappointment
- Annoyance

I then ask them to choose the relevant ones underlying their distress at that moment. This can be a life-changing experience. For the first time in their lives, they identify and name specific emotions relevant to them. They can then focus on their unhealthy negative emotions, which I suggest they list in order of importance. I explain to them that emotions are the signposts to our inner world and can greatly assist in exploring our thoughts and behaviours. Learning how to create such a menu is the first step towards acquiring emotional resilience.

The Emotional Menu Exercise

At this stage, I would like to ask you, the reader, to carry out the following exercise, where you learn how to create your own emotional menu:

1. For the next four weeks I want you to carry a notebook and whenever something distresses you, write down the triggering event.
2. Then use the menu laid out above as a guide to explore which emotions were triggered. Are you feeling anxious, depressed, hurt, frustrated or simply sad or annoyed?
3. If several emotions are triggered, list them in order of importance to you, at that moment.
4. Pay special attention to your unhealthy negative emotions.
5. Do not be concerned about how to interpret or manage your emotions. It is just important, at this stage, to identify them.

The more you perform this exercise, the more accurately you will begin to identify your emotions. This is an important first step towards developing emotional resilience. If you can identify your emotional responses to a stressor, then coping with it becomes easier. This exercise will also teach you how often several emotions are triggered by the same stressor. Learning to identify which emotions are involved when you are exposed to difficult situations also removes much of the confusion. You can now identify emotionally why you are so distressed.

The next step on our journey is to explore the body's internal system, which controls your physical and psychological responses to stress. Understanding its role in emotional resilience is essential.

The Role of Our Stress System

As mentioned above, emotions are frequently associated with secondary physical symptoms. The classic examples are anxiety and depression. These physical symptoms have their origin in our stress system. Stress has physical as well as psychological components. Resilience has as much to do with managing the former as the latter. So how does stress manifest itself in the body and why?

As human beings evolved, survival was the priority. Threats were initially mainly physical, so the body developed lightning-fast reflexes to be able to detect and deal with the dangers inherent in its environment. The whole body had to be able to gear up instantly to face such threats, and evolution created our internal stress system to organise such a response. Sometimes the threats would go on for longer periods, so we had to be able to keep this system on high alert during such episodes. We also had to be able to switch it off for periods, so we could eat and relax.

In general, a person's stress system dealt well with these situations during our ancestors' time. Firstly, they might encounter a threat to their life or that of their family, and would have to stand and fight. Secondly, they might encounter situations where they would clearly be fearful for their life if they hung around, so they would flee. Thirdly, they might be under sustained threat for a longer period – whether that involved looking for food or being under sustained attack from enemies. In all cases, the stress system had to be able to switch on the appropriate response, the main thrust of which was to keep them and their family alive. The central controller had to be the brain. It had the job of deciding when to activate or calm down their responses to such stressors.

Whenever we encounter any form of stress, either acute or more prolonged, the body initiates a cascade of automatic internal physiological responses.

The Brain's Response

We all have a 'logical brain', situated at the front of the brain, called the prefrontal cortex and an 'emotional brain', in the middle of the brain, called the limbic system.

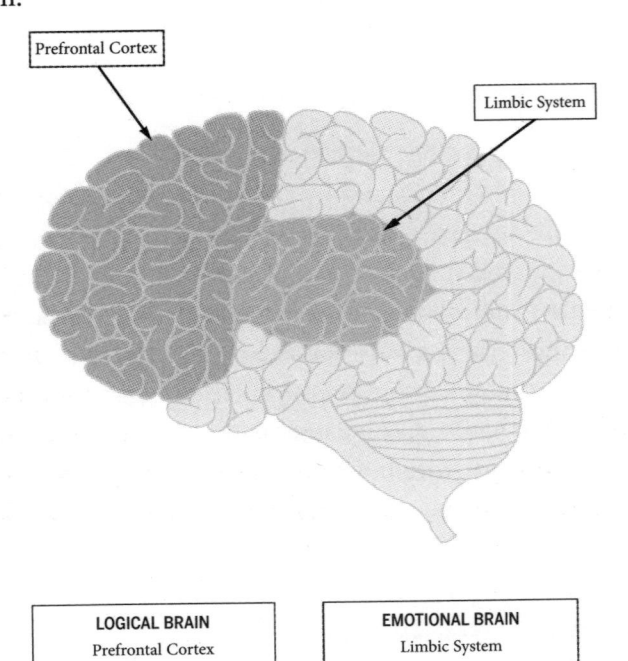

Figure 1: The logical brain and the emotional brain

Our lives are controlled by the flow of information between the two. The coordinator of our stress system is the stress box, called the amygdala, which is a key player in our emotional brain.

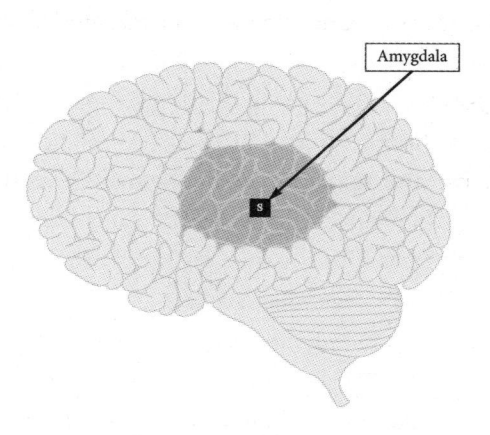

Figure 2: The stress box

When under attack from any internal or external stressor, the amygdala swings into action to activate the body's responses. How we choose to respond will depend sometimes, but not always, on the outcome of the conversation within the brain between our emotional and logical centres. Once decided, the amygdala activates two systems within the body itself. One will involve an internal nervous system response and the second a hormonal one. Let's look at these in more detail.

The Nervous System Response

The nervous system response is carried out by a crucial internal system of nerves activated by the brain and involving almost every organ in the body. This is called the autonomic nervous system (ANS). Every second of the day, the activity of most of the organs in the body, including our heart, lungs, gut, glands, is being monitored and altered by this involuntary internal system. Without it, we would not function. Because the ANS is so important in relation to our stress system, it is worth examining it in more detail.

There are two parts to the ANS with almost diametrically opposed functions – one to 'hype the body up' to prepare for the stresses of every day and the other to calm it down and give it a 'breather'.

The first is called the sympathetic nervous system (SNS) and is the main player in activating our acute reactions to stress. It causes the heart to beat more quickly, the mouth to go dry, the pupils to dilate and the skin to sweat. It also inhibits digestion. It is all about activating the body in the face of a threat to either fight, freeze or flee.

The second is called the parasympathetic nervous system (PNS) and its job is to calm us down when not under stress. It causes the heart to beat more slowly, encourages digestion in the gut, constricts the pupils and makes our muscles feel more relaxed – the so-called 'rest and digest' functions.

The activity of the SNS in response to stress is a straightforward one, with the nerves directly activating all the relevant organs, such as the heart and lungs. As we will see, it also leads to an indirect secondary hormonal response by activating the adrenal stress gland. In everyday life, it is the SNS that also keeps us alert, activated and 'on the ball'. While this function is critically important, we would struggle if the brain and body remained constantly on such high alert. This is where the PNS comes in. Its task is to assist us to calm down, eat and digest our meals, to take time out to rest and, in general, just chill out. For example, all of us can relate to how relaxed we feel after sitting down to a nice meal with our family or friends. These sensations are partly to do with our PNS firing. It is helping us to take a breather from the hustle and bustle of life.

This downtime is critically important, as our mental and physical health require a balance between our SNS and PNS.

The Hormonal Response

The hormonal response is activated within the brain itself when the stress box or amygdala sends messengers to the hormone control box, the hypothalamus/pituitary gland.

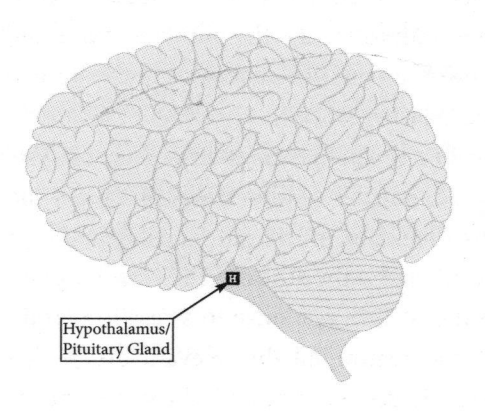

Hypothalamus/
Pituitary Gland

Figure 3: Hormone control box

This, in turn, sends hormones into the bloodstream, which travel to two glands situated over the kidneys, our adrenal glands. These lie at the heart of our stress response. The adrenal gland is divided into a central core and an outer shell, called the adrenal medulla and adrenal cortex. The former is the source of two of our key acute stress hormones, adrenaline and noradrenaline. It is strongly activated by the SNS. The latter, on the other hand, is strongly activated by the hormones sent from the brain and produces the chronic stress hormone glucocortisol. These hormones are then released into the bloodstream and travel around the body to activate all the various organs like the heart, lungs, gut and so on – all of which are involved in the stress response.

It is worth examining the difference between the two acute stress hormones (adrenaline and noradrenaline) and the chronic stress hormone (glucocortisol), as all play different roles in the stress response.

Adrenaline is released in large amounts when we encounter an acutely stressful situation where we feel mainly fear, and our natural response is to flee from the stressor. For example, if we are confronted by a drug addict with a knife and decide to run for it. The physical symptoms we experience from an adrenaline rush are a pounding heart, difficulty breathing, a stomach in knots, shaking, sweating, a dry mouth, a constricted throat, weakness and dizziness.

Noradrenaline is released in large amounts when we encounter an acutely stressful situation where our response is to get mad and stay around to fight. So if, for example, we were threatened by the same addict but chose (unwisely) to try to wrestle the knife from him.

Glucocortisol is released in larger amounts when we encounter a stressful situation that looks as if it is going to last for a longer duration. In situations of chronic stress, high levels of this hormone cause symptoms such as fatigue, poor concentration, feeling wired all the time, sleep difficulties and a greater incidence of cold sores, mouth ulcers and other infections.

The role of our PNS is to allow the stress system to take a breather and encourage the body to relax and take time to digest its meals, and so on. Without it, we would live in such a state of acute stress that we would quickly burn out. As a general principle, the more activated our PNS is in our lives, the calmer and less anxious we feel. Those who have developed emotional resilience will find themselves living mainly in this space. Those who struggle with anxiety and frustration will find themselves living in the world of the SNS. It's not a good place to be, as we will explore later.

What Are Skills and How Do We Acquire Them?

Since this book is about developing key emotional resilience skills, let's first explore what exactly a skill is. A skill is the ability to master an area of expertise. Traditionally, we associate skills with tradesmen, such as carpenters or electricians. But all of us have an innate capacity to acquire skills in a multitude of areas. Before acquiring any skill – for example, driving a car, cooking, dancing or learning the piano – it is necessary to progress through several stages.

1. The first stage involves learning or developing the skill. This may involve acquiring information and techniques from somebody skilled in the area. As this information is new and strange, it requires significant mental concentration to absorb. It can also feel awkward, initially, putting it into action. Just think of the first few lessons with a driving instructor to visualise these feelings.

2. The second stage involves practising the skill repeatedly until it becomes

more familiar. We feel increasingly comfortable putting it into action.

3. The third stage is reached when application of the skill in everyday life becomes routine and automatic. We no longer consciously think about using this skill in practice. It is embedded in our unconscious mind, one more skill we have mastered.

4. The final stage arrives when we become sufficiently experienced to pass on the skill to others, and so the cycle begins again.

It is important to note that the right side of our brain is most engaged while learning a new task. This is also the side of our brain most activated when we are anxious. It is no surprise, therefore, that we equate anxiety with learning a new skill. The good news is that when, through learning and practice, we have developed a skill, everything then moves to the left side of our brain. This has the job of managing routine, automatic tasks. As this is the side of the brain associated with positive emotions, we are often much calmer when automatically performing routine skills. Let's take the example of learning to drive. We are often extremely anxious for the first few months while acquiring the skill, but nine months later, when the skill has become automatic, we are much calmer when driving.

When acquiring specific emotional resilience skills, the process is similar. You will initially learn the skill, often with the assistance of somebody experienced in the area or through a manual. You will feel anxious and awkward at the beginning, and this is normal. The next step involves practising the skill repeatedly in everyday life. The more you practise, the more automatic the skill will become, until any initial anxiety gradually disappears. Finally, the skill becomes part of us. We no longer consciously think about it, we just do it.

It is also exciting to realise that as we are learning and acquiring new skills, something amazing is occurring in our brains. We begin to increase the amount of myelin around the neuron tracts involved in this process. Myelin is important in speeding up and making these tracts in the brain more efficient. It makes our brains increasingly effective. It also explains why the more often we practise the skill, the easier we find it to apply it. We are literally rewiring our own brains.

What Are Emotional Resilience Skills?

Emotional resilience skills can transform the lives of those prepared to learn, practise and master them. Many of the people struggling with anxiety, depression and other mental health conditions who I have worked with over the decades found that using these skills improved their mental health dramatically. Others found a new confidence in themselves, and that their ability to cope with stress increased significantly. Their capacity to problem-solve expanded. Their interpersonal relationships improved. Their social skills evolved. They became wiser and often more compassionate towards themselves and others. They became more realistic and pragmatic about life and themselves.

In summary, they learned how to become emotionally resilient.

It is also worth noting that once a learned skill becomes automatic, it is embedded in our memory bank for life. Think of learning to drive a car or riding a bicycle. We may allow the skill to fall into disuse, but how quickly it can be resurrected if we reactivate it. So, too, are the skills of emotional resilience there for life, once we have learned them.

But as with anything of value, learning these skills involves dedication, hard work and practice. We are often anxious, even frustrated, when first attempting to develop these skills, but it is worth the effort. The prize is substantial. Those with strong emotional resilience skills will achieve much in their lives.

Emotional resilience skills are, of course, slightly different from routine skills such as driving a car. The latter is more about specific motor skills, while the former focuses on learning and practising specific cognitive and behavioural skills. But the principles remain the same. The skills must be developed and practised repeatedly until they become instinctive.

We can divide the emotional resilience skill set into three groups:

1. Personal: the resilience skills required to manage your personal life.
2. Social: the resilience skills required to cope with your social world.
3. Life: the resilience skills required to cope with life itself.

Personal Emotional Resilience Skills

These include how to:

- develop unconditional self-acceptance
- deal with the physical symptoms of anxiety
- deal with the uncertainty of life
- manage discomfort
- cope with failure and success in life
- stop oneself catastrophising
- challenge perfectionism
- cease procrastinating
- practise mindfulness
- problem-solve

Social Resilience Skills

These include how to:

- develop and practise empathy
- read and interpret non-verbal cues
- become comfortable in social interaction situations
- deal with performance anxiety
- develop the art of conversation

Life Resilience Skills

These include how to:

- cope with the unfairness of life
- develop a healthy work/life balance
- resolve personal conflicts
- become more pragmatic about life
- cope with stress

There is inevitable overlap between the three skill sets. But, in general, the emotional resilience skills required for each group are subtly different, as we will see later.

Why Have these Skills Been Chosen?

You might be surprised by the skills that appear in the list above, while optimism, altruism, meaning, gratitude, hope, structure and personal responsibility, among others, have not been included. Some of these can indeed play a major role in increasing our emotional resilience, and they can nourish and greatly enrich our emotional and mental health.

But emotional resilience, if built to last, must be built on solid foundations. These must be created, in turn, by developing the core personal, social and life skills detailed above. Without these basic skills, it becomes increasingly difficult to journey any further towards our goal of making ourselves truly independent and emotionally resilient. There is little point, for example, in discussing the importance of a concept such as gratitude unless we have first learned how to accept ourselves unconditionally. Or to discuss the importance of personal responsibility or self-discipline unless we have learned how to manage discomfort.

Once we have laid these foundations and developed these more fundamental skills, we can then complete the task of developing full emotional resilience by exploring the 'higher order' insights, such as meaning and gratitude, and putting them into practice in our lives.

Before moving on to explore these essential skills, let's first briefly discuss the importance of cognitive behavioural therapy (CBT) as a tool to assist us in our task of acquiring emotional resilience.

2.

COGNITIVE BEHAVIOURAL THERAPY (CBT)

What Is Cognitive Behavioural Therapy?

When we talk about cognitive behavioural therapy (CBT), 'cognitive' refers to mental processes such as thoughts, ideas, perceptions, memories, beliefs, the ability to focus attention, reason and problem-solving; 'behaviour' refers to what we do and what we avoid; and 'therapy' refers to an approach used to deal with a problem or illness.

CBT is based on two simple but profound concepts: first, that our thoughts influence our emotions, which influence our behaviour, so what we think affects what we feel and do; and second, that it is not what happens to us in life that matters but how we choose to interpret it. These concepts form the basis of all therapy disciplines within CBT.

What Is Its Relevance to Emotional Resilience?

Throughout the rest of this book, we will regularly apply CBT concepts and exercises to assist us in developing many of the skills that are essential to emotional resilience. We will also discuss clinical scenarios where the application of these concepts and exercises is shown to transform the lives of those who lack such skills. It is, therefore, essential that we explore the origins of this form of therapy and see how it is used in practice. It is not necessary for you to understand CBT in any detail, but simply to have an overview of this important talk therapy.

When we are discussing skills such as how to develop unconditional self-acceptance, challenge perfectionism, deal with failure or cope with the unfairness of life, it will become increasingly obvious just how valuable such CBT techniques are in practice. To truly appreciate them, however, we need to understand the concepts underlying this therapy.

CBT stems from the relationship between cognition – how we interpret our environment – and behaviour. This relationship has been known for centuries. The Greek stoic philosopher Epictetus (AD 50–135) stated, 'Men are disturbed not by things but the view which they take of them.'

The theory behind CBT is based on the concept that people with anxiety and depression develop persistent negative thoughts over time, which in turn lead to unhealthy negative emotions and destructive behaviour patterns.

In CBT, the psychologist/therapist highlights the negative and dysfunctional thoughts the person experiences when feeling depressed or anxious, and the concomitant negative behaviour patterns. By challenging these erroneous attitudes and explanations, and rationalising them, the person's thoughts and behaviour become more logical and positive. This technique owes much to the pioneering work of two great therapists, Aaron Beck and Albert Ellis.

Recognising Our Thoughts, Emotions and Behaviour: The ABC Model

The person credited with transforming the way in which we link thoughts, emotions and behaviours is Albert Ellis, arguably one of the greatest psychotherapists of the last hundred years. It was he who came up with the simple ABC model.

We have already described the world of emotions in Chapter 1, but let us now define what our thoughts and behaviours are.

Thoughts

These are best defined as the words, images, ideas, memories, beliefs and concepts that flow in and out of our conscious mind. Just because a thought comes into our mind, that does not mean it is true. Thoughts rarely come individually. Usually they come in a flow, one quickly after another, in a cascade.

Thoughts can be very visual, sometimes logical and sometimes emotional. Thoughts influence emotions, which in turn influence behaviours. They play a crucial role in the formation of our memories.

There is a major emphasis on positive versus negative thoughts in dealing with harmful stress and mental health in general. Perhaps realistic thoughts should be the goal. We will be dealing with this subject later in the book, when we examine the world of pragmatism.

Emotions

We explored briefly the world of emotions in the Introduction. Emotions are important as they are the junction points between our thoughts and behaviour, and it is worth exploring these links further.

Emotions play a major role in our behaviour. If we are sad, our response might be to cry or to avoid other people. If we are angry, we might become aggressive. If we are jealous, we might constantly check our partner's phone.

Decisions made in life are more influenced by emotions than logic. Modern therapists believe that suppressing our emotions is unwise. They recommend that we accept and embrace them. Because we often emphasise the role of negative emotions in illnesses like depression and anxiety, we can forget how powerful positive emotions like love, hope, joy, compassion, wonder, trust and forgiveness can be in our lives. We hear about the power of positive thinking, but we need to hear more about the power of positive emotions.

Many emotions ascribed to thoughts and events are sourced in unconscious emotional memory banks, developed during our upbringing and in our adult life. They may be triggered by internal or external events.

Emotions and thoughts are intimately interconnected, tightly woven together, creating the beautiful web of our lives. Many assume that our emotions control our thoughts, and, at first glance, this seems to be true. But many seemingly completely emotional responses to situations have their base in the thoughts or beliefs lying dormant in our mind. It's the balance between these two pathways that will often decide our mental health and also decide how we will cope with the major stressors that life will send our way.

Behaviour

This is best defined as what we do or how we respond to events occurring in our internal or external environment. It can be influenced by both logic and emotion and can be on different occasions either healthy or unhealthy. Typical examples of the latter would be: not exercising, misusing alcohol, self-harming in depression, avoidant or perfectionist behaviour, misusing tranquillisers in anxiety, or violent behaviour in anger.

The Approaches of CBT Founding Fathers Albert Ellis and Aaron Beck

The Ellis Approach

Ellis's highlighted what had been known for thousands of years: 'It is not what happens to us in life that upsets us and causes us so much grief, but rather how we interpret it.' He believed that the latter is based on simple inbuilt belief systems we develop as human beings, mainly due to our experiences when growing and maturing.

A simple way of looking at this is that we pick up 'viral beliefs' as we travel through life. Like many physical viruses, we may not be fully aware of when and where we picked them up. We can, however, recognise them by the way they begin to influence our lives – emotionally and behaviourally.

Ellis also demonstrated that the resulting emotions and accompanying physical symptoms we may feel have behavioural consequences. It is often the physical symptoms or negative behavioural consequences that we experience as a result of our emotions that may encourage us to finally look for help.

Ellis developed a simple ABC formula.

A

'A' stands for 'activating event'. This is an event that sets up a chain of thoughts, emotions and behaviour. It can refer to an external event – either present or future – or an internal one, such as a memory, mental image, thought or dream. A useful way of examining the activating event is to divide it into the 'trigger' – the actual event which starts the ball rolling – and the 'inference' we assign to the trigger – how we view the event. In many cases, this involves assigning a 'danger' to the triggering event.

B

'B' stands for 'belief', an all-encompassing term that includes our thoughts, our demands on ourselves, the world and others, our attitudes and the meaning we attach to internal and external events in our lives. It is through our beliefs that we assess and interpret the triggers.

Ellis divided them into rational and irrational beliefs. Rational beliefs – which lead to healthy negative emotions like anger, concern and sadness – are self-limiting, problem-solving and empowering. They help us adapt to life's events. Irrational beliefs – which lead to unhealthy negative emotions like rage, anxiety and depression – are self-defeating, problem-generating and disabling. They inhibit our ability to cope, making matters more difficult.

I regard these beliefs as a lens through which we focus on our internal and external worlds. In practice, they often present as demands we make of ourselves – some reasonable, some not.

C

'C' stands for 'consequences', an all-inclusive term that can include the emotional and physical experiences, and the behavioural responses that result from A and B.

Ellis's ABC Model in Action
A simple example of this would be when Sara discovers a work colleague has been let go. Her ABC would look like this:

A   Activating Event:
- Trigger: her work colleague has been let go
- Inference/danger: she might be next

B   Belief/Demands: 'I must not lose my job. If I do, I won't be able to cope with being unemployed.'

C   Consequences:
- Emotional reactions: anxiety
- Physical reactions: stomach is in knots; tension headache; sighing constantly to relieve the tension
- Behaviour: stops eating; tries excessively to please her boss; constantly ringing a friend in personnel, seeking reassurance she is not next in the firing line; begins to investigate future job options; constantly checking her finances in fear she will go bankrupt because of losing her job

We will revisit Sara's story later, in the final chapter.

In general, we use Ellis's techniques to help us deal with general anxiety, social anxiety and depression. This involves challenging irrational beliefs and behaviour.

The Beck Approach

Beck's major contribution was to highlight how cognitive interpretation of events in our lives could lead us to be emotionally distressed, and how this in turn could lead to unhelpful and self-perpetuating behaviour patterns. He felt that we all had 'core beliefs', or ways of looking at the world, which lay underneath those interpretations, and definite 'rules for living', which arose out of the unhelpful and self-perpetuating behaviour patterns. In general, once he had identified the main emotion and behaviour, Beck would always try first to challenge our interpretation of events, getting us to logically dispute them. Only if he was unable to reach the person through this approach would he progress to examine and dispute their core beliefs/rules for living.

In general, we use Beck-type approaches when dealing with panic attacks and most phobias. This involves challenging the interpretation of events and the person's behaviour.

In this book, we will draw primarily on the wisdom of Ellis, but on occasions we will use some of Beck's techniques, especially when dealing with the physical symptoms of anxiety.

A Summary of CBT and Emotional Resilience

- Our thoughts influence our emotions, which influence our behaviour.
- It is not what happens to us in life that causes us distress, rather how we interpret it.
- We can learn simple techniques to change our thinking and behaviour.
- These techniques will form the basis of the skills necessary to develop emotional resilience.

The Power of the Written Word

The simplest, most effective technique to help the brain to challenge and reshape the mind is to embrace the concept of writing things down. I use this technique regularly. When an issue is disturbing our emotional mind, our logical mind often struggles to become involved. This is because the emotional brain is more powerful than the logical brain. But in writing things down on paper, the more logical, rational parts of the brain are switched on, so we can examine the issue with greater clarity. This can be a powerful tool when combined with CBT techniques to reshape people's thinking and behaviour.

For many people, it is a game-changer to put down on paper, in their own writing, what it is that's going on in their emotional mind. Sometimes we do not grasp just how irrational our thinking and behaviour can be until we write it down and, in the cold light of day, rationally analyse what we have discovered through this process.

The left prefrontal cortex is more associated with language and cold, hard analysis, so we will be recruiting this part of the brain to assist us in analysing

– and in providing potential solutions to – information that surfaces through the simple act of writing things down.

In this book, as in *Anxiety and Panic*, you will notice that the written word forms an *essential* part of my approach. I have felt for years that a combination of the written word and CBT techniques is the shortcut to developing the key skills necessary to acquire emotional resilience.

So, acquire a notebook! You will be using it regularly while performing many of the exercises laid out here.

Equipment for the Journey

Before embarking on any journey, it is important to decide on the necessary equipment. You will require the following:

- An open mind
- Commitment
- A notebook
- A sense of humour

A Final Thought

As you progress through this book, you will observe how I have set up the CBT sessions exactly as carried out in real life. Most of the exercises suggested are simple and straightforward, if, on occasion, challenging. They are also easy enough to put into practice. If you find the concepts and exercises helpful and you put them into practice yourself, your journey will have been particularly worthwhile. If you are struggling to put them into practice, possibly because of some mental health difficulties, I suggest finding a trained CBT therapist to assist you.

You will also note how the emotional resilience skills I explore are built on one another and are regularly interlinked. Some of you may prefer, as discussed in the introduction, to go straight to skills of greater relevance to you. Or you may find it more useful to explore them in the order laid out. My preference is for the second option. It is more likely to lead to a fuller, deeper understanding of the skills necessary to survive in the world in which we find ourselves.

With these provisos in mind, let's begin.

PART TWO

Personal Resilience Skills

3. SKILL ONE

UNCONDITIONAL SELF-ACCEPTANCE
Becoming Comfortable in One's Own Skin

Why Is this Skill Important?

Unconditional self-acceptance is a key emotional resilience skill. For decades, mental health has been dominated by the importance of self-esteem, the suggestion being that developing skills to improve self-esteem should form the cornerstone of any modern resilience programme. In fact, the whole thrust of modern psychology is focused on how to boost your self-esteem. Countless self-help books and programmes purport to demonstrate how best to achieve this objective. The idea is based on the concept that we can make value judgements about ourselves and, if not content with the result, conjure up skills to increase our self-worth.

I am going to argue that the whole concept of self-esteem is flawed. I am suggesting a different path, easily within your reach. I am going to teach you how to 'accept yourself without conditions', or, simply, 'how to be comfortable in your own skin'. To do this, we must challenge conventional wisdom – that boosting self-esteem or self-worth is essential for emotional resilience and positive mental health.

Society is comfortable with the world of judgement and rating. Social media is built on this platform. It is a short step from this to believing that human beings can be rated by themselves or others.

Underlying anxiety and depression is the world of negative self-rating. If permitted, our internal emotional mind will mercilessly flagellate us in every way imaginable. I constantly listen to wonderful people describing themselves as weak, worthless, failures, useless and of no value. They assume that human beings can be described as such. My task is to assist them to challenge such beliefs and to become comfortable in their own skins.

I have always believed that the shortcut to true peace is unconditional self-acceptance. It is the bedrock of emotional resilience. We could all benefit by developing this skill and practising it repeatedly until it becomes automatic. Acquire it, and your life will be truly transformed.

Before we show you how to develop unconditional self-acceptance, we must consider the world of self-esteem and rating.

Can We Increase Our Self-esteem?

This was a question the great psychotherapist and father of CBT Albert Ellis attempted to answer decades ago. In answering it, he acquired a critical insight. He had been exploring how best to assist patients increase their self-esteem with conditions such as depression. This led him to analyse what the term meant, and therein his journey of discovery began. He realised that the issue was not how best to increase self-esteem, but rather the belief that it could be defined or measured at all. Ellis's insight was that we are attempting to define and measure something that is non-existent. And we are making ourselves anxious, depressed and ashamed in the process.

Despite this insight, we continue to use words like self-worth and self-esteem as if they are definable or measurable concepts. If asked to define on paper the term 'self-worth', it should be a simple task. Is it not obvious? Is it not how we value ourselves as human beings, and therefore easy to measure and improve? Let's explore this concept further.

The Rating Exercise

This is a wonderful exercise to challenge our whole concept of self-rating. It is an exercise I regularly request that individual patients and large groups of people do. The results are astoundingly disparate. Let's see how you do.

1. On a sheet of paper, draw a straight line. At one end of the line, write '1' and at the other, '100'. Now rate yourself as a human being between one and a hundred, with the former being useless and the latter, fantastic.
2. Having marked in the score for your personal rating, now mark in where others would rate you.
3. Next, imagine you were recently diagnosed with depression and are on medication. With this information, where would you now rate yourself on the scale.
4. Then, mark in where you think others would rate you on hearing this news.

How Did You Do?

The results of the first part of this exercise will impart some important information about yourself. If your personal rating is, for example, ninety-five to a hundred, you are clearly setting the bar extremely high, and are thus more likely to become anxious or frustrated if not constantly achieving these levels. If your personal rating is under twenty, you may feel you are not making the grade in life, and are thus more likely to suffer from conditions like depression. Most of us rate ourselves somewhere in between these extremes.

Reviewing your assessment of what others think of you can also be revealing. If the 'others' rating is extremely high, you may constantly feel under pressure to match up to other people's perceived high expectations. This can also lead to us becoming anxious. If extremely low, this may suggest that others do not think much of us, so you may be prone on occasion to feel depressed or ashamed. Once again, most people mark themselves comfortably between the two extremes, assuming others have a reasonable opinion of them.

Now for the results of the second part of this exercise. How many 'changed' their rating when asked to visualise the situation where they were diagnosed with depression and requiring medication? My own experience from performing this exercise over many years is that some will mark their self-rating down but not their 'others' rating. The majority will mark down both. This underlies the shame and stigma surrounding depression and other mental health conditions.

Did You Fall into the Trap?

In my experience, almost everyone falls into the trap! They immediately begin to rate themselves as human beings. They also allow others to rate them. In addition, they will frequently vary their rating depending on circumstances.

Now for the sting in the tail.

On what grounds or using what scale did you apply these ratings to begin with? Most of us, on reflection, admit that we cannot answer this question. In practice, no such scale exists.

It becomes more complex. Suppose I put five of your friends or colleagues in a row, requesting you rate them as human beings, each against each other, detailing the grounds on which you have awarded your scores. Which scale did you apply? It is an impossible task to perform, as no such grounds or scales exist.

This is because of the wonderfully individual nature of every human being. All of us are special, unique and totally undefinable. There is no scale or book to measure our worth as human beings. Yet we constantly fall into the trap of believing that people can be measured, as such, either by ourselves or others.

The Members Only Club

To counteract this tendency to play the rating game, join me in a special Members Only club. This is a highly exclusive club, of which I have been a fully paid-up member for many years. There are three important criteria for membership:

1. We are not allowed to rate ourselves as human beings.
2. We are not allowed to accept others' ratings of us as human beings.
3. We can rate our behaviour (which includes our skills), but not ourselves.

This Members Only club is based on a concept created by my colleague, leading CBT psychotherapist and author Enda Murphy, loosely based on Ellis's insights. By becoming a member of the club, you are separating who you are as a human being from your behaviour. You are now free.

Never again do you need to worry about your 'worth' or how others view you. We, as members, accept that there is no scale to measure worth, but we do accept that we are responsible for our behaviour and can challenge it, if necessary. We also accept that others have the right to challenge our behaviour.

If you are a member, you must accept that we all mess up in terms of our behaviour, but we cannot be defined by it. Our only task every day is to do our best in terms of our behaviour and our skills. What Ellis teaches us is that we must learn to accept ourselves without conditions, while remaining free to rate and challenge our behaviour.

Fully paid-up members of the club will find their lives transformed. All of us play the rating game. We spend our lives matching up to some illusory idea of who we should be or who others think we should be, and so find ourselves anxious, depressed or ashamed. We need to be kinder to ourselves, stop living in the world of rating and simply accept responsibility for our behaviour. This is true self-acceptance, a skill worth learning and practising. I have seen this emotional resilience skill revolutionise lives.

But how can we develop and put this skill into practice? Like most skills, it is easy to learn and understand the concepts behind it, but more difficult to integrate it into our everyday lives.

One of the primary reasons that most people struggle to develop unconditional self-acceptance is that we all have a critical voice in our mind called our 'pathological critic'. Let's explore this arch-enemy of self-acceptance further.

The Pathological Critic

We are all familiar with this 'inner voice', constantly nagging and berating us for even the smallest mistakes in our everyday lives. It is the pathological critic that drives our tendency to rate ourselves. The pathological critic is, of course, our internal emotional mind. Normally the rational brain and mind attempt to control the emotional brain, with limited success. When anxious and, especially, depressed our pathological critic can really turn against us. We begin to truly 'believe our own bull'!

Imagine a so-called good friend who rings you daily, gleefully informing you of your shortcomings. Eventually you begin to believe that he must be telling the truth. Now visualise this friend ringing you incessantly throughout the day with these relentless, deprecatory comments. This is what occurs when the pathological critic gets out of control, as it does in depression. We all hear this voice, at times, with its snide comments suggesting you are 'useless', 'weak', 'a failure', 'worthless' or 'abnormal'.

The main reason the pathological critic wins the internal battle is that our rational brain and mind are powerless to control it if the conflict is occurring solely in our minds. But if we can teach ourselves to write what it is saying down and learn to challenge it on paper, it becomes much easier to put the voice back in its box. This is because our rational brain and mind can, on paper, challenge the pathological critic messages, which are of course false and without foundation. This concept is central to the following exercise, which forms the basis of how to develop the skill of self-acceptance.

The Unconditional Self-acceptance Exercise

To develop this skill, I want you to perform the following self-acceptance exercise:

1. For the next three months, I want you to carry a notebook around with you.
2. Whenever you find yourself rating yourself, I want you to write down the trigger and what your emotion was. The typical example might involve somebody at work, or a family member or friend criticising something you have said or done.
3. Later in the day, when free to do so, write down on a sheet of paper what the pathological critic was telling you – for example, you are a failure, or you are useless, or worthless.
4. Then, on that paper, challenge what the pathological critic is telling you using the techniques that we will now explore.

How to Challenge Your Pathological Critic

The real key to developing unconditional self-acceptance is to learn how to challenge that inner voice using the rules of the Members Only club as a guide. As we have already observed, your emotional mind is much more powerful than your logical mind. If the pathological critic is pouring out venom, it is difficult for you to challenge it in your emotional mind. But on writing down its 'comments' on paper as detailed above, your logical mind can now challenge their content.

'I Am Useless'

Suppose the comment or rating is that you are useless, and we wished to dispute this on paper. You would then ask the following questions:

1. What does this statement really mean in practice?
2. Can I or indeed any human being be defined as 'useless' or of 'no value'?
3. Is this not just another attempt to rate myself?

Now write down the rules of the Members Only club.

You can quickly see on paper that the statement 'I am useless' is a form of rating yourself as a human being, and so you need to discard it. Can a human being be really defined as a 'useless' or 'useful' person? Of course not! However, you can rate your behaviour or skills as useful or useless, and if somebody wishes to assess or rate either of these, you are free to debate with them whether it is true or false. This enables you to distinguish between who you are as a human being and your behaviour.

'I Am a Useless Mother'

Imagine you are a mother. Somebody makes a throwaway comment which implies you are a bad or useless mother. Your pathological critic takes over: *Maybe they are right, and I am useless.* You write this down in your notebook and then later challenge it on paper as follows.

Your pathological critic is implying that you are a useless mother, which is of course another form of rating, as it suggests you are a useless person. But is this true? Can a human being be defined as a useless person? Of course, not! By accepting this is not the case, you are now free to progress the discussion to an assessment of parenting or mothering skills. Now you are on much safer ground. It is easier to debate on your strengths and weaknesses as a mother. Most mothers know that they are doing their best, as are you.

'I Am Weak'

So, too, with the belief that you are weak. Imagine you did not stand up for yourself when a work colleague challenged you. Later, your pathological critic begins to castigate you as being a weak person. Once again, you would write down the trigger and your rating of yourself into your notebook. Later you would challenge on paper those comments as follows.

Can a human being be rated as weak or strong? Is this yet again another form of rating? Can a human being be rated in this manner? Of course not! As members of the Members Only club, such expressions of self-rating are no longer allowed.

Human beings cannot be defined as weak or strong, for no such rating scale exists. Can you rate your behaviour or skills? Of course you can. We all have strengths and weaknesses in relation to skills and behaviour, and are free to debate these with ourselves or others. So, in this case you could challenge your handling of your colleague's comments and decide how to deal with them in the future. By challenging in this manner what the pathological critic is errone-ously trying to convince you to believe, you will gradually learn to distinguish between who you are as a human being from your behaviour.

The same applies to other beliefs suggesting you are abnormal, a failure, worthless or any other term which involves self-rating. We deal with them all in a similar manner, by challenging them on paper, using the rules of the Members Only club. You will eventually learn to be kinder to yourself, which is the essence of what it means to be truly mentally healthy.

By practising this exercise daily, you will gradually begin to accept yourself as you are, without imposing any conditions. You will become more realistic about behaviour and skills, and more honest in appraising which areas of either you may need to improve on. Eventually, after months of this exercise, you will automatically begin to stop rating yourself or accepting others rating you. When this occurs, you have finally achieved the holy grail of mental health by becoming comfortable in your own skin.

MARY'S STORY

Mary, a thirty-five-year-old mother of two with a history of what she describes as 'low self-esteem' attends an appointment with Dr Jim. She was raised in a negative household, by a mother suffering bouts of undiagnosed depression, and a father who was rigid and authoritarian. Mary and her siblings were subjected to a barrage of criticism and negativity. By twenty-five, she had ex-perienced several bouts of major depression, requiring medication. Although happy in her job and in a good relationship, she struggled with persistent in-ternal ruminations – a steady flow of negative thoughts – implying she was worthless. She had attended several therapists, who had explored her past. But none could assist her in dealing with her ruminations. She explains to Dr Jim how, despite the absence of major life stressors, she struggles to shake off these relentless negative internal self-critical thoughts and feelings of low mood.

Dr Jim offers to use CBT techniques to assist her and she agrees. First, he explains the role of rational and irrational beliefs, how they are the lens through which we view everything that happens to us in life. He also explains the ABC concept and how they will use this system to locate her irrational beliefs. He then asks her for a concrete, everyday example that would typically trigger her low mood.

Mary gives him an example of a neighbour rushing by her in the super-market and not acknowledging her presence. Following this, she began to feel depressed. 'So, the trigger was your neighbour seemingly ignoring you in the supermarket and your emotion was depression,' says Dr Jim. 'How did you feel physically and what was your behaviour when you felt depressed?' he then queries.

Mary noted that she had become fatigued, subsequently losing her appetite, interest and drive. In terms of behaviour, she isolated herself for several weeks. 'I just went to work, returning straight home afterwards. I couldn't face another person blanking me like that,' she adds. 'I also found myself struggling with concentration and unable to stop the negative thoughts flying through my head.' She also admits to excessive drinking and withdrawing into her shell at home.

'What was it about being apparently blanked by your neighbour,' asks Dr Jim, 'that caused you to become depressed?'

'It was obvious she did not want to stop and chat to me,' replies Mary.

'And why would this bother you?' he asks.

'Because it confirmed what I believe about myself, that I am worthless and not worth spending time with,' she replies. 'It also proved that I am useless and a failure.' She admits these were typical thoughts triggered by such incidents.

'So, to summarise why it bothers you,' Dr Jim concludes, 'it was your neighbour blanking you in this manner that confirmed you were not worth stopping to talk to. Even worse, it suggests you are worthless.'

Mary agrees with this assessment.

'Let's examine what irrational belief was triggered by this situation and the interpretation you assigned to it,' says Dr Jim. After a long discussion, they conclude her belief was that because she had been blanked by her neighbour, she was worthless.

They put this information into her ABC.

A   Activating Event:
- Trigger: being blanked by her neighbour
- Inference/danger: that her neighbour had purposely blanked her; they did not feel she was worth stopping for, which confirmed her own impressions that she was indeed worthless

B   Belief/Demands: 'Because I was blanked by my neighbour, I am worthless, useless and a failure.'

C Consequences:
- Emotional reactions: depression
- Physical reactions: significant fatigue, difficulties with appetite, concentration and memory
- Behaviour: ruminates constantly about how worthless and useless she is; isolates herself socially; eats poorly and stops taking exercise; drinks excessively at home; becomes increasingly withdrawn and quiet at home

'Now we understand, Mary, what made you feel depressed on this occasion and your resulting behaviour, let's help you to reshape your thinking and behaviour in relation to this. Because, if we're successful in this instance, we can apply the same concepts to similar situations in the future,' says Dr Jim. 'We could dispute or challenge your "A", or your interpretation that your neighbour chose to blank you,' he explains, 'and your evidence that this interpretation was true. We could argue whether your neighbour even saw you in the first place, or was hurrying home to some family or other emergency and unable to stop because of this.'

Dr Jim continues: 'What is more effective is to challenge the "B" and the "C". What we mean by this is to challenge your irrational belief and the emotional and behavioural consequences of this belief.'

He begins by challenging Mary's behaviour. They discuss the unhealthy habits she had fallen into. 'They are what I regularly do in such situations,' she admits. Following a frank conversation, Mary agrees that stopping exercise, heading for the wine bottle, eating poorly and isolating herself socially and domestically were not of assistance. They visit positive behaviours, like increasing exercise, improving nutrition, avoiding alcohol as a crutch and challenging her tendency to isolate herself at such times.

'Let's now challenge your "B", or your irrational belief,' says Dr Jim. 'This took the form of an absolute belief that you are worthless. Is this belief rational or irrational, Mary?' he asks.

She admits it was probably irrational.

Dr Jim then asks her to rate herself between one and a hundred as a person.

'I could only give myself twenty at best,' she replies.

'And where do you think others rate you?'

'A little higher, maybe forty.'

'And when your neighbour blanked you, where did you rate yourself?' asks Dr Jim.

'Zero,' Mary replies, with tears in her eyes.

'And where do you think others would rate you if word went out that this had occurred?'

'Very low, maybe five to ten,' she replies.

Dr Jim empathises with her, as she is clearly distressed by this exercise. But he then asks the following question: 'Can we rate a human being? Where's the measuring tool?' Mary, on reflection, agrees that we can't, as human beings are too complex. Dr Jim then introduces her to the Members Only club and its rules.

Mary exclaims, 'But who else is a member of this club and how do I join? It sounds great.'

'The other members of the club are the rest of humanity. All of us are fallible and imperfect. We must learn to accept ourselves unconditionally. To join is easy, membership is free and makes us invulnerable to the arrows life shoots at us.'

Mary begins to smile, grasping the power of the allegory. 'I would like to join,' she decides.

'One of life's greatest resilience skills is discovering how to accept ourselves without conditions,' says Dr Jim, 'a skill easy to learn but requiring regular practice to become second nature.'

'Our irrational beliefs are very strong,' he explains further, 'so we usually end up constantly searching the environment for evidence that these beliefs are true, ignoring all evidence to the contrary.'

Mary begins to understand. 'Are you suggesting that I automatically as-sumed my neighbour was blanking me, so ignored all other possibilities that this might not be the case?'

Dr Jim agrees. 'This comes from a false belief that human beings can be rated. But, as a newly minted member of the Members Only club, only your behaviour can now be rated, not you. So, whatever the reasons for your neighbour's behaviour, they are no longer relevant, as you now accept yourself without conditions.'

Mary experiences a lightbulb moment and she feels a great weight has been lifted. She seeks advice on how to put this newly discovered skill of unconditional self-acceptance into practice in her life. Dr Jim then introduces her to the pathological critic. She can readily identify with this critical voice in her emotional mind. She can especially relate to the devastating comments telling her that she was useless, weak, a failure, worthless and abnormal. She even throws 'boring' on to the list.

Dr Jim then asks her to define on paper what a worthless person is. This leads to a debate as to whether a human being can be classified as such. Isn't this only another form of rating? He then asks her to define self-worth and self-esteem. Following further discussion, they agree these terms are equally impossible to define. 'Human beings are indeed too special and unique to be classified as such,' he explains, 'yet we continue to use these terms in everyday life.'

They then go on to consider the difference between who we are as human beings and our behaviour or skills. Mary begins to understand, for example, that she can be useless at doing something but can't be defined as a 'useless person'. The bullying statements generated by her pathological critic are indeed false and need to be challenged on a regular basis. Dr Jim elaborates further: 'When simple things happen to us during the day that trigger our pathological critic into action, and self-deprecatory thoughts flood our emotional mind, we require some simple techniques to challenge them.'

He continues: 'I suggest you write down in a notebook when such comments enter your mind. When you have some spare time, write down on a page what the pathological critic was attempting to bully you into believing. On an opposite page, write down the rules of the Members Only club. Then challenge on paper what the voice is saying. You will find that the bully rapidly retreats once your rational mind faces it down.'

Mary agrees to put this exercise into practice. Initially she finds it intimidating and on occasions becomes quite anxious. But day by day, week by week, she faces down her pathological critic. With constant practice, her newly found self-acceptance skill becomes automatic. On a subsequent visit to Dr Jim, she notes her mood is now significantly improved. She is also more peaceful and acceptant of herself. She has become increasingly resilient in the face of difficulties that arise. She has taken her first and most important step towards acquiring emotional resilience. She has at last become comfortable in her own skin!

Key Learning Points

There are some useful learning points from this chapter:

1. Self-esteem is a myth, as it implies that human beings can be rated by themselves or others.
2. In practice, there are no criteria for rating, judging or measuring ourselves as human beings.
3. We can learn to rate our behaviour and skills and accept that other people are entitled to rate or judge these. We are, of course, entitled to challenge such assessments if we feel they are inappropriate.
4. The greatest gift we can give ourselves is to learn the skill of how to accept ourselves as we are, or to become comfortable in our own skins.

4. SKILL TWO

THE FLOODING TECHNIQUE
How to Deal with the Physical Symptoms of Acute and General Anxiety

What Is Flooding?

Flooding is a mental health technique designed to combat the physical nature of anxiety. It involves developing the skill of experientially accepting and going with the physical symptoms of anxiety. This technique is most effective in helping us to deal with acute anxiety, especially panic attacks and phobias. We use a modified version to deal with the symptoms of general anxiety.

Why Is this Skill Important?

Anxiety is an innate part of the human condition as we combat the stresses of life. The physical nature of anxiety is, however, often overlooked. This lack of understanding causes chaos for many people.

We are currently in the throes of an anxiety epidemic for reasons too numerous to detail here. Technology and social media are playing their part. Many are familiar with the 'worrying' side of anxiety, but fail to grasp its physical dimension. In *Anxiety and Panic*, I explained how to quickly conquer panic attacks, phobias and social anxiety, and diminish the effects of general anxiety. Flooding is an essential technique to assist us in managing the physical symptoms so prevalent in these conditions.

It is also important to mention the role of the physical symptoms of acute anxiety in adolescents presenting with self-harm. According to the Child and Adolescent Self-harm in Europe (CASE) study (2010), over 9 per cent of Irish children of school-going age self-harm. This figure is mirrored throughout

51

the developed world, in the UK, Europe and the USA. This study identified anxiety as one of the underlying causes. Another study on self-harm among 15–16-year-olds in Scotland (O'Connor, 2009) found that 13.8 per cent of respondents had self-harmed within the previous twelve months, with several noting that anxiety was an underlying factor.

The inability of this school-going age group to recognise anxiety and a dearth of appropriate skills to manage the accompanying physical symptoms are two of the most common underlying causes of this mental health crisis. These skills should ideally be taught to all children and adolescents, not only to reduce risks of self-harm, but to prevent them growing into adults with lives blighted by easily manageable conditions such as panic attacks.

Adults, too, can benefit from developing and practising this skill. As life, on occasion, threatens to engulf us, anyone may experience distressing periods of acute anxiety. Those trained in the flooding technique will cope better with such periods. They can also assist others struggling with these physical symptoms. Learning to cope with the physical nature of anxiety will also increase our emotional resilience.

Before advancing further, let's explore what happens *physically* in the body during a bout of anxiety.

The Physical Nature of Anxiety

To understand this process, we must first distinguish between fear and worry. Fear relates to a perception of some immediate danger present in our environment, presenting itself as an extreme threat to our safety. If, for example, we heard sounds of an intruder in the middle of the night, it would usually trigger an immediate feeling of the emotion of fear. We could also experience such feelings if attacked by a wild animal. Fear is a sensible emotional response in such situations to a clear environmental danger which has suddenly become manifest. It is also associated with major physical bodily responses. Panic is a state of acute fear.

Worry is where we begin to reflect on and become anxious about possible dangers or unpleasant possibilities that might happen in the future. This, too, can be accompanied by associated secondary physical responses.

The common denominator between fear and worry is that in both cases the emotion is brought about by the perception of some danger. In fear and panic, the danger is seen as being present in the immediate; in worry, the danger is perceived as something that might happen in the future. In both cases, there are associated physical responses. In fear, these are usually quite pronounced and obvious; in worry, they are lower key but often more persistent.

We explored our stress system and its role of seeking out danger and reacting accordingly in Chapter 1. Here, we will review its role in anxiety and panic.

The Role of the Gunslinger in Acute Anxiety

When faced with an acute danger, the boss of the stress system, the amygdala, fires, sending information to our adrenal stress gland to pump adrenaline into our bloodstream. This is our flight hormone. Its job is to prepare us to run by making our heart rate increase, our breathing become shallow and faster, and our muscles tighten up; it also makes our mouth dry and our stomach clench, and we experience weakness, and an overwhelming sense of dread and danger. These symptoms are incredibly uncomfortable but not dangerous. It is the job of the amygdala to seek danger both internally (within our own mind and brain) and externally. But this structure is quite ancient and primitive. Its motto is 'Act first and let someone else (i.e. our rational brain) do the thinking'.

In acute situations, the amygdala, which I call 'the gunslinger' due to its lightning-fast reflexes, will fire without consulting our rational brain if it senses any significant danger. It then enters complete survival mode. When this occurs, we experience an adrenaline rush and the resulting symptoms noted above. All that occurs in acute anxiety is that the gunslinger senses acute danger and reacts, as it is trained to do, producing the unpleasant physical symptoms so familiar to those suffering from panic attacks and phobias.

The gunslinger has a very long memory for danger, which explains why we become increasingly fearful of experiencing further panic attacks and of situations such as planes, lifts, motorways, crowds and so on, in phobias. It does not do talk therapy. It only responds to experiences. But it does, however, have a potential to 'change' its memory. It is this capacity that we feed into when applying the technique of flooding. When our gunslinger fires acutely, as occurs in a panic attack, it will trigger an adrenaline rush normally lasting for five to eight minutes. If, however, we try to prevent it firing, the attack can last from thirty to sixty minutes.

In more chronic forms of anxiety, such as general anxiety and post traumatic stress disorder (PTSD), the amygdala is also active but in a lower-key, persistent manner. We will briefly explore later how flooding can be applied to these conditions. First, let's focus on how to learn and apply the flooding technique in acute anxiety. We will focus primarily on how to apply it during panic attacks, but similar principles apply to all phobias.

How to Develop and Practise this Skill

When experiencing the acute physical symptoms of anxiety, as one feels during a panic attack – heart pounding, shallow, fast breathing, stomach in knots, shaking, sweating and so on – there are two approaches to dealing with them. You can fear them, regard them as dangerous and carry out multiple safety behaviours to bring them to a halt. In this scenario, as in the middle of a panic attack, you may attempt to stop the symptoms – leave the area, use breathing exercises, seek assistance from those close to you, visit your GP or A&E.

In this situation, you are assigning a danger to the physical symptoms. Because your amygdala is geared to look for danger, the more you assign a danger to such symptoms, the more it fires, causing further surges of adrenaline to be released. This, in turn, increases and prolongs the physical symptoms you are so desperate to eliminate. This is the vicious cycle in which many people become enmeshed during panic attacks and in their phobias.

The alternative approach in a period of acute anxiety, as you are experiencing the physical symptoms, is to apply the flooding technique.

The Flooding Technique
1. Visualise in your mind that you are stuck to the floor or seat and unable to move.

2. Allow the uncomfortable physical symptoms to wash over you like a wave, without trying to stop them.
3. Do not apply any safety behaviours to try to stop these physical symptoms – just go with them.
4. Accept that a typical adrenaline rush is only going to last five to eight minutes.
5. Adapt the philosophy of 'bring it on' in relation to these uncomfortable physical symptoms.
6. Accept that these physical symptoms are uncomfortable but not dangerous.
7. You are only allowed to move when the symptoms have subsided.

You will notice when you first apply this technique that the acute physical symptoms quickly settle. If you constantly apply the same exercise each time, you will notice the symptoms gradually decreasing and eventually, in many cases, rapidly disappear. Most people will only need to apply this technique four or five times before this happens.

To learn and practise the skill of flooding, you must accept the essential information that the physical symptoms created by an adrenaline rush are extremely uncomfortable, but not dangerous. You are not going to suffer a heart attack or stroke, lose control or go mad when experiencing them. It is the function of your stress system to keep you safe, not harm you. So, it is really the discomfort you are desperate to avoid.

Fooling the Gunslinger

If you apply the flooding technique instead of the safety behaviours when you feel acute anxiety, you are playing the gunslinger at its own game. For as you apply flooding, experiencing but accepting the uncomfortably physical symptoms of anxiety, the amygdala changes its memory. It recognises you are no longer assigning danger to these symptoms, but instead just going with them. Since its job is to sense danger and it is no longer picking danger up, it quickly shuts down the adrenaline rush. The physical symptoms cease and the gunslinger recalibrates its memory for future similar episodes. It turns the dial down.

This is the key to the management of panic attacks and phobias. If you would like to read about the exact neuroscientific basis of this technique, please read *Anxiety and Panic*.

If you develop and practise this skill, never again will you be concerned about the physical symptoms of acute anxiety. What a boost to your emotional resilience and future mental health. Panic attacks and phobias will become a distant memory!

The Role of Flooding in Managing General Anxiety

Before discussing how best to apply flooding techniques in general anxiety, it is important first to recognise that the brain is geared to tuning up or down our responses, depending on how much we focus its attention on something. Most of us fail to notice how often this happens in everyday life. This is because the brain does this automatically and seamlessly. To show how this works in everyday life, I recommend the following exercise.

The Radio Exercise
1. Sit in a quiet space, on your own, with your phone turned to silent.
2. Tune the radio to a channel you are comfortable with.
3. Have with you whatever novel or non-fiction book you are reading at the moment.
4. For five minutes, leave the book closed in your lap. Listen intently to the sounds coming from the radio. Notice how loud they seem.
5. Now for the next five minutes, open your book and focus on it alone, completely ignoring the sound coming from the radio. Do you notice how the more engrossed you become in the book, the more the sounds seem to fade into the background? This is because the brain has shifted its attention away from the aural sounds towards the visual information contained in your book. The radio has now become background noise. This is an example of the brain's extraordinary ability to change or

adapt to new stimuli and suppress the ones that have now become less relevant.

The Role of the Gunslinger in General Anxiety

In acute anxiety, the gunslinger is firing at red-alert level. It is sensing an acute major danger and causing adrenaline surges as a result. This could be interpreted as the stress system's equivalent to an emergency services response to a 999 call. In general anxiety, it is firing at a much lower intensity but for longer periods of time. This leads first to outpourings of smaller amounts of adrenaline. These give rise to similar symptoms as in acute anxiety, but more persistent and of lower intensity. Secondly, and more importantly, it leads to outpourings of glucocortisol, the chronic stress hormone we discussed in Chapter 1. This is the hormone which leads to the chronic physical symptoms so prevalent in general anxiety. These include fatigue, irritable bowel, tension headaches, teeth-grinding and many more. People with general anxiety become worn out by these low-grade physical symptoms.

In general anxiety, the gunslinger is firing, as always, because it is sensing danger. In this case, the dangers are associated with what is going on in our emotional mind. Later, we will explore the world of catastrophising. The right side of our brain, especially the prefrontal cortex, is where we catastrophise. It has a direct link to the amygdala. So, the more we catastrophise for example, the more irritable the gunslinger becomes, and the more we experience the above physical symptoms.

Calming Down the Gunslinger in General Anxiety

How do we deal with these more chronic, low-grade physical symptoms created by our irritable gunslinger? The answer is twofold. Firstly, we use CBT skills and techniques, some of which we will explore later in this book, to calm down our catastrophising emotional mind. This has an immediate effect in calming down the gunslinger. Secondly, we use a modified version of flooding to deal with the actual physical symptoms themselves.

The Modified Flooding Technique

To apply this technique when you encounter the chronic physical symptoms of general anxiety, follow these steps:

1. Never try to stop the physical symptoms of general anxiety. This only causes them to become more pronounced and persistent.
2. Instead, practise the lessons learned from the radio exercise and treat the symptoms as background noise.
3. If you choose to treat them like music playing in the background while you are getting on with your life, your brain can tune them out. If, however, you choose to listen intently to them, like sounds emanating from the radio, your brain will zoom in and heighten your awareness of them.
4. Go with these uncomfortable low-key physical symptoms. Treat them as background noise. This frees you up to get on with your life.

By treating our irritable gunslinger in this manner in general anxiety, and simply going with the physical symptoms, we remove its power over us. The brain begins eventually to tune them down or out. This is what we mean by using modified flooding techniques in general anxiety. It is amazingly effective at reducing the distress such symptoms can cause. If you would like to explore these concepts further, you can read more about them in *Anxiety and Panic*.

PETER'S STORY

Peter is twenty-nine and working in the media. His job is stressful, but he enjoys the challenge. Alone in his flat while working on his computer, he becomes aware of his heart pounding. This is followed by a shortness of breath. Thoughts of dying alone from a heart attack flash into his mind – 'This is it!' Suddenly, his whole body is shaking and his mouth becomes dry. He struggles to breathe. His heart is now thumping at an alarming rate, his stomach is clenched in knots. The sweat pours out and he feels weak and dizzy. Every muscle in his body is tense.

Terrified he would be unable to access medical help in time, he struggles out of the apartment, banging on the door of his neighbour. They find him distressed and gasping for air, and immediately call for an ambulance. Peter has just experienced his first panic attack.

In A&E, his symptoms finally settle. But he experiences several more attacks over subsequent weeks. His GP refers him to Dr Jim, to seek further assistance.

Dr Jim listens carefully to his story and then asks, 'Has anyone explained to you what happens during a panic attack?' Peter admits that nobody had. Dr Jim takes out an ABC sheet and explains the ABC system.

'Now,' says Dr Jim, 'let's revisit your first panic attack and examine it, in minute detail on paper, using this model. Without understanding what happens in your body and mind during a panic attack, it's difficult to eliminate them.'

He begins by asking Peter, 'What was the first physical symptom you noticed when the panic attack began?'

'I was on my computer, when I noticed my heart pounding,' he answers.

'And what was your emotion at the time?'

'Panic.'

'And what symptoms did you notice when you became panicky?'

Peter lists the physical feelings he experienced at the time.

'Now we are building up a picture of what happened on the night,' explains Dr Jim. 'We know the trigger, we know your emotion, which was panic, and we know the physical symptoms created by the latter. Returning to the initial trigger, where your heart was thumping – what danger did you associate with these symptoms at the time?' he asks.

'I felt I was going to die,' Peter answers.

'So, what demand were you making in relation to these initial physical symptoms?' asks Dr Jim.

'I just wanted the symptoms to stop,' Peter replies.

'And what happened when you tried to stop them?' asks Dr Jim.

'It got worse,' he answers. 'I became more panicky and fearful. It was awful. I've never experienced such feelings of absolute terror. The more I tried to stop the symptoms, the worse they became.'

'Now,' says Dr Jim. 'A final but important question: what did you do or what was your behaviour when the full panic symptoms arrived?'

'My first action was to seek immediate help from my neighbours before I lost consciousness and died. They immediately contacted the emergency services and I was transferred by ambulance to the local A&E department.'

When probed, Peter admits that, following further episodes, he has seen his GP, used tranquillisers and even tried breathing exercises but nothing has worked.

Together they put together the following ABC:

A Activating Event:
  * Trigger: heart pounding in chest
  * Inference/danger: I am going to have a heart attack and die

B Belief/Demands: 'These symptoms must stop.'

C Consequences:
  * Emotional reactions: panic
  * Physical reactions: thumping heart, difficulty breathing, sweating, muscle tension, stomach in knots, weakness, dizziness, dry mouth, shaking
  * Behaviour: left apartment to seek immediate help on first attack; sought urgent assistance from emergency services in the form of ambulance, oxygen and transport to hospital; had full hospital screening but was discharged home none the wiser; later attended GP for further screening and reassurance; had trial of tranquillisers; attempted breathing exercises during the actual attack

'What caused the distressing physical symptoms you experienced during this panic attack?' asks Dr Jim.

'I assume it was the feelings of panic that triggered them,' replies Peter.

Dr Jim agrees. 'But what happened in your body to cause these symptoms?'

Peter struggles with this question, so Dr Jim explains that the emotional brain oversees our stress system, whose job it is to protect us from danger. He elaborates: 'When our emotional brain senses danger in any form, it activates two adrenal stress glands in our abdomen, instructing them to release our fear hormone, adrenaline.'

He then introduces Peter to the amygdala, which he describes as an ancient structure, around since the time of the dinosaurs. It is the boss of his stress system and its job is to scan his internal and external environment for danger. If it senses danger, it activates the freeze, fight or flight response. It is this part of Peter's emotional brain that activated the release of adrenaline.

Dr Jim adds that the amygdala, which he calls the gunslinger, is trigger-happy, with razor-sharp reflexes and a long memory for danger. He tells Peter that the gunslinger's motto on sensing danger was 'Act first and allow more rational parts of the brain to decide if the danger was real or not'. So, it was not particularly 'smart'! They also discuss the function of adrenaline: how it prepares the body to escape danger; how, when adrenaline is released, it prepares the person to run by increasing their heart rate and breathing, and diverting blood from gut and mouth to their muscles; and that these physical symptoms were not dangerous, but were uncomfortable.

'During your panic attack,' Dr Jim asks him, 'do you now accept that the physical symptoms experienced were due to an amygdala-driven adrenaline rush?' When Peter agrees, Dr Jim goes on: 'Were the symptoms you experienced dangerous?' By now, Peter is beginning to see the light.

'No,' he replies, 'I realise now they were not dangerous.'

'But were they uncomfortable?' asks Dr Jim.

This time Peter replies without hesitation: 'Yes, they were extremely uncomfortable.'

Dr Jim then asks Peter to write down and remember the crucial maxim: 'The physical symptoms of anxiety and panic are uncomfortable, but not dangerous!' He then enquires, 'How long do your panic attacks usually last for?'

'They could often last for an hour.'

Dr Jim explains that this is common, and queries why the symptoms took so long to settle. Peter struggles with this. Dr Jim explains further: 'It was your safety behaviour that was preventing the body's stress system from returning to normal.' He then demonstrates how Peter was in fact keeping the panic attack going through his behaviours – by going to A&E, seeking out assistance from neighbours or work colleagues, not going into public areas, or attempting to stop the panic attack by breathing exercises.

'The amygdala is quite used to perceiving danger and triggering an adrenaline rush. But upon realising there is no obvious danger present, it shuts down this adrenaline rush often within ten minutes.' Peter, through his safety behaviour, continued to imply to the amygdala that there was still significant danger present. As a result, it continued to trigger a flow of adrenaline. So, the panicky physical symptoms continued on unabated.

'Suppose you were in the middle of a panic attack and I stuck your shoes to the ground so you couldn't move. What do you think would happen?' Dr Jim asks.

Peter visualises this scenario in his head. 'I would find that scary,' he replies.

'But what would actually happen?' insists Dr Jim.

'Well, I understand now that nothing serious is going to happen. So, I assume that eventually the physical symptoms would subside,' says Peter.

'How long would this take?' asks Dr Jim.

Peter guesses that it might take up to half an hour. Dr Jim explains that, in practice, the symptoms created by the adrenaline rush would be gone after ten minutes if Peter did absolutely nothing. He elaborates further: 'The difficulty most people experience with panic attacks is that they believe the physical symptoms are dangerous. They keep trying to make them stop. It is this demand and safety behaviour, such as going to emergency departments, leaving the scene of shopping centres, trying to escape into fresh air, breathing exercises and so on, that keeps the panic attack going.'

Dr Jim asks Peter to visualise going down to the local beach and facing the sea. 'Then put up your hand and try to stop the tide coming in.'

Peter laughs. 'I would look a little foolish.'

'But that is what people in the middle of a panic attack are attempting to do,' explains Dr Jim, 'because trying to stop an adrenaline rush is like trying to stop the tide. Just as the tide comes in, so it will also go back out. So, too, will an adrenaline rush, if we don't interfere with the process through safety behaviours.'

Peter reflects on this. 'But won't enduring these symptoms be uncomfortable and unpleasant?' he asks.

'Now we come to the nub of the issue,' replies Dr Jim. 'These physical symptoms are extremely uncomfortable, therefore hard for us to bear. This explains why sufferers try so hard to stop them. We all hate discomfort, and avoid it at all costs. I am going to share with you a mental health technique called "flooding", to help you to manage these physical symptoms.

'Visualise, Peter, when a panic attack arrives, that you are stuck to the seat. Then allow these uncomfortable physical symptoms to sweep over you like a wave. Surrender yourself to these sensations like water flowing over you in a shower, draining down the plughole. Imagine yourself saying to them, "Come on, let's be having you. You have five to eight minutes to do your worst!" Once you accept them as not dangerous, just uncomfortable – a nuisance – you will rapidly lose your fear of them. Instead of trying to get rid of the sensations, simply embrace them.'

Peter is still concerned that he will be overwhelmed by the discomfort. Dr Jim then asks, 'Is it in your interest, Peter, to learn how to deal with panic attacks once and for all or to experience lifelong discomfort from living in a permanent state of fear and dread?'

Peter quickly acknowledges that, no matter how difficult, it is preferable to banish panic attacks for life. 'In that case,' Dr Jim goes on, 'you must put these ideas into practice. The more you embrace and challenge the physical sensations by practising flooding, the less the emotional brain is bothered about them, and the quicker the adrenaline rush and physical symptoms completely subside.'

He explains how once the amygdala learns there is no real danger associated with the physical symptoms in panic attacks, its emotional memory banks are reshaped for the future.

'What happens in panic attacks,' Dr Jim concludes, 'is that we become physically anxious, possibly due to being subconsciously stressed by work or other life issues. This may lead to a physical symptom such as our heart beating faster. We then assume this physical symptom is dangerous and we demand it goes away. This leads to the emotions of panic and the subsequent cascade of physical symptoms that are so well known to the sufferer.'

In practice, the physical symptoms of anxiety, such as Peter's presenting ones, were never dangerous. 'They do not cause us to suffer heart attacks or strokes, to collapse or to die. They are simply the normal physical symptoms of anxiety – uncomfortable but not dangerous.' By avoiding safety behaviour and using his flooding technique, Peter will help his amygdala to recalibrate its memory and banish panic attacks from his life.

Two weeks later, when Peter comes back to see Dr Jim, he is incredulous that he has had no further panic attacks. He still gets physically anxious but is no longer concerned about it. He is no longer fearful of future panic episodes, as he now has the skills to deal with them.

Six months down the line, he has remained panic attack-free. His fear of fears is gone. He has conquered and reset his amygdala. Most of all, he has developed an important emotional resilience skill which he will retain for the rest of his life.

Key Learning Points

1. The physical symptoms of anxiety are uncomfortable, but not dangerous.
2. They are caused by our amygdala (the gunslinger) – the boss of our stress system – inappropriately sensing danger and releasing the stress hormones adrenaline and glucocortisol into the bloodstream.
3. Learning the flooding technique skill, which teaches us to go with the physical symptoms of anxiety, can assist us to rapidly reduce and often banish many of these symptoms.
4. Through this technique, we can reset – sometimes for life (in the case of some forms of acute anxiety, such as panic attacks and phobias) – our gunslinger's memory for danger.

5. SKILL THREE

HOW TO DEAL WITH UNCERTAINTY
The Toss of a Coin

Why Is this Skill Important?

Rationally, we accept uncertainty as a part of life. Yet our emotional mind seems determined to convince us that it is otherwise. Anxiety is one of the most common mental health conditions in our twenty-first-century world. Frequently underlying this condition is a hidden demand for absolute certainty. It is often a core demand in general anxiety, PTSD and obsessive-compulsive disorder (OCD). Many people with depression also struggle with the uncertainty surrounding the condition. The same can be said for numerous physical health and other challenges we face in life.

It is therefore essential to develop the skill of how to deal with uncertainty. Each one of us will encounter periods of stress throughout our lives, with accompanying uncertainty. Those who master this skill will be emotionally more resilient to such stressors, which will automatically reduce the mental health challenges such periods can engender.

One could say that chance favours the prepared mind!

How to Develop and Practise this Skill

If you are constantly struggling with a demand for absolute certainty in some, or all, areas of your life, I suggest the following exercise, which was first shared with me by CBT therapist and colleague Enda Murphy. It will require a sense of humour, a burning desire to banish this demand and, on occasion, the enlisting of assistance from those close to you.

The Coin Exercise

Let's begin by asking you to write down on a piece of paper a list of personally enjoyable activities. Here is a typical list:

- TV and Netflix programmes
- Shopping
- Going out to a movie
- Going out with a partner for a meal
- Different forms of exercise
- Having a glass of wine with a meal
- Social media
- Reading an enjoyable book
- Meeting up with friends in a pub

When drawing up this list, be totally honest, only putting down activities you really enjoy. Otherwise this exercise will be ineffective.

Now for the fun part!

For the next four weeks you are going to become very au fait with a simple coin. Heads mean yes, tails mean no. This coin is now going to remove all certainty from your everyday life.

Let's begin with TV and Netflix. For the next four weeks, every single episode of any series or soap, together with every movie and football match you were planning to watch, becomes dependent on the toss of a coin. Because . . . before each episode or programme you are anxious to watch, you must toss a coin! Heads you can watch it, and tails you can't, and you are not allowed to watch it on catch-up. (I can hear the groans already.) If you are honest in performing this exercise, you will feel anxious before tossing the coin, jubilant if it turns up heads and completely frustrated if turns up tails.

If you are anticipating a glass of wine with your meal, toss the coin. Heads you can have it, tails and it is going to be water. If you are socialising with friends, heads you can drink, and tails you can't. If you are enjoying a good book, heads you can read it and tails, you must wait until the following day to see how the protagonist gets on. If you're out shopping and you find a dress, suit or sweater that really looks good on you, again, toss the coin. Heads you can take it home, tails you leave it behind.

When it comes to exercise routines the pattern is similar. You must get ready to exercise, but just before you go, toss the coin. Heads you can go and tails you can't. Or even worse, if you like a brisk walk or a run, heads you can go ahead as normal, tails you must walk at a snail's pace. It is amazing how frustrating this can be.

If you are planning to go out with your partner to a meal or movie, firstly explain the purpose of the exercise to them so that they are on board. You both get ready, but as you are going out the door, you must toss the coin. Heads you can go and tails you can't. You may not be popular, but this must be done with a joint sense of humour.

Now for the daddy of them all, namely social media. If you are serious about banishing uncertainty from your life, this can really get the message across. Each day, you must toss a coin. Heads you can check your social media for the day, and tails you must disengage for twenty-four hours. Now I really can hear the groans!

You can decide on your own list. The key is to be honest. Only write down activities you find pleasurable. You also have to genuinely follow through on the 'tails' part of the exercise. No cheating, please, or the exercise is a waste of time.

Lest you assume I am joking about this exercise, let me good-humouredly inform you I am deadly serious.

What Is the Purpose of this Exercise?

Why ask you to cede control of your everyday life for four weeks to the whim of a coin? The answer is that we all fall into the trap of assuming we have absolute control over our everyday lives. What time we get up at, what we will have for our meals, when we exercise, check our social media, read, watch TV and Netflix, socialise, and so on. In other words, we are absolutely certain of how our normal, everyday life will pan out.

We then assume this is how life should be, in relation to more serious matters, such as health, finances, relationships, and so on. We are seeking 100 per cent certainty that our demands in these areas are met. If we examine this demand in more detail, it is clearly irrational.

Is anything in life 100 per cent certain other than death? (And the cynic would add taxes!) Of course, this demand is impossible to achieve and leads inevitably to anxiety or frustration.

The key to the coin exercise is how you adapt when things do not go your way. What do you do when you are really frustrated, unable to view a programme, check social media or read your latest book? How do you change your behaviour? What do you do instead? This is a microcosm of real life.

By the time you have repeatedly performed the coin exercise over a four-week period, uncertainty will be embedded in your emotional mind as the norm. You will no longer seek absolute certainty in relation to more serious concerns. You will have become more realistic about life. You will discover an inner resilience and capacity to adapt when matters are not going your way, when life – as it is wont to do – goes pear-shaped. By the way, if towards the end of this four-week exercise you are still seeking absolute certainty, continue for a further four weeks. The penny will drop quite quickly if you are aware of this possibility. It is amazing how this exercise focuses the mind.

SUSAN'S STORY

Susan presents to Dr Jim with a long history of anxiety. She is twenty-eight, happily married and a mother of two active boys. She is obsessed with the thought of developing some serious health condition that will remove her permanently from her family. Dr Jim empathises, and suggests some CBT approaches to deal with her anxiety. He explains to Susan about rational and irrational beliefs, how they are the lens through which we view everything that happens to us in life. He then explains the ABC concept to her and how they will employ this system to locate and challenge her irrational beliefs. He asks for an example of a situation that has triggered a bout of anxiety. Susan mentions a recent telephone call, informing her that a work colleague had developed breast cancer. Following the call, she became extremely anxious. 'And how did you feel physically?' asks Dr Jim.

'I felt awful,' she replies. 'Stomach in knots, difficulty breathing and my heart was beating faster. I felt weak and shaky, my muscles were tense and the tiredness was overwhelming. I also had terrible nightmares that night. The following morning, I ended up with soreness in both jaws from grinding my teeth.'

'And what was your behaviour when anxious, following this phone call?' Dr Jim asks.

Susan admits to constantly checking her breasts, seeking reassurance from her husband, checking Dr Google for information, which made matters worse. She also found herself in tears when gazing at her sons, contemplating their future without her.

'What was it about this phone call, Susan, that caused you to become so anxious? What danger were you assigning to the news that this work colleague had developed breast cancer? What did you visualise was going to happen?'

Susan admits to being convinced she is next. She can visualise the scenes in her mind. Surgery followed by chemotherapy and radiotherapy. She can see where it is going to end. 'At times, I can see myself laid out in the coffin,' she explains, with tears in her eyes. 'My husband left on his own. My two children not really understanding what has happened to their mother . . .'

'Now let's examine what irrational belief was triggered by this situation and the danger you assigned to it,' says Dr Jim. 'This usually takes the form of some absolute demand you are making about the trigger. So, what demand were you making of yourself after this telephone conversation?'

Susan replies: 'I was demanding that I must not develop breast cancer.'

They then put together the following ABC:

A Activating Event:
   • Trigger: telephone conversation with a friend and hearing a work col-
     league has developed breast cancer
   • Inference/danger: she is going to be next to develop breast cancer;
     if this happens, she will end up with surgery, radiotherapy and

chemotherapy; she might eventually die, and leave her husband and two children behind without a wife and mother

B   Belief/Demands: 'I must not develop breast cancer and die. I must not leave my husband and two children without a wife and mother.'

C   Consequences:
- Emotional reactions: anxiety
- Physical reactions: stomach is in knots, difficulty taking a deep breath, heart beating a little faster, shaking, muscle tension, teeth-grinding at night and significantly increased tiredness and fatigue
- Behaviour: constantly checks breasts for lumps; seeks reassurance from husband; checks internet for information on breast cancer; attends GP seeking reassurance; drinks more wine than usual; has nightmares and is grinding her teeth in her sleep; spends hours replaying numerous visualised scenarios in her mind as to what would happen if she died

'So now we understand, Susan, what made you so anxious about this event and what the resulting behaviour was, let's reshape your thinking and behaviour in relation to it. Because if we're successful in this instance, we can apply the same concepts to similar situations in the future,' says Dr Jim. 'We could dispute or challenge your "A", or your interpretation of the telephone conversation with your friend. And we could dispute the evidence that you were actually going to develop breast cancer. But that wouldn't help if next week you felt you might develop a brain tumour. It is more effective, Susan,' Dr Jim continues, 'to challenge your irrational belief, the real driver of your anxiety, and the emotional and behavioural consequences of this belief.'

First, Dr Jim takes her through the unhealthy behaviours they have uncovered, exploring how she can challenge them. 'Let's examine and challenge your "B", or your irrational belief. This took the form of an absolute demand that you must not develop breast cancer. Is this demand rational or irrational, Susan?' he asks.

She agrees that it is irrational. Dr Jim then asks, 'What would be a healthier demand?' After some discussion, they both agree that a more rational or healthier demand might be that she would prefer not to develop breast cancer, but this was out of her control.

This leads to a discussion on the importance of control in Susan's life. Dr Jim then asks her what can she control in her life. After a few attempts to answer this, she admits she can control very little. Dr Jim elaborates that when seeking control, we are usually looking for absolute certainty, order, security and perfection. In Susan's case, she is looking for absolute or 100 per cent certainty.

Susan can immediately relate to this demand: 'It is all I have sought since my teens,' she exclaims. 'All my life, I have struggled to cope with uncertainty.' After a conversation about the impossibility of achieving 100 per cent certainty in relation to anything in life, Susan finally accepts that, rationally, this is an impossible demand to fulfil. 'But how can I stop it?' she exclaims. 'It is so ingrained.'

Dr Jim agrees that it is difficult to shake off irrational beliefs once they become entrenched. 'I am, however, going to suggest an exercise to assist you in dealing with uncertainty,' he adds. He explains that while Susan might understand cognitively that absolute certainty is a myth, she needs to grasp this concept emotionally. 'You have to understand it in your gut as well as your head,' he explains.

He then asks her to write down a list of activities she finds pleasurable. This is easy: she loves TV, Netflix, social media, going out with friends, having a glass of wine with her meal, going out with her partner to the theatre or for meals, and especially her daily yoga routine. Dr Jim then lays out the coin exercise and what it will entail. Susan is aghast when she realises that her life will be determined by the toss of a coin for a whole month. But she agrees to put it into practice to the best of her ability.

The following month is one of the most challenging periods of Susan's life. Her whole organised world is turned on its head, and she grows to hate that coin! By the end of the second week, however, Susan begins to get the point. She learns to accept emotionally that she has no real control over her everyday life. By the end of the month she realises she can indeed deal with uncertainty and is now able to adapt if the coin does not go her way.

On a return visit to Dr Jim, she admits to feeling a lot less anxious and that she is no longer seeking absolute certainty in her life. He advises her that any-time she finds herself struggling to deal with uncertainty in relation to health, or indeed any other matter, she should repeat the exercise for a further month. Susan good-humouredly assures him that this threat was enough to banish the fear of uncertainty from her life for good! Whenever the demand for certainty did, in practice, try to reassert itself, a few days of the coin exercise quickly assisted her in putting the ogre back in its box.

Key Learning Points

1. One of the most common causes of anxiety and frustration is a demand for absolute certainty.
2. If you find that you are struggling to deal with uncertainty, then apply-ing the coin exercise to common enjoyable activities can teach you that a demand for 100 per cent certainty is, in practice, impossible.
3. If we can learn to deal with uncertainty in our everyday lives, it is easier to accept this concept in relation to the bigger events in life.
4. The 50/50 toss of a coin is truly a metaphor for real life.

6. SKILL FOUR

HOW TO DEAL WITH DISCOMFORT
Short-term Pain for Long-term Gain

Why Is this Skill Important?

Discomfort is and always has been an integral part of human existence. Most of us accept this as a fact of life and build into our lives relevant coping mechanisms to deal with it. However, some of us really struggle to deal with this harsh reality and do everything in our power to avoid it. Managing discomfort is especially relevant for modern society. Why is that so?

It is because not knowing how to manage discomfort leads to intense frustration. This, in turn, underlies many mental health problems, especially anxiety conditions such as panic attacks and phobias, and depression. These conditions create significant discomfort, something we dislike, but, for example, as we explored in Chapter 4, the chapter on flooding, accepting the discomfort of the physical symptoms of acute anxiety is essential. There are also strong links between frustration and most addictions. The behavioural response to a demand that one should not suffer discomfort is, in the case of the addict, to seek out substances and addictive behaviours to ensure that this is not experienced.

It is also relevant in toxic stress. While some of us will become anxious and release adrenaline when stressed, others will become frustrated. This is important, as frustration can lead to the body pouring out noradrenaline, our aggression hormone, rather than adrenaline, our more benign fear hormone, when we are anxious. There can be significant physical health consequences if this outpouring of noradrenaline is persistent or prolonged. If you are interested in this topic, you can read more about it in *Toxic Stress*.

Alongside mental health conditions, one must also be deeply concerned at the high levels of frustration within modern society. The media constantly informs us that we live in an age of anxiety. Rarely is it mentioned that we also live in an age of frustration. Consider road rage on the motorways, queues at the airport, boorishness in restaurants . . . Experiencing and managing discomfort is a skill older generations were forced to develop through necessity. This is no longer the case in our present-day, fast-moving, technologically driven society. Discomfort is regarded as something not to be tolerated, something to be avoided at all costs. In some situations, our response when frustrated is to lash out verbally, to succumb to road rage, forget our manners, be brusque, and a host of other unpleasant behaviours.

Parallel with this desire to avoid discomfort is an increasingly prevalent belief that everything should be 'instant'. That includes all forms of self-gratification. The concept of 'I should get what I want, when I want it' can be translated into 'I deserve to have this pleasure now, not later.'

This demand for everything to be instant is seeping insidiously into the current generation, fed such a menu from childhood. Parents may also assume it is their task to ensure the lives of their children are less stressful than theirs were, by sheltering them from potential discomfort. This removes a key resilience building block integral their children's future happiness. Once they have reached the exam years and beyond, a young person may struggle to cope with the problems that real life will begin to throw at them.

The consequences of these changes can be seen right across society, where frustration is growing at an exponential level. The basis of this frustration is a growing sense of entitlement that we should live in a world where discomfort is either absent or reduced to a minimum.

Of course, this is a false reality, as life is full of discomfort. If we fool our adolescents and young adults – and indeed ourselves – into believing discomfort is not a part of life, we risk exposing them, and ourselves, to significant mental health consequences, many of which we are already experiencing as a society.

Dodging discomfort is bad for your mental health. So, learning how to deal with discomfort is a skill we all need to learn, practise and, ideally, pass on to our children. It is a critically important emotional resilience skill.

Learning How to Deal with Discomfort

Underlying the emotion of frustration is the irrational belief 'I should not have to suffer discomfort'. This is often backed up by similar demands, such as 'The world must change to suit me' or 'Everybody else must change, not me'. As I often good-humouredly say to patients, 'Good luck with those demands!' It is useful to redefine frustration as 'disturbance/discomfort anxiety' in order to distinguish it from 'ego anxiety'. In the latter, we are making some demands on ourselves. In the former, we are making some demands on the situation. When frustrated about something, we are usually demanding that other people or situations change so that we don't have to suffer discomfort. This relieves us of the burden of having to change something in ourselves, or of accepting that it is not always possible to change circumstances, and that we must learn to adapt.

Low Frustration Tolerance

To develop this skill, we must introduce another term: 'frustration tolerance'. This defines our capacity to suffer discomfort. None of us likes discomfort but we all have different endurance or tolerance levels. Those with high frustration tolerance levels can accept short-term pain for long-term gain. Those with low frustration tolerance (LFT), however, are not prepared to put up with short-term pain, yet still desire long-term gain. A simple example of this might be where I might remain frustrated with my fitness regime, yet refuse to get off the couch.

So, the real key to developing the skill of how to manage discomfort is to acknowledge that frequently in life we must learn to accept short-term pain if we wish to achieve long-term gain. Once you learn how to put this concept into practice in your everyday life, you will no longer struggle to deal with discomfort or expect the world or life itself to change to suit you.

To learn how best to achieve this objective, I suggest the following two frustration exercises.

Frustration Exercise One

In the first exercise, we are going to challenge your low frustration tolerance as follows:

1. For the next eight weeks, I want you to carry a notebook around with you.
2. Whenever you encounter a situation where you find yourself feeling extremely frustrated about something, write down in your notebook what the trigger was and what your emotion was.
3. When you have a few quiet moments, take out your notebook and write down on paper your answers to the following three questions:

   What was your long-term aim or what did you want to achieve?
   What short-term discomfort were you trying to dodge?
   Did your behaviour worsen the situation and, if so, how could you change it?

4. Finally, having honestly answered these questions, decide on how you are going to put the proposed changes into action.

What you will usually discover through this exercise is how often either you were demanding that something or someone must change to avoid you having to experience discomfort, or you were avoiding or dodging the discomfort and hassle of dealing with the issue yourself. Once you have identified on paper the discomfort you were trying to avoid and detailed how you will now deal with the issue, put this solution into practice. This may involve having a difficult conversation with someone to resolve a situation, or taking on something which might be challenging. You may have to change how you view a situation or accept something which cannot be changed. These solutions not only challenge your frustration, but make you more resilient.

Frustration Exercise Two

The second frustration exercise involves the coin exercise described in the previous chapter on uncertainty, Chapter 5. For four weeks, I suggest you repeatedly perform the coin exercise until you learn how to cope with the frustration created when the coin turns tails, messing up your previously organised, controlled, everyday life. Initially you will hate and despise that coin, as it has removed control from your grasp. Bit by bit, however, you will notice yourself becoming more resigned to when the coin turns tails.

The key to this exercise is of course that to achieve your long-term objective of learning how to deal with discomfort, you must put up with the short-term pain of missing out on many pleasurable activities. You will notice after a month of this exercise that you have a greater acceptance of and adaptability towards situations not going your way. Your frustration levels will fall and your capacity to accept discomfort will gradually increase.

If you haven't got the message after four weeks, I find that repeating the exercise for a further four weeks will usually consolidate the concept!

If you carry out these two exercises as outlined, the effects on your life can be transformative. You will solve problems more efficiently and with less hassle; you will cease to be aggressive, irritable and demanding. Instead, you will be calmer and more tolerant of discomfort and acceptant of the fact that discomfort is part of life. You will realise, finally, that learning how to manage discomfort is one of the genuine shortcuts towards developing greater emotional resilience in your life.

MICHAEL'S STORY

Michael is a married thirty-five-year-old, and a father of three small children, working in a job he hates. He feels unappreciated and that his skills are underused, and he dislikes the team he works with. He has become unhappy, irritable and moody at home. His wife, Jill, is increasingly concerned about his mental health and convinces him to visit Dr Jim to rule out depression. Dr Jim listens carefully to Michael's story, reassuring him that depression is not the culprit.

He empathises with Michael in relation to his work situation, and suggests some CBT approaches that might be of assistance. He explains what rational and irrational beliefs are and how they will use the ABC concept to locate them. He then invites Michael to provide an example of a recent typical situation that they could use as a trigger. 'Having to go to work tomorrow morning,' he replies with a rueful smile. 'I just can't stand the thought of getting up and facing the ordeal of another day!'

'And how does this make you feel emotionally?' asks Dr Jim.

'Frustrated,' replies Michael.

'So now we have the trigger and the emotion,' says Dr Jim. 'What is it about having to present yourself for work tomorrow that is making you feel frustrated?'

'Where do I begin?' replies Michael. 'There are so many things frustrating me. I am totally overqualified for the job, so I find it extremely boring dealing with the mundane tasks assigned by my manager. He is younger and less experienced, and yet I must report to him. He does not appreciate his good fortune in having somebody as experienced as me to perform these tasks. I find my two co-workers even more irritating to deal with. I should, of course, be better paid and dealing with more challenging projects, but I am forced to eke out each day, performing mind-numbing tasks.'

'Anything else about this work situation causing you to feel frustrated?'

'I want the situation to change, but they do not seem to understand my frustration. No matter how many hints I drop, they continue to ignore my obvious talents,' replies Michael.

'And have you considered moving?'

'I would need to do further training to move on to a different company.'

'And why have you not considered this?' asks Dr Jim.

'It would be so much hassle. And why should I have to? All I want is for my employers and fellow colleagues to change their approach and I would be content where I am,' he replies. 'Anyway, even if I did move on, it would probably be more of the same.'

'And what do you do when you become frustrated?' asks Dr Jim.

Michael admits to becoming extremely irritable with his work colleagues and manager. 'It doesn't stop there,' he adds. 'I am so moody and grumpy at home. I don't know how Jill puts up with me. I even take it out on the children and I feel bad about that.'

On further probing, he admits to ruminating constantly about the situation, becoming increasingly stressed as day in, day out nothing changed. 'I even began to drink more at night and stay up later,' he adds.

'And how do you feel physically when you get very frustrated?' asks Dr Jim.

'I just feel all my muscles go rigid with tension. I often feel like lashing out at somebody to release it. I am also having tension headaches, and I feel tired but wired every evening,' he replies.

'So now let's examine what irrational belief was triggered by this situation and the interpretation you assigned to it,' says Dr Jim. 'What absolute demand were you making of yourself about the situation?'

'I just wanted them all to change,' Michael replies testily. 'If they changed, I would not have to experience this hassle and disturbance. It's that simple,' he adds. 'I should not have to put up with all of this discomfort.'

'Any other demands?'

'I should not have to carry out such mundane tasks!'

Together with Dr Jim, Michael completed the following ABC:

A Activating Event:
- Trigger: the thought of having to go to work the following morning
- Inference/danger: he is overqualified for his current job; he finds the tasks he is assigned mundane and boring; having to report to a manager younger and, in his opinion, less experienced than himself; he could consider moving to a different company, but that would involve a lot of hassle and discomfort; he would not have to consider this if everybody at work saw things the way he did, and changed accordingly

B Belief/Demands: 'I should not have to carry out boring mundane tasks. My work colleagues and manager should change to ensure I am not having to endure any discomfort. I should not have to suffer discomfort.'

C Consequences:
- Emotional reactions: frustration
- Physical reactions: muscle tension; tension headaches; feeling wired
- Behaviour: persistently irritable and moody at work and at home; on occasions feels like lashing out physically; ruminates constantly about the situation; drinks more at night; stays up later at night

'So now we understand, Michael, what made you so frustrated about this event and your resulting behaviour, let's see if we can reshape your thinking and behaviour in relation to it. Because, if we are successful in this instance, we can apply the same concepts to similar situations in the future,' says Dr Jim. 'We could dispute or challenge your "A", or your interpretation, but what is more effective is to challenge your irrational belief, the real driver of your frustration and accompanying physical and behavioural consequences.'

He explains how the physical symptoms of frustration were created by the aggression hormone noradrenaline, and how this could cause physical health difficulties for him in the future if he did not learn how to manage his frustration.

He also takes Michael through his unhealthy behaviours and discusses how to challenge them. How could being persistently irritable and moody at home and at work, for example, advance the situation? Michael agrees that, in practice, this was making his life more difficult.

'Let's now examine and challenge your "B", or your irrational belief,' says Dr Jim. 'This took the form of absolute demands that you must not suffer discomfort and that your work situation should change to accommodate you. Is this belief rational or irrational, Michael?' he asks.

'Of course, it is rational,' Michael replies indignantly. 'Why should I have to put up with discomfort because they won't change their behaviour?'

'But suppose I told you it is completely irrational,' challenges Dr Jim.

Michael was taken aback. 'Are you suggesting I should have to put up with this discomfort? And that it's not their responsibility to change to suit me?'

This leads to a discussion of what was rational versus irrational. They agree that 'I would prefer not to suffer discomfort and that other people should change to suit me, but "Hello, life!"' would be a more rational belief.

Michael began to see the humour in the situation. 'You would like me to understand that I am expecting the world to change to suit me,' he says, 'but in real life, this is unlikely to happen.'

Dr Jim agrees.

'But that doesn't sort out my dilemma,' says Michael. 'In fact, I feel even more frustrated that I must return tomorrow to face the same difficulties.'

'Don't worry,' reassures Dr Jim. 'I have a simple solution to your current situation.'

Michael is puzzled. 'I can't wait to hear it.'

'This evening, I want you to write out a letter of resignation to the company,' answers Dr Jim, with a twinkle in his eye.

Michael is completely taken aback. 'But why would I do that?' he asks.

'Well, you have explained how impossible the situation at work is and how you just can't stand it. This is the only possible solution to getting rid of your discomfort. You will no longer have to face your manager or co-workers, or any of that hassle. Neither will you have to deal with those mundane tasks.'

'But what will I do instead?' Michael enquires. 'And what about the bills and the mortgage? How will I cope with no money coming in?'

'But this would sort out your immediate concerns,' answers Dr Jim. 'You wouldn't suffer any further discomfort in the short term. There would, of course, be some long-term difficulties, such as the ones you have detailed, but your current trials would be over.'

Michael begins to understand. 'You are suggesting that I can't have it both ways.'

Dr Jim agrees.

This leads to a discussion about frustration tolerance, how those with low frustration tolerance sought long-term gain but wanted to dodge short-term pain. 'There is one important question to ask yourself, Michael, when feeling frustrated about anything,' explains Dr Jim. '"What discomfort am I trying to dodge?" So, how could you apply this concept to your present situation?'

'I suppose I am trying to dodge the hassle of looking for a new job,' Michael answers. 'Instead of insisting my work colleagues change, it is up to me to make things happen.'

'What, then, should your long-term gain be?'

'That I find myself in a new job, in which I am challenged but in a more positive working environment.'

'And what will be the short-term pain?'

'I suppose staying where I am until I find a suitable alternative,' replies Michael.

'And what are the long-term gains of this decision?'

'I would have a place to go, money coming in to pay the bills and time to seek out an alternative.'

Dr Jim sees that Michael is grasping the message. 'In life, we all would like to dodge discomfort. It would be wonderful if people and situations changed to suit us.' They both agree with a laugh that this was not going to happen any time soon! Dr Jim also explains how learning the skill of managing discomfort in his life would ensure Michael became more emotionally resilient. Dr Jim then suggests some frustration exercises to achieve this objective.

For Michael, these are a game-changer. He begins to perform the first frustration exercise detailed above, finding multiple opportunities to challenge himself at home and at work. The coin exercise, in turn, teaches him how to manage frustration in his everyday life. He accepts that this was how he had lived his life to date, always looking for the quick fix, always looking for others to change. At the heart of it all was Michael not wanting to put up with the discomfort of having to change matters himself.

He begins in earnest to challenge his demand that the world must change to suit him and thus his behaviour alters at work and at home. Because of this, he begins to interact better with work colleagues and his manager, and starts to find his current job less stressful. He is still bothered about the mundane nature of his employment, but he begins to accept that it is paying the bills.

Michael also starts attending a night course to upgrade his skills. One year later, he transfers to a larger company, where he finds himself constantly challenged and fulfilled. The increased salary is a welcome bonus. More importantly, he has become increasingly emotionally resilient. He has finally come to accept that life is indeed full of discomfort and dodging it is no longer an option. His new mantra had become 'Short-term pain, long-term gain'.

Key Learning Points

1. Discomfort is part of life and something we must all learn to deal with. Trying to avoid this reality can lead to intense frustration and unhealthy behaviour patterns, such as intolerance and road rage.
2. Underlying frustration is the unhealthy demand that situations, people and life must change so that we do not have to suffer discomfort.
3. Learning to accept the concept of short-term pain for long-term gain is the shortcut to learning how to manage discomfort.
4. Some simple frustration exercises can teach us how to achieve this goal.

7. SKILL FIVE

HOW TO COPE WITH BOTH FAILURE AND SUCCESS

'If you can meet with Triumph and Disaster
And treat those two impostors just the same'
RUDYARD KIPLING, 'If—'

Why Is this Skill Important?

We all fail in life. Most of us do so regularly and, on occasion, spectacularly! Failure is an innate part of living, but we often struggle to cope with this reality. After many years of assisting people with mental health conditions, it has become increasingly obvious to me how essential this skill is. Inability to cope with failure regularly underlies anxiety, depression, self-harm, eating disorders and addiction.

Success, equally, presents its own set of difficulties. Many of us assume that being successful protects us from the realities of life. In practice, it doesn't. Paradoxically, it can trigger similar mental health conditions as failure. Some might succumb to anxiety. Depression is quite common, as is addiction. Many misuse or abuse alcohol, substances or gamble to withstand the pressure of staying at the top. When depression and addiction combine in such situations, self-destruction sadly and inevitably follows.

Underlying personal failure and success is the world of rating. When we fail in any aspect of life, whether it is in academia, sport, relationships, business or professionally, many of us rate ourselves as failures. This can lead to a second assumption that others will also rate us as failures. Similarly, when successful, we rate ourselves as a success, assuming others will hold similar opinions. This puts us under pressure to continue performing at unrealistically high levels.

This tendency to rate oneself as a success or failure underlies many of the difficulties besetting modern life. With the advent of social media, both success and failure are rapidly and exponentially exaggerated. The consequences are to be seen at all ages, but most significantly in our children and adolescents, who are being brainwashed into believing that success should be the only goal, with failure something to be dreaded.

This has led to an epidemic of anxiety and depression in these age groups, along with concomitant self-harm, addiction and misuse of substances. If you believe 'I am a failure' when things go wrong, or 'I am a success' when they go well, disaster beckons. Both place intolerable stress on your mental health.

All of us struggle with success and failure, because the rating game is now an integral part of modern life. Those who can challenge these two 'impostors', putting them firmly back in their box, will discover the challenges of life easier to handle. If your goal is emotional resilience, this skill is essential.

Failing versus Failure

Firstly, let's explore the concept of failing at something versus being a failure as a person – that if you are not successful at a task you have set yourself, then you are a failure. Suppose you are struggling to conceive a child, as is the case for one in six couples. Once again you attempt IVF, but sadly it results in another miscarriage. This is the scenario facing many couples. They become extremely anxious. Underlying this is the belief that they must conceive and have a child, and are failures if they can't.

When we explore this belief, it is completely irrational. The first part of the demand suggests we can control all factors leading to the arrival of a healthy baby into our lives. However, like most of life, we cannot control the multiple factors underlying this process. As we discussed in Chapter 5, the chapter on uncertainty, there will always be an element of uncertainty whether we can achieve this or any other goal set in life.

The second part of the demand suggests the belief that one can be considered a failure at all. Can a human being be a failure? Of course not. But many of us fall into the trap of believing this to be possible. As we explored in Chapter 3, the chapter on unconditional self-acceptance, a human being is far too complex, special and unique to be rated. When we call ourselves failures, this is exactly what we are doing. Calling myself a failure implies that I, as a human being, can be described as such.

Let's return to the concept of the Members Only club detailed in Chapter 3. You may remember the important criteria for membership:

1. We are not allowed to rate ourselves as human beings.
2. We are not allowed to accept others' ratings of us as human beings.
3. We can rate our behaviour (which includes our skills), but not ourselves.

By becoming a member, we separate who we are as human beings from our behaviour. So, we cannot regard ourselves as failures as this would imply human beings can be rated. Neither can we allow others to rate us as failures, for the same reason. We and others can, however, rate our behaviour and our skills.

If someone has set their heart on having a child, and an IVF intervention is not successful, then technically that person has failed at this task on this occasion. But there are other factors involved, out of their control, which will decide if they are successful at this or any other task. This does not mean they are a failure as a person, as many end up believing. Rather that they are a special, unique person who, often with the assistance of a loving partner, has attempted a procedure which has failed on this occasion.

The Skill of Managing Failure

We can fail at something, but we can never be a failure as a person. This is a critical distinction. If you fail at a task, you have been unsuccessful, on this particular occasion, in achieving your objective. The further implication is that you can try, on subsequent occasions, to reach your goal. That is what happens in real life.

Few top business people or sportspeople reach their goal without travelling the long, arduous road of repeated failure. In the USA, for example, the heads of most successful companies can relate to this reality. Many have clambered back to their feet after bankruptcy to try again. Similarly, with great sportspeople, many experience humiliating failures before achieving that elusive gold medal or trophy.

Having had the privilege of meeting some of those sportspeople, the message conveyed to me was simple: the only failure is not getting back up again. Therein lies an important lesson about how best to deal with failure. As human beings, our only task is to do our best in relation to our skills and behaviour. We will fail, and we will do so regularly. But this should form part of a learning process that assists us to finally achieve whatever our desired goal is. If we adapt our attitude, accepting that we cannot control the variables but persisting nevertheless, we will often succeed. This, of course, is one of the real secrets to emotional resilience.

Successful versus Success

What about success? Many top celebrities and sportspeople encounter the same difficulties as those who regard themselves as failures. If you believe 'I am a success', the implication is that 'you' are the one who is a success. This is a personal rating where you are rating yourself, highly. This puts huge pressure on you, the person. You now see yourself only through the eyes of success, and you assume others see you likewise.

For this high rating to be maintained, you must continue to be successful. But what happens when you struggle to stay at the top? You will now think positively or negatively about yourself depending on whether you, at that moment in time, are successful or failing. If failing, you fall back into the belief 'I am a failure' and feel badly about yourself. If successful, you are elated by how wonderful 'I am', which is equally unhealthy. The pressure of remaining at this impossibly high level eventually leads to the consequences outlined at the beginning of this chapter.

The Skill of Managing Success

If you are struggling with success, join me in the Members Only club. Just as with failure, membership of this club means we are banned from rating ourselves as a success, because this is a form of self-rating. We are permitted, however, to rate our behaviour or skills as being successful, and we are allowed to work on both our skills and our behaviour so that we can attain whatever levels we hope to achieve in an activity or sport. As part of this club, we can also constantly reassess our behaviour in terms of the 'cost' of achieving our objectives. This can often lead to reappraisal of whether such a cost is worth it in the long run, or if it is too high in terms of our mental and physical health. This is how we teach ourselves to deal with the world of success.

How to Practise this Skill

Coping with Failure Exercise
If you are struggling to come to terms with failure in your life, I suggest the following exercise:

1. For the next two months, I want you to carry a notebook around with you.
2. Anytime something happens which triggers the thought that you are a failure, write down in your notebook what the trigger was (what did you fail at?), your emotional response (usually anxiety or depression) and your rating of yourself.
3. It may be that you do not do as well in an exam or project as you had expected, you make an error at work, you struggle in a relationship, you feel you are a bad parent or you fail at sport. The list of possible opportunities is endless, as we all fail regularly, in so many aspects of our lives.
4. Later, when you have some free time, take out your notebook and begin on paper to challenge the belief that you are a failure.
5. Begin with the question: 'Do you regard yourself as a failure as a person because you failed in this task?' If the answer is yes, ask yourself: 'On what

grounds can you or any other human being be regarded as a failure? Is this not another form of rating?' Examine the rules of the Members Only club again. Very quickly, you will see that you may have failed at a task, but you cannot be a failure as a person.

Now focus on the effort put into achieving your goal and rate yourself on this, rather than on the result. Once freed from the burden of rating yourself as a person, you can accept that on this occasion your efforts were unsuccessful.

You can then concentrate on the last link in the chain. How you can improve your skills or behaviour to achieve your stated objective. In other words, it's time to get up and try again.

Coping with Success Exercise

If you are struggling to deal with success in any area of your life, I suggest you carry out the following exercise:

1. For the next two months, I want you to carry a notebook around with you.
2. Anytime something happens which triggers the thought that you are a success, write down in your notebook the trigger (what were you successful at?), your emotional response (usually anxiety) and your rating of yourself.
3. It may be that you are extremely successful academically or that you are a top athlete, sportsperson, musician or business person. But now you feel under extreme pressure to maintain the often impossibly high levels expected by both yourself and others.
4. Later, when you have some free time, take out your notebook and begin on paper to challenge the belief that you are a success.
5. Begin with the question: 'Do you regard yourself as a success as a person because you were successful in the area in question?' If the answer is yes, ask yourself: 'On what grounds can you or any other human being be regarded as a success? Is this not another form of rating? And one that is putting you under extreme pressure?' Examine the rules of the Members Only club again. Very quickly, you will see that you can be successful at a skill or task, but you cannot be a success as a person.

Now focus on the effort put into achieving your goal and rate yourself on this, rather than on the result. Once freed from the burden of rating yourself as a person, you can accept that, on this occasion, your efforts were successful.

Finally, this frees you to explore the cost of achieving these elevated goals and assess whether you are comfortable with paying this price for continued success in your skill or career. Some may be happy to do so. Others, on reflection, may decide that they are no longer content to do so. The choice is yours. If the price of remaining at a high level of achievement (whether in academia, sport or your career) is the destruction of your mental health, then you should strongly review your current situation.

By performing these exercises repeatedly over a two-month period, you will learn how to separate who you are as a person from your success or failure at a specific task or skill, and begin to treat the twin impostors of success and failure with the disdain they both deserve!

SIMON'S STORY

Simon is a twenty-seven-year-old man who has been referred to Dr Jim following a serious self-harm episode, triggered by his girlfriend Jane ending their three-year relationship. A highly successful businessman, his world came crashing down when poor investments made during a boom period failed badly, putting him under significant financial pressure.

Simon is a high-flier. He has always made the right choices in business and has always been equally successful in his relationships. But for the first time in his young life, failure has entered his world.

When Jane entered his life at twenty-four, all was rosy. The future was bright. But within two years, his financial affairs fell into crisis. As the stress built, he became irritable and difficult to live with. Thus began a pattern of rows, followed by apologies, followed by further rows. Jane, although she loves Simon, has run out of road and broken off the relationship. His world has imploded. He has begun to drink more and isolates himself from friends and family.

Underlying this is his sense of absolute failure. How could he have allowed matters to come to this? He, who has been so successful, has now failed totally in business and in love. Things come to a head and, one night following a heavy binge, Simon takes a serious overdose. Only an unexpected visit from a family member prevents a tragedy.

Dr Jim empathises with his story and feels that Simon's inability to cope with failure underlies his difficulties. He suggests that some CBT techniques might be of assistance and Simon agrees. Dr Jim then explains what rational and irrational beliefs are and how they will use the ABC concept to locate them. They decide to use the breakdown of his relationship as the trigger. 'And how did this make you feel emotionally?' Dr Jim asks.

'I felt very depressed,' Simon replies.

'How did this make you feel physically?'

'Extremely fatigued.'

'And what was it about Jane leaving you that made you feel depressed?'

'I felt such a failure,' he says. 'Not only had I made a mess businesswise, but I had pushed away the one person who cared about me.' He adds: 'All my life, I have been successful. They called me the man with the golden touch. Look at me now, "The man even his girlfriend does not want to touch!" I am just a loser.'

'And what did you do when you became depressed about the breakdown?' asks Dr Jim.

'I just fell to pieces, drank like a fish, cut myself off from everybody and couldn't get out of my own head. I was beating myself up mercilessly,' Simon replies. 'Finally, I just wanted to end it all.'

'So now let's examine what irrational belief was triggered by this situation and the interpretation you assigned to it,' says Dr Jim.

After some discussion, Simon decides that it was his belief that he was a failure that was really triggering his emotion of depression, and Dr Jim agrees.

They then put together the following ABC:

A   Activating Event:
  - Trigger: his girlfriend, Jane, leaving him
  - Inference/danger: he is a failure in business and in his relationship

B   Belief/Demands: 'Because I have failed in business and in my relationship, I am a failure.'

C   Consequences:
  - Emotional reactions: depression
  - Physical reactions: fatigue
  - Behaviour: drinks excessively; ruminates constantly about being a failure; withdraws socially; attempts self-harm

'So now that we understand, Simon, what made you so depressed about this situation, let's assist you in reshaping your thinking and behaviour in relation to it. Because if we're successful in this instance, we can apply the same concepts to similar situations in the future,' says Dr Jim.

'We could dispute or challenge your "A", or your interpretation,' Dr Jim explains, 'but it's more effective to challenge your "B", or your irrational belief, and your behaviour.' Dr Jim asks Simon to consider how withdrawing socially, drinking excessively or attempting self-harm, for example, could advance the situation.

Simon agrees that they could not, and so he and Dr Jim explore some healthier alternatives.

'Let's now examine and challenge your irrational belief,' says Dr Jim. 'This took the form of an absolute belief that, due to your relationship breaking down, you are a failure. Is this belief rational or irrational?'

Simon feels it is quite rational. 'Am I not a living embodiment of the word "failure"?' he asks.

'But suppose I told you it is completely irrational?' queries Dr Jim.

Simon is puzzled: 'But am I not a failure because my relationship has failed?'

Dr Jim asks Simon to fill in the rating scale laid out in Chapter 3, the chapter on self-acceptance. As expected, his rating is quite low. Dr Jim then asks: 'Can a human being be rated? Where's the measuring tool?'

After some discussion, Simon agrees that there is no such tool. Dr Jim then introduces him to the Members Only club. 'This is a highly exclusive club. There are three important criteria for membership:

1.   We are not allowed to rate ourselves as human beings.
2.   We are not allowed to accept others' ratings of us as human beings.
3.   We can rate our behaviour (which includes our skills), but not ourselves.

'With this concept in mind,' says Dr Jim, 'can a human being be defined as a failure?'

Simon struggles with this question, so Dr Jim introduces him to his inner pathological critic, which we also discussed in Chapter 3. He explains to Simon how this voice is dominating his emotional mind. Simon begins to grasp the power of his inner emotional world to influence his thinking and behaviour. It is his pathological critic convincing him to define himself as a failure.

This leads to a discussion of the reality of success and failure.

'What you are suggesting is that I cannot be a failure or a success as a person. But I can fail or be successful at some task or skill?'

Dr Jim agrees. 'We can be successful at a specific moment in time, in achieving our goal of being a good business person, performer, sportsperson, and so on. But we cannot be defined as a success as a human being, as this is a form of rating. And the same goes for failure. It is also important to accept that we all fail regularly, and that this is a part of life.'

This is a watershed moment for Simon. He realises that he has fallen into the trap of rating himself as a success or failure, rather than rating his skills and behaviour. 'But how can I change?' he asks.

Dr Jim suggests that for the following three months, Simon carries a notebook around with him and performs the exercise described earlier in this chapter. Simon proceeds to do this, and finds it transformative. He is especially empowered by the concept that the only failure is not getting back up again.

Because of this exercise, and following further visits with Dr Jim, Simon becomes determined to get back on his feet and restart his life. He restructures his portfolio and, over time, significantly improves his financial situation. More importantly, following a long conversation with Jane, with whom he shares his newly found insights into success and failure, they decide to reignite their relationship. Two years later, they are happily married and Jane is expecting their first child.

Key Learning Points

1. Learning how to manage failure in life is one of the most important emotional resilience skills to develop. This is because failure is an integral part of life.
2. The key to managing failure is to accept that we can fail at some task or skill or activity or career at any moment in time, but that we cannot be a failure as a person, as this is a form of rating. The only real failure in life is not getting back up again to have another shot at whatever it is we failed at.
3. Learning how to cope with success in life is also a key skill to develop. This is because success appeals to our ego and can become addictive, but the cost of staying at the top in any area can be high.
4. The key to managing success is to accept that we can be successful at a skill or task or activity or career at a moment in time, but that we cannot be a success as a person, as this is a form of rating. We must also learn to constantly re-evaluate the price of remaining at the top.

8. SKILL SIX

HOW TO CHALLENGE
CATASTROPHISING
The Worst-case Scenario

Why Is this Skill Important?

We all, on occasion, catastrophise about possible negative outcomes in life situations. This involves visualising the worst-case scenario, convincing ourselves this will inevitably occur. At the same time we assume that if this scenario were to happen we would simply be unable to cope.

Our rational brain, especially the right prefrontal cortex, developed over aeons the ability to project forward and explore negative scenarios that could arise, if certain courses of action were undertaken. This has been of great evolutionary value in the past, in predicting and avoiding potential dangers that might occur. But what happens when this useful ability to visualise such scenarios develops a life of its own?

This is what happens when we regularly catastrophise. It usually takes the form of a cascade of progressively negative thoughts, leading to the person becoming increasingly anxious. Let's take the example of Paul: Paul, who constantly catastrophises, is informed that somebody close to him has developed cancer. The 'washing machine' in his head turns on and the negative catastrophic cascade begins. 'Maybe I am next. I can see myself requiring surgery. Maybe I will need chemotherapy or even radiotherapy, like Vincent. I will be constantly sick. What will happen to the children if I end up dying? Julie will struggle to bring them up on her own. It is going to be so sad. Just awful!'

From a mental health perspective, such a catastrophic thinking cascade is most commonly associated with anxiety conditions such as general anxiety.

An example is health phobia. Many people with this condition spend their lives catastrophising how awful it would be if they were to develop a major illness. One interesting study by Gautreau et al. (2015) showed the catastrophising of bodily or physical symptoms over time was what drove health anxiety. In this scenario we become anxious, develop the physical symptoms of anxiety as laid out in Chapter 4, and then begin to catastrophise about them, thus creating a vicious cycle. It is also frequently present in depression and toxic stress. Learning the skill of challenging catastrophising can be life-altering for those with these conditions. We can all can benefit from developing this skill.

Life is stressful. There will be occasions where your inner reserves will be seriously challenged. You may become toxically stressed, which can trigger a bout of catastrophising, which in turn might lead to anxiety. Those who have developed and practised this skill will cope better with such stressful periods and are generally more emotionally resilient.

How to Challenge Catastrophising

First, let's revisit the world of the emotional brain versus the logical brain. For decades, we have known that the emotional side of the brain is more powerful than the rational one. It comes as little surprise, therefore, that your emotional mind is also more powerful than your rational mind. Imagine passing your favourite fast-food restaurant while struggling with your weight. Your rational mind will argue that a takeaway is going to worsen the situation. Your emotional mind is smelling the delicious aromas emanating from the restaurant. Which wins? It is usually your emotional mind.

When your emotional mind catastrophises about something that might happen in the future, it is like a dog with a bone. It simply won't stop chewing on the bone, defying all attempts made by your rational mind to switch it off. This is the scenario facing someone who is constantly anxious through persistent catastrophising. The negative thinking cascades continue unabated.

To change this pattern, we must allow the rational mind to become more involved in analysing the accuracy of the frequently erroneous conclusions of the emotional mind. This is the concept underlying the following exercise.

The Spilt Milk Exercise

Imagine a glass of milk in front of you on the table. What would you visualise if I said 'spilt milk'? Most of us immediately visualise a complete mess, with milk all over the place. We may even visualise the smell of it if it's not cleaned up quickly. But suppose I asked you to tip the glass gently so a simple drop of milk appeared on the table. Is this not spilt milk, too?

This tendency for the emotional mind to visualise spilt milk as a complete mess is, on occasion, endemic in us all. But for the person who catastrophises, all they will see is a puddle. Their emotional mind can only visualise a mess. Their rational mind, which might have suggested the possibility of a drop, is silenced. With this concept in mind, let's challenge catastrophising using the following steps:

1. For the next eight weeks, I want you to carry a notebook around with you.
2. Anytime something negative happens and you find yourself catastrophising, with a cascade of worst-case-scenario thoughts, write down the trigger and the content of these thoughts in your notebook.
3. Later, when you have some free time, take out your notebook and write down one by one on paper the catastrophic conclusions you arrived at.
4. Then challenge on paper the accuracy of each catastrophic conclusion. Where is your absolute proof that this is going to happen? Unless you can prove on paper that this catastrophic thought is true, then it is only a drop of spilt milk and not a puddle.
5. You will quickly note just how difficult it will be to prove that these thoughts are true, and how rarely there will be evidence of a puddle.

Writing such thoughts down *on paper* allows you to extract them from your emotional mind. The action also has the secondary effect of allowing your rational mind the opportunity to properly analyse their content. Many people, in my experience, are shocked on seeing their catastrophic thoughts on paper. 'I didn't actually write that down' is often the stunned reaction. 'I cannot believe that I was accepting such conclusions. They don't make sense!'

This is because your rational mind is a pragmatic person when allowed to assess situations, quite dispassionate in his analysis, often presenting a completely different perspective. When something is written down on paper, he becomes rapidly engaged in such analysis.

Putting the Exercise into Practice

Suppose you were someone with a health phobia, like Paul, whom we met at the beginning of the chapter. Having written down your cascade of catastrophic thoughts in your notebook, you would later peruse them, one by one, challenging their veracity. Can you prove on paper that the content of each thought is true? Can you, for example, prove on paper that just because your friend developed cancer the same will happen to you? Where is your evidence? Have you attended a specialist, who has performed tests and informed you that this is the case? Even if you developed cancer, where is your proof that you would need surgery or chemotherapy? Or that you would inevitably die and leave your children without a father?

You will rapidly discover that proving on paper the veracity of any of these catastrophic conclusions is impossible. Your rational mind will, one by one, discard them as unfounded. If you develop the skill of writing down and challenging such thoughts in this manner, your catastrophic thinking will slowly but surely begin to fade away. You will need to practise this exercise repeatedly, even for the simplest of everyday occurrences. Everything that triggers such a cascade must be written down and challenged, until it becomes automatic for you to rationalise such thoughts.

If you practise this skill repeatedly over several months, you will observe how you are soon catching and challenging these thoughts in your head before they grow wings. Your reward will be a significant reduction in anxiety levels and a more pragmatic approach to bad news. You will also become increasingly emotionally resilient and able to manage stressful situations in your life.

PHILIP'S STORY

Philip grew up in a household where both his parents were extremely anxious. His father was especially prone to catastrophising. By his teens and early twenties, Philip found himself falling into a similar pattern. He became increasingly anxious, with catastrophic thinking.

Now in his mid-forties, he is married, with several children, and is managing a major retail outlet. Following a stressful period at work, he experiences the physical symptoms of general anxiety in the form of significant fatigue. His GP recommends some time off work. His occupational health department subsequently refers him to Dr Jim.

Philip reveals to Dr Jim that he is constantly consumed by thoughts that something terrible is going to happen. 'I am just exhausted by these thoughts,' he explains. 'I relate them back to my upbringing. My father was especially anxious and a worrier, like me.'

Dr Jim empathises, agreeing that this tendency to catastrophise may have stemmed from Philip's upbringing, but suggests some CBT exercises might be of assistance. He then explains what rational and irrational beliefs are and how they will use the ABC concept to locate them.

Dr Jim asks for an example of a recent situation which has triggered Philip's catastrophising. 'I got a call last Thursday morning from my manager to attend a meeting with him later that day,' replies Philip.

'And how did that affect you emotionally?' asks Dr Jim.

'I became extremely anxious.'

'And physically?'

Philip says his stomach was in knots, he had difficulty taking a deep breath, his heart started beating a little faster, he was shaking, his muscles tensed up, and his fatigue increased significantly. 'I also had a real sense of dread,' he adds.

'So now we have the trigger, the emotion and how it made you feel physically,' says Dr Jim, 'but what is it about you having to present yourself for this meeting that made you feel so anxious? What danger were you assigning to it?'

'I felt like my whole world was about to implode,' he replies. 'There could only be one reason for such a call. To inform me of some major error at work. I could see it happening before my eyes. My job was at risk. What would I do if I was let go? I would be unable to pay my bills. The house would be at risk. How would I tell my wife, Maura? And as for the children . . .'

'So now let's examine what irrational belief was triggered by this situation and the danger you assigned to it,' says Dr Jim. 'This usually takes the form of some absolute demand you are making about the trigger. So, what demand were you making of yourself after this request to meet the boss?'

After some discussion, they agree his demand was that he must not lose his job and that, if he did, he would be a failure for letting it happen.

'And what was your behaviour when you became anxious after this phone call?' asks Dr Jim. Philip admits to seeking reassurance from work colleagues; checking back over his previous month's work, looking for evidence of errors; ringing his wife, who tried to calm him down; and constantly worrying and catastrophising about how awful it would be if he was let go.

Dr Jim and Philip then put together the following ABC:

A   Activating Event:
- Trigger: telephone call from head office requesting he attends meeting with boss
- Inference/danger: he has made some major error at work; as a result, he is going to be let go; if this happens, he will be unable to meet his financial commitments; he may not be able to hold on to his house and may end up homeless; his wife and children would suffer as a result

B   Belief/Demands: 'I must not lose my job. If this happens, I am a failure for letting it happen.'

C   Consequences:
- Emotional reactions: anxiety
- Physical reactions: stomach in knots, difficulty taking a deep breath, heart beating a little faster, shaking, muscle tension, significantly increased fatigue
- Behaviour: goes back over his previous month's work, seeking out

evidence of mistakes; seeks reassurance from work colleagues and wife; spends hours replaying numerous visualised scenarios in his mind if worst fears are realised

'So now that we understand, Philip, what made you so anxious about this situation, let's help you to reshape your thinking and behaviour in relation to it. Because if we're successful in this instance, we can apply the same concepts to similar situations in the future,' says Dr Jim.

He continues: 'We could dispute or challenge your "A", or your interpretation of the telephone call from head office. We could probably dispute whether there was proof that you were going to be fired. But what is more effective is to challenge your irrational belief and behaviour.'

First, Dr Jim and Philip discuss how to manage the physical symptoms of anxiety using flooding techniques, which we explored in Chapter 4. Dr Jim also takes him through the unhealthy behaviours they have uncovered and how to challenge them. They agree that spending hours checking back on his previous month's work and seeking reassurance from colleagues and his wife is destined to make him feel more anxious.

'Let's now examine and challenge your "B", or your irrational belief,' says Dr Jim. 'This took the form of an absolute demand that you must not lose your job. Is this demand rational or irrational, Philip?'

Philip agrees that it was probably irrational.

Dr Jim then asks, 'What would be a healthier demand?'

After some discussion, they agree a more rational or healthier demand might be that he would prefer not to lose his job, but this was out of his control.

This leads to a discussion on the importance of control in Philip's life. They focus especially on his difficulties in dealing with uncertainty. Dr Jim suggests that Philip performs the coin exercise described in Chapter 5 to help him manage this. They also discuss his belief that he would be a failure if he were to lose his job. Can any human being be defined in such terms? Dr Jim introduces Philip to the Members Only club, and he is more than happy to join.

Dr Jim then focuses on Philip's tendency to catastrophise. 'Which is more powerful,' Dr Jim asks, 'your emotional or logical mind?'

'I assume your logical mind,' replies Philip.

'That is what many assume, but in real life the emotional mind is much more powerful than the logical mind.' Dr Jim then gives examples of this in practice. Next, he asks, 'What do you visualise when I say "spilt milk"?'

Philip answers with a laugh: 'A complete mess. I have spilt milk myself on many occasions, and I can confirm that it goes all over the place.'

'But suppose I told you that it could also be just a drop of spilt milk?' says Dr Jim. 'That is what we do in our emotional mind. We assume it is a mess without considering other possibilities.'

Philip can see where this is going: 'You mean our emotional mind will always assume the worst without proof to the contrary? But how can we stop this from happening if it is such a strong tendency?'

Dr Jim suggests the best way to counteract the power of the emotional brain is to write down the cascade of catastrophic thoughts and challenge them on paper. 'If something is going on in your emotional mind, the rational mind struggles to get in on the action,' he explains. 'When we write it down on paper, our rational mind is engaged. It can now challenge the content and conclusions of such thoughts.'

Philip begins to understand. 'So you would then apply the spilt milk analogy to what you have written?'

Dr Jim agrees. 'Unless you can prove on paper that the catastrophic conclusions you have come to are true, it is only a drop of spilt milk.'

Together, they apply this approach to the various catastrophic thoughts Philip had assigned to the meeting in the run-up to going to see his boss at head office. When examined on paper, Philip can immediately see there was no proof that any of these things were going to happen. 'So, I assumed it was going to be a puddle of spilt milk,' he laughs, 'but it was only a drop.' He then reveals that his boss had simply wanted to congratulate him on a work project he had been engaged in, where an important customer had commented positively on his efforts. 'I felt so stupid afterwards,' Philip admits. 'All of that worry with no basis whatsoever for my panic.'

Dr Jim suggests that Philip carries a notebook around with him for the next month or two. If anything triggers a cascade of catastrophic thoughts, he is to note the trigger and include a brief description of the thoughts. Later, when he has some free time, he should sift through the content of the thoughts written down and challenge them on paper. Where is his evidence that they are true? If he cannot prove on paper that his catastrophising is true, then once again it is only a drop of spilt milk and not a puddle.

Philip carries out this exercise over the following months. Gradually, he begins to recognise and challenge the thoughts in his mind before writing them down. Slowly but surely, his tendency to catastrophise diminishes. His anxiety and stress levels significantly reduce. His emotional resilience to managing stress soars.

Key Learning Points

1. Our emotional mind is more powerful than our logical mind, so if we begin to regularly catastrophise or visualise the worst-case scenario, our lives can turn into a constant battle with anxiety.
2. This can lead to a catastrophic cascade of thoughts every time something negative happens in our life.
3. We can learn to decrease this tendency by writing down and challenging the veracity of each catastrophic cascade conclusion.
4. This is best done by practising the spilt milk exercise, where we must decide in each case whether the thought is a drop or a puddle of spilt milk.

9. SKILL SEVEN

HOW TO CHALLENGE PERFECTIONISM
When 99 Per Cent Is Not Enough

Why Is this Skill Important?

It is healthy to set reasonable, achievable goals. It is also completely acceptable to set high standards and to strive to reach them. Athletes, footballers, rugby players and golfers set such standards, sacrificing much to achieve them. So, too, do those who work in creative, artistic worlds, such as writers, artists and musicians. If our goal is to improve our skills, then striving to attain high standards is both healthy and admirable.

But what happens when we set impossible personal goals and standards? Or identify ourselves with the achievement of such goals? This is the world of the perfectionist, a world in which their sense of themselves is intrinsically bound up with achieving those standards. Perfectionism is not just an ideal, but a way of life. The consequences of living a life where everything must match up to some personally created, impossible-to-achieve standard can be devastating.

Perfectionism has as much to do with our thinking as our behaviour. It can take many forms. Some people may be obsessed with achieving perfection in relation to their physical body. The modern obsession among young men of seeking a perfectly toned muscular body is a good example of this. This has led to the misuse of anabolic steroids, which is neither healthy nor desirable. Others seek perfection in their facial appearance or body shape. Social media, with its emphasis on superficial looks, has added to the pressure of having to present the perfect body, face, clothes and, indeed, life. Our obsession with Botox, plastic surgery and the whole cosmetic industry feeds into this demand for perfection. We are a long way from being comfortable in our own skin.

For others, perfectionism takes a different form. It may be related to achieving impossible demands academically, artistically or on the sports field, where our rating of ourselves is totally dependent on achieving these standards. The annual anxiety epidemic before major state-education and university exams is experienced not just by those anxious they might fail, but also by high achievers seeking perfection. Perfectionism may relate to your home or it might find expression in the workplace. While employers might see this as an admirable trait, the cost of achieving this objective can be high.

Perfectionism exacts a heavy toll on our mental health. It can also lurk behind depression, especially among high achievers. This is not surprising, since depression is associated with relentless, negative self-rating. If you base your sense of yourself on whether you can achieve some impossibly high standards, then trouble may be lurking around the corner.

Perfectionism is also a common theme underlying general anxiety, at the core of which is a tendency to make impossible personal demands and rate ourselves as failures when we can't achieve them. Since perfectionists apply a demand for total perfection to some or all aspects of their lives and rate themselves as failures if they can't match up, anxiety is almost an inevitable consequence. Recent research data by Handley et al. (2014) has consolidated the links between general anxiety, pathological worry and perfectionism. Perfectionism-driven anxiety and low mood are also often found lurking behind self-harm in adolescents and young adults.

A potentially serious form of perfectionism is the demand for the perfect body image, which underlies eating disorders such as anorexia nervosa and bulimia. The consequences can be tragic. Anorexia nervosa has one of the highest rates of suicide of all mental health conditions. Recent research (Riley et al., 2017) has consolidated the strong links between perfectionism, demands for control and eating disorders.

There is also recent evidence (Smith et al., 2017) consolidating the links between perfectionism and risks of self-harm and suicide. This meta-analysis was one of the most comprehensive studies to date on the subject and identified some of the typical characteristics of the perfectionist such as over-striving, constant self-criticism, periods of intense psychological pain and a constant struggle to deal with failure. These go some way towards explaining the links with suicidal ideation. The research also noted that those perfectionists who feel the weight of other people's expectations were most at risk.

Learning how to combat perfectionism can be a useful skill for all of us to acquire. There can be an underlying whiff of perfectionism to each of us. It may appear in different forms, whether to do with home, work, sport or social media. How many are obsessed, for example, with presenting the perfect image and life online through various social media platforms? A significant proportion of the population rates themselves if their social media world is not perfect in their eyes or in the eyes of others. Nowhere is this more prevalent than in the adolescent population. They have been brainwashed into believing that perfection is something achievable and worth striving for.

How to Challenge Perfectionism

There are two core elements to perfectionism.

1. The first element is a demand for absolute or 100 per cent perfection in some or all aspects of our lives. This is, of course, a completely unachievable goal.
2. The second element is an irrational belief that we are a failure if we cannot achieve this demand. Many perfectionists rate themselves very highly, sometimes as high as 99 per cent on the rating scale we discussed in Chapter 3. If they cannot stay at this high level, they consider themselves a failure.

If you are struggling to deal with perfectionism, both this demand and this belief must be challenged.

How to Challenge the Worlds of Rating and Failure

In Chapter 3, we explored the skill of how to challenge the belief that a human being can be rated at all. This involves developing unconditional self-acceptance by becoming a member of the Members Only club. For those who live in the world of perfectionism, this represents a significant challenge, often because of their excessively high self-rating.

The key is to accept that we can rate our behaviour or skills, but not ourselves as human beings. If you are someone who 'lives for your rating', it can be humbling to learn that you are actually just one of us! This implies that you are not perfect, and that you will mess up, like we all do, and regularly struggle to achieve targeted goals.

We also dealt with the concept of failure in Chapter 7, and that while we can fail at an activity or goal, we cannot be failures as people, as this is a form of rating. If you can learn to let go of self-rating, accept yourself unconditionally and cease to believe that you can ever be a failure as a person, the mental health benefits that you reap will be immense. For those struggling with perfectionism who live for their rating or struggle with failure, I suggest you revisit the relevant chapters.

How to Challenge Your Demand for Perfection

For the rest of this section, we are going to focus on the skill of managing your demand for 100 per cent perfection. This demand and the concomitant unhealthy behaviours are stubbornly resistant to change. Both will need to be challenged in your everyday life. This will involve developing increased awareness of how much you seek absolute perfection in different aspects of your life, and your tendency to seek out imperfections, ignoring all of the positives. To identify and challenge this demand for 100 per cent perfection, I recommend the following two exercises.

The Perfection Exercise
1. For the next two months, carry a notebook around with you.
2. Each time you notice yourself seeking absolute perfection in relation to any aspect of your life, however insignificant, write down the trigger, your emotions (usually anxiety, frustration or depression) and your perfectionist demand. Also note any unhealthy resulting behaviours.

3. Later, when you have some free time, I want you to challenge on paper your demand for total or 100 per cent perfection. Is such a demand achievable in any area of life, when rationally analysed on paper? Are you only seeking out imperfections, ignoring all of the positives? Is this not irrational?

4. Finally, analyse what your behavioural response was. Did you excessively strive to achieve your goal, no matter the cost to self or others? Did you procrastinate, for fear of the result not being perfect?

5. Challenge any unhealthy behaviours that you have unearthed. Why are they unhealthy? What can you do to change them?

Let's suppose you have just finished a project but are struggling to hand it in, because in your mind it is not completely perfect. You become increasingly anxious. In this scenario, you would write down in your notebook the trigger, which is your project, your demand for absolute perfection and your emotion, which is anxiety.

You would then challenge this demand on paper. Is 100 per cent perfection achievable? Of course not! Are you constantly scanning the project, ignoring all the fine work you have done and concentrating solely on the small imperfections that you have picked out? Is this helpful or rational? Next, you would challenge your behaviour, which is to procrastinate.

If you carry out this exercise regularly, you will notice your thinking and behaviour slowly begin to change and that you become more realistic about life. You will learn to accept that both life and you can never be perfect.

The Chaos Exercise

For the next eight weeks, I am going to introduce total chaos into your perfect life through the following exercise:

1. Every day, I want you to mess up something small on purpose. It might be putting some mismatched pieces of clothing together. It might be non-matching colours, or a tie that clashes with your shirt. Don't shave for a day if this makes you self-conscious. Leave your hair untidy. Leave off some cosmetics for the day.

2. You must live with this 'imperfection' for the day. How did you cope? In the beginning, it will drive you crazy. You will spend much of the day constantly aware of this imperfection. But by the end of the day, you will notice that you are gradually adjusting, that the imperfection has faded into the background.
3. Another option is to load something on to your social media showing you up as imperfect.
4. Leave your desk at work untidy for twenty-four hours. Ask your partner to mess up a room in the house that you would otherwise prefer ordered. You then must live with this for twenty-four hours. This drives perfectionists totally crazy, or so they tell me.

The possibilities to cause chaos in this manner are endless. Each person can identify small opportunities that would bother them. I recommend you come up with your own list (what drives you nuts?) and put this exercise into practice.

If you are perfectionist in nature, you will initially struggle to live with these minor imperfections and you will become anxious and frustrated. But after repeatedly performing this exercise, you will notice that you are coping better with these imperfections and are less anxious as a result.

The thinking behind this exercise is to demonstrate that you can indeed live with imperfection, learn to adjust and let go. It also teaches you to develop a sense of humour about yourself and life. The world is not going to end if imperfections are present. Once you stop seeking out imperfections, you will also begin to cease your demand for absolute perfection.

If you have carried out these exercises, learned to challenge your demand for absolute perfection and ceased to live in the world of rating, you will experience significant mental health benefits. You will become more realistic about life and cope better with imperfections in yourself and others. You will feel less anxious and less prone to bouts of depression. You will also become more emotionally resilient to the slings and arrows of life.

CLAIRE'S STORY

Claire is a forty-two-year-old mother of two, working part-time in a local business. She presented to her GP with a history of persistent fatigue and irritable bowel symptoms but, following investigation, her doctor has diagnosed anxiety and referred her to Dr Jim.

She grew up in a perfectionist household, where both parents demanded and expected high standards from all three children. Claire spent her childhood and adolescence living up to these standards, rating herself mercilessly if failing to do so.

After some discussion with Claire, Dr Jim feels that perfectionism might lie at the root of her anxiety, which in turn is causing her physical symptoms. He suggests some CBT approaches to deal with it. He then explains what rational and irrational beliefs are and how they will use the ABC concept to locate them. He then asks Claire for an example of a situation which has triggered her perfectionism.

'Recently I invited four of my friends to my home for a meal and became incredibly anxious before the event,' she replies.

'So now we have the trigger and the emotion,' says Dr Jim. 'How did it affect you physically?'

'I was a nervous wreck,' Claire replies. 'My stomach was in knots, I was hyperventilating, my heart was thumping, my muscles were tense and I had a persistent tension headache. I was also so tired. I even thought of cancelling the meal.'

'What was your behaviour, other than considering cancelling the meal, when you became anxious about this event?' asks Dr Jim.

Claire admits to having spent hours cleaning and recleaning the house, even though it was already spotless. She spent ages preparing exotic and complicated dishes to impress her friends. She also found herself catastrophising as to what might go wrong on the night, seeking constant reassurance from her partner about the proposed menu and drinking several glasses of wine to calm herself down.

'What was it about the upcoming party, Claire, that caused you to become so anxious? This usually means that you were assigning some danger to the trigger. In this case, what danger were you assigning to preparing this simple meal for your friends? What did you visualise was going to happen?'

Claire tells Dr Jim that she visualised that the meal would not be perfect; that this would ruin the night for everyone, and that she would feel a complete failure.

'So now let's examine what irrational belief was triggered by this situation and the danger you assigned to it,' says Dr Jim. 'This usually takes the form of some absolute demand you are making about the trigger.'

With Dr Jim's help, Claire identifies that her main demand was that the meal must be perfect, otherwise she would be a failure.

They then put together the following ABC:

A Activating Event:
  • Trigger: preparing a meal for her friends
  • Inference/danger: the meal might not be perfect; her friends would be disappointed; if this happened she would feel she had failed

B Belief/Demands: 'The meal must be perfect. If not, I am a failure.'

C Consequences:
  • Emotional reactions: anxiety
  • Physical reactions: stomach in knots and loose stools, heart pounding, tension headache, muscle tension, increased fatigue
  • Behaviour: tries to ensure the house is perfectly tidy; spends ages trying to pick the right menu; catastrophises how awful it will be if the meal does not turn out well; seeks reassurance from her partner that all will go well; drinks more wine than usual

After reviewing the ABC, Claire acknowledges that this is a typical scenario for her. 'I seek perfection in everything I do,' she exclaims. 'No wonder I am so exhausted all the time!'

'Now that we know what made you so anxious about having your friends over for a meal, let's help you to reshape both your perfectionist thinking and your behaviour in relation to this. Because if we're successful in this instance, we can apply the same ideas to similar situations in the future,' says Dr Jim. 'We could dispute or challenge your "A", or your interpretation, but what is more effective is to challenge your irrational belief, the real driver of your anxiety, and the emotional and behavioural consequences of this belief.'

First, Dr Jim talks Claire through how to deal with the physical symptoms of anxiety using the flooding technique, which we discussed in Chapter 4. She finds this very helpful. 'I have always wondered why I developed these physical symptoms,' she says. 'It's a relief to realise that they are simply caused by my stress hormones.'

'Let's now examine and challenge your "B", or your irrational belief,' says Dr Jim. 'This took the form of an absolute demand that the meal must be perfect. Is this demand rational or irrational, Claire?'

She reluctantly agrees it is probably irrational.

Dr Jim then asks, 'What would be a healthier demand?'

After some discussion, they both agree that a more rational or healthier demand might be that she would prefer if the meal was a success on the night, but that this was out of her control.

This leads to a discussion on the importance of control in Claire's life. Dr Jim asks her what she can really control in her life. After a few attempts to answer this, Claire realises that she can control very little. Dr Jim explains that when we are seeking control, one of the four things we are looking for is 100 per cent certainty. The other three are 100 per cent order, security and perfection. 'So, what were you looking for here?' asks Dr Jim.

Claire decides that she was seeking 100 per cent certainty that the meal would go well and 100 per cent perfection! Following discussion, she accepts that it is unrealistic to demand 100 per cent certainty about this or indeed anything in life. To teach her how to challenge this demand, Dr Jim suggests that over the course of the next month, she performs the coin exercise detailed in Chapter 5.

He also challenges her irrational belief that she would be a failure if the meal did not turn out as successfully as hoped. Would she be a failure as a person or would she have simply failed on this occasion, in relation to this task? Dr Jim asks Claire to fill in the rating scale, discussed in Chapter 3. She automatically rates herself at ninety-nine. 'I have always thought I must be the best,' she explains, 'so that I retain a healthy opinion of myself.'

'And where do others rate you?'

'I assume they would also rate me very highly, say around ninety.'

'And if the meal went badly, where would you rate yourself?'

'I would probably have to drop my rating to ninety,' Claire replies, glumly. 'I would feel like such a failure!'

'And where would others rate you if they discovered you had made a total mess of the meal?'

'I think that their rating would drop to eighty.'

'I can see why you are struggling with perfectionism,' Dr Jim tells her, good-humouredly. 'You have an extremely high self-rating. But on what grounds can you rate a human being?'

Claire struggles with this, as she has never asked herself this question before. After some more discussion, they agree that there is no criteria to rate a human being. Dr Jim introduces her to the Members Only club; she can only join it if she agrees that she is not allowed to rate herself or to allow others to rate her. If she belongs to this club, she can only rate her behaviour or skills.

'Are you saying I am not allowed to rate myself?' she asks, sadly. 'I live for my rating.'

'Then why are you here?'

Claire begins to laugh. 'You have a point. It is not helping me much in my life.'

Dr Jim agrees. 'It is this tendency to rate ourselves as human beings that underlies perfectionism. Many people with this condition tend to rate themselves highly. It then becomes impossible to live up to this rating, and so they begin to rate themselves as failures.'

Dr Jim and Claire have a long discussion about unconditional self-acceptance, and the difference between failing at something and being a failure as a person.

Claire begins to realise that she has to stop rating herself personally, and start focusing more on her skills and behaviour. She promises to practise the skill of unconditional self-acceptance over the following months.

Dr Jim then turns their attention to Claire's biggest difficulty, namely her tendency towards perfectionism. 'I don't know how to change my behaviour,' she admits. 'No matter how often I attempt to change, I revert to the same pattern.'

Dr Jim empathises with Claire, and proposes a new approach to challenge her perfectionism. Firstly, he asks her to carry a notebook around with her for the next two months. She is to note down anytime she seeks absolute perfection in some area of her life, detailing the trigger, the demands, her rating of herself and the resulting behaviour. Later, when she has some free time, she should take out her notebook and challenge on paper her demand for total perfection. Is total perfection not just a myth? She should also challenge any self-rating thoughts as above. Finally, she is to review her behaviour and explore what needs to change. If she performs this exercise repeatedly, it will greatly assist her to challenge her perfectionist thinking and behaviour.

Dr Jim then introduces Claire to the chaos exercises detailed earlier in this chapter. They decide to focus on her appearance, in the form of cosmetics and mismatched clothes, and that Claire will encourage her partner to mess up the kitchen and living room on a regular basis. Claire blanches at the thought of such chaos and disorder. It will challenge her core being, but she promises to carry out the exercises faithfully.

Over the following months, Claire puts everything she has learned into practice. She applies the flooding techniques to her physical symptoms and begins to challenge her perfectionist thinking and behaviour. In the beginning, the exercises make her extremely anxious and frustrated. She finds the daily chaos exercise especially trying, but she perseveres. She also performs the coin exercise, to deal with her demand for absolute certainty, with the assistance of her partner. He finds them equally demanding – he is a man with extremely low frustration tolerance!

The combination of the perfection, coin and chaos exercises goes a long way towards banishing her perfectionist thinking and behaviour. But what really makes the difference is her gradual acceptance of herself without conditions. Her days of living for her 99 per cent rating are over!

Six months later, when Claire visits Dr Jim again, she is a new person. She no longer battles with perfectionism and has learned to develop a sense of humour about herself and life. Her anxiety levels have significantly reduced and her fatigue has vanished. She is on the road to emotional resilience.

Key Learning Points

1. In perfectionism, we demand 100 per cent perfection in some or all aspects of our lives, and rate ourselves as failures if we cannot achieve this demand.
2. We also spend our lives seeking and finding small imperfections and ignoring all evidence to the contrary.
3. To combat perfectionism, we must challenge our demand for absolute perfection and our belief that we can be rated or considered a failure.
4. With the assistance of relevant exercises, we must also learn to live with the reality that imperfections are a normal part of life.

10. SKILL EIGHT

HOW TO CHALLENGE PROCRASTINATION

What Is Procrastination?

All of us tend to put things on the long finger. How often do we decide to do something, yet still have not got around to it days later? We are adept at finding excuses, too busy with other tasks, or could it simply be laziness? But for some people, putting tasks on the long finger, called procrastination, becomes the norm. This creates chaos in their lives, as problems pile up, until they become seemingly unsurmountable.

What Lies Beneath Procrastination?

Firstly, procrastination is a behaviour, and all behaviour has a purpose. That purpose is to satisfy some underlying emotion. So, if someone is sad, they may cry. Or if they are anxious about something, they may avoid it. To understand procrastinating behaviour, we must dig deeper to reflect on the emotions underlying it, which are usually anxiety and frustration. Underlying these emotions are the thinking patterns or irrational beliefs already discussed. We will explore these further later on.

Why Is this Skill Important?

This skill is important because of the potentially negative consequences of procrastination on our mental health. You may be surprised that this seemingly innocuous behaviour can lead to great difficulties, but I have observed many people become paralysed because of it. People with general anxiety, for example, learn to dread starting or finishing tasks. They consequently allow them to build up, becoming increasingly stressed and anxious. This relentless spiral ends with them feeling constantly exhausted, and rating themselves as a failure for not getting on top of things. The situation is worsened when someone with this condition also suffers from persistent fatigue. They learn to 'hoard' energy reserves, using procrastination to prevent them becoming depleted.

People suffering from bouts of depression can also experience similar difficulties. They, too, lack the energy and motivation to carry out tasks, so they procrastinate and once again find themselves swamped by those tasks piling up. This in turn leads to further procrastination. The mountain gets higher, and they start rating themselves as failures, while their mood drops further. In some cases, this may lead to self-harm, as the person can see no route out of this vicious circle. A recent study by Flett et al. (2016) also suggested that procrastination may in itself increase our vulnerability to bouts of depression.

For others, where the underlying emotion is frustration, a similar pattern emerges. But in this case, they also hold the belief that they should not have to carry out these tasks in the first place. The combination of tasks building up and their refusal to deal with them results in them becoming increasingly stressed and irritable. None of this is good news for their mental or physical health.

The classic example of procrastination is addiction. The addict always wants to stop tomorrow. Unfortunately, for many, tomorrow never arrives. Their behaviour is triggered by a combination of anxiety and, more importantly, frustration.

Procrastination is also a common feature present in those struggling with toxic stress. The reasons are obvious. The more anxious or frustrated a person becomes when stressed, the greater the likelihood that they will procrastinate, as they are too 'tired but wired' to cope with them. This increases our toxic stress, placing us at risk of yet more physical and mental health difficulties. A recent meta-analysis study on the links between procrastination and burnout (Hill et al., 2015) confirmed strong links between them, especially in the domain of work.

But apart from the significant mental health problems created or worsened by procrastination, we all can benefit from some retraining techniques as to how best to tackle this behaviour. There is a streak of procrastination in us all.

There are also clear links between procrastination and self-control. This was highlighted by recent research (Duckworth et al., 2017) into the area of self-control which supported the importance of young people developing this skill as early in life as possible. It highlighted how a capacity to self-regulate our emotions and behaviour as students was a better predictor of academic success than general intelligence.

If you want to become emotionally resilient, you must learn how to challenge your natural tendency to delay tackling tasks requiring your attention. Otherwise you may end up being a bystander in your own life, rather than an active participant.

Once again, this is a skill we need to acquire ourselves and pass on to our young people. Too often, our motto is 'Why do today what you can put off until tomorrow?'

The primary reason for acquiring this skill is to learn and apply self-discipline to our lives. For some of us, this goes against the grain. However, if we are honest with ourselves, we will accept that there are significant benefits to applying such a discipline. Train yourself to deal with the main tasks of the day before going to sleep each night, and major benefits will accrue. By challenging your natural tendency to procrastinate, you will find yourself less stressed, anxious or frustrated. You may also notice that you will have more, rather than less, time for pleasurable activities, and that you find it easier to cope with difficulties when they arise because you are able to apply the same disciplined approach.

The message is clear. Those who wish to be truly emotionally resilient must challenge the long finger of procrastination in their lives!

How to Deal with Procrastination

If you are struggling with procrastination, I recommend the following two exercises.

Procrastination Exercise One

The purpose of this exercise is to learn what thinking patterns and emotions underlie your tendency to procrastinate, and how best to manage them.

1. For the next month, carry a notebook around with you. Whenever you have a task to perform and find yourself procrastinating, write down the task in question and the emotions triggered. The most common emotions are anxiety, frustration and, less frequently, depression.
2. Later, take a sheet of paper and tease out the situation as follows. Begin by identifying the principal emotion. Once identified and written down, it becomes easier to understand why you delayed or struggled to complete the task in question, within the required timeframe.

If your emotional response to the task or decision is anxiety, ask yourself the following questions:

Are you struggling to deal with uncertainty surrounding the result of the task to be performed?

Are you demanding perfection in all aspects of life, and now applying this unachievable demand to the task in hand?

Are you catastrophising about the potential outcome of the task or decision? Are you unable to cope with the possibility of failure?

Are you concerned that the energy required to complete the task will devour your limited, valuable reserves?

Are you struggling with the world of rating in relation to yourself or others?

In almost every case where procrastination is due to anxiety, the answer to a number of the above questions will be yes. Identify the questions that are relevant to you and add them to your sheet.

If your emotional response to the task or decision is frustration, then ask the following questions:

Are you frustrated that you must perform the task at all?
Are you trying to dodge some discomfort by not proceeding with the task?
Do you believe the task is someone else's responsibility?
Are you simply lazy and having a good time, and so rebelling against the hassle of applying the discipline necessary to proceed with the task?

Once again, identify the relevant questions and add them to your sheet.

The skills necessary to deal with uncertainty, rating, perfectionism, catastrophising, failure and frustration have been explored in earlier chapters. I recommend you revisit the relevant ones. If you are dealing with uncertainty or frustration, you may end up performing the coin exercise. If you are struggling with rating or the possibility of failure, then challenge your self-rating and join the Members Only club. If you are struggling with catastrophising, then the spilt milk exercise will be of assistance.

Once you have identified and challenged these underlying irrational beliefs and demands, the next step is to develop a skill-based strategy to deal with the behaviour itself.

Procrastination Exercise Two

For the next month, carry a notebook around with you. The purpose of this exercise is to learn how to manage tasks without falling into the behavioural trap of procrastination. Let's assume you have a specific task or project to complete. I want you to take the following five steps:

1. The first step is to establish a timeframe for completion of the task in

question. Write this date into your notebook.

2. The second step is to establish a 'personal deadline' time or date for the task to be completed. This should always be a date chosen ahead of the true one. For example, if you are required to have a project or assignment ready in four weeks, then make your personal deadline three weeks. This mobilises you to finish the task ahead of time.

3. The third step is to divide the task into three or more parts, allotting a specific timeframe for each one. In the case of the project mentioned in step 2, this would mean assigning a week to complete each of the three parts. This prevents you catastrophising about the work involved, as you won't be attempting to bite off the whole assignment in one go. Now you only need to focus on a third of the assignment for that one week. This immediately reduces stress, as the goal is eminently achievable.

4. The fourth step is to pull together the completed sections, edit them and hand the project in well ahead of the scheduled deadline.

5. The final step is to organise in advance something pleasant for when the task is finished. This will encourage you to complete it. The emotional mind and brain love a reward. Linking together the completion of a task with such a reward assists us to retrain our mind and brain.

Decision-making Exercise

We may have a similar tendency to procrastinate when making decisions. Many people not only procrastinate about a specific course of action, but also the decision preceding it, meaning they can become paralysed by indecision. We can apply a similar skill technique when dealing with this difficulty.

1. Write down the proposed decision and timeframe in your notebook.

2. Once again, identify and write down the emotion, which will usually be anxiety, and the underlying demands driving it. The most common demands relate to uncertainty and fear of failure – 'I must be certain I make the right decision. If I don't I am a failure.' We have already detailed how best to challenge these on paper.

3. Now write down the pros and cons of the decision, and decide on a course

of action based on your conclusions, together with a clear timetable. Don't be afraid to research information or look for assistance when making your decision.

4. Having decided on an appropriate course of action and timeline, apply the same steps detailed above. Break up the task into three parts, assign a timeframe for each and an overall timetable, and assign a finish date ahead of the actual deadline. Once again, allow yourself a treat once the task is complete.

This is how you develop the skill of dealing with the scourge of procrastination, which blights so many lives. You must practise this skill repeatedly, as procrastination is another behaviour that is stubbornly resistant to change. If you are prepared to integrate the above blueprint into your life, the results will be life-changing.

KATE'S STORY

Kate is thirty-five and in a relationship of five years. On several occasions, her partner Thomas has suggested they might take the next step of getting married and having children. But as with many areas of her life, Kate keeps procrastinating over this decision. She struggles with anxiety and long-standing difficulties with perfectionism and fear of failure, the roots of which go back to her childhood. She is a personal assistant to a busy executive, and she is constantly under pressure. Her boss relies on her for assignments to be ready on time and well researched. She attends her family doctor, complaining of persistent fatigue, tension headaches and irritable bowel symptoms. Following investigation, her GP clarifies that her symptoms are due to anxiety and refers Kate to Dr Jim for assistance.

Kate reveals her long battle with procrastination, how it is crippling her life. 'I just become so anxious if I have to make a decision, or start or finish a task,' she explains to Dr Jim. 'I end up constantly exhausted and don't know how to break the cycle.'

Dr Jim empathises, and suggests that they might try some CBT approaches.

He then explains what rational and irrational beliefs are and how they will use the ABC concept to locate them. He asks Kate for an example of a situation where she has become anxious and has procrastinated. She mentions a request from her boss to research and put together a brief for an important client. She immediately felt anxious. 'And how did that make you feel physically?' asks Dr Jim.

'I found my heart was beating faster, my stomach was in knots, I had a dry mouth, my muscles were tense and I felt very shaky. Over the following days, the tension headaches became unbearable and I was just totally exhausted.'

'What was your behaviour on becoming increasingly anxious about this task?'

Kate admits lapsing into her usual behavioural pattern of procrastination. 'I knew the deadline was in ten days,' she explains, 'but every time I considered putting the brief together, I found another reason to delay the task.'

'Any other behaviours?' Dr Jim asks.

'I found myself deflecting queries from my boss as to my progress,' she answers. 'I ended up becoming even more anxious.'

'What was it about your boss's request, Kate, that caused you to become so anxious? What danger were you assigning to preparing this brief? What did you visualise was going to happen?'

Kate tells Dr Jim the danger was that she might make a complete mess of the brief, and would feel a complete failure if this happened. 'I am such a perfectionist,' she adds. 'I would have to be comfortable I had covered every possibility in the report. I couldn't handle making a major mistake.'

Kate acknowledges a tendency to catastrophise about everything. 'I can only see the worst-case scenario at all times!' She reveals that her visualisation is that the report would be a mess. She would make the wrong suggestions, her boss and the client would be annoyed, and she could end up losing her job.

Kate admits to drinking more alcohol that week, to calm her anxiety, adding that she ended up working day and night for the last two days before the deadline, putting the final report together. 'All because I delayed and procrastinated for so long before beginning.'

'So now let's examine what irrational belief was triggered by this situation, and the danger you assigned to it,' says Dr Jim. 'This usually takes the form of some absolute demand you are making about the trigger.'

After some discussion, they decide her main demands were that she must not make any mistakes in the brief. It must be perfect; if not, she would be a failure. She must also have the brief ready in time.

They put together the following ABC:

A   Activating Event:
  - Trigger: request from her boss to prepare a brief
  - Inference/danger: the report might not be ready in time; it might not be done perfectly; the recommendations she makes might be incorrect; if this happened her boss and the client would be extremely unhappy; as a result, she might lose her job

B   Belief/Demands: 'I must not make any mistakes in the report. If this happens I am a failure. The report must be ready in time and must be perfect.'

C   Consequences:
  - Emotional reactions: anxiety
  - Physical reactions: stomach in knots, heart beating a little faster, shaking, muscle tension, increased fatigue
  - Behaviour: constantly procrastinates about beginning the brief; reassures her employer all is well while struggling to do the report; catastrophises about how awful the report will be, with long-term consequences of losing her job as a result; attends her GP because of fatigue; drinks more wine than usual; has a frantic rush to put the report together in the final days before deadline

'Now that we understand what made you so anxious about preparing this report and the resulting procrastinating behaviour, let's help you to reshape your thinking and behaviour. Because if we are successful in this instance, we can apply the same concepts to similar situations in the future,' says Dr Jim. 'We could dispute or challenge your "A", or your interpretation, and we could probably dispute whether there was proof that you might not have the report ready in time or that you might make recommendations that turn out to be incorrect. We could also challenge whether you would definitely lose your job if this happened.

'What is more effective, Kate,' continues Dr Jim, 'is to challenge your irrational belief, the real driver of your anxiety, and the emotional and behavioural consequences of this belief.'

He begins by discussing how to manage the physical symptoms of anxiety using the flooding technique discussed in Chapter 4. 'Let's now examine and challenge your "B", or your irrational belief,' says Dr Jim. 'This took the form of an absolute demand that you must have the report ready in time and must make the correct recommendations. Is this demand rational or irrational, Kate?'

Kate accepts that it is irrational.

Dr Jim then asks her, 'What would be a healthier demand?'

After some discussion, they agree that a more rational or healthier demand might be that she would prefer to have the report ready in time and that the recommendations would turn out to be accurate. But whether this happened or not was out of her control.

This leads to a discussion on the importance of certainty in Kate's life. 'Can you realistically demand 100 per cent certainty that you will always make the best recommendations in this or any other briefing report?' asks Dr Jim.

Kate accepts that this is indeed a bit unrealistic. 'But I find myself falling into this trap every time.' To teach her how to challenge this demand, Dr Jim sets Kate the coin exercise described in Chapter 5 to perform in the following month. He also challenges her irrational belief that she would be a failure if the report did not turn out to be as accurate as her employer requested. Was she a failure as a person or would she simply have failed on this occasion, in relation to this task? Dr Jim introduces her to the Members Only club, and she embraces the concept. They also discuss her perfectionism, agreeing to return later to this issue.

Dr Jim then turns their attention to Kate's biggest difficulty, namely her tendency constantly to procrastinate. 'I don't know how to change this behaviour,' she admits. 'No matter how often I resolve to change, I slip backwards into the same pattern.'

Dr Jim empathises, and suggests a new approach to challenging her procrastinating behaviour. He demonstrates how to write down and break any task into sections as detailed earlier.

Kate is excited by this new approach. 'I like the idea of breaking up a task like this!' she exclaims. 'So much of the time, I look at the mountain of work to be carried out and consider throwing in the towel before I have even begun.'

Dr Jim suggests that she should arrange some small reward for her hard work following the completion of her task. 'Our emotional brain will be more enthusiastic about completing a task if it senses something pleasurable on the horizon,' he explains.

Dr Jim recommends that Kate begins by applying this skill to small tasks in her everyday domestic life before extending it to more significant areas. 'Teach yourself to apply this skill on a daily and weekly basis to simple chores that you regularly procrastinate about. It then becomes easier to put into practice when encountering more complex work projects.'

Kate applies herself to learning this skill with determination. Each day she writes out the main chores to be carried out, sets clear timelines and breaks down the individual chores into timed sections. At the end of more difficult tasks, she allows herself a small treat. Gradually, she is getting through her to-do list faster and more efficiently, resulting in more spare time for herself. She begins to apply the same technique to her work situation. Her boss comments on her increased efficiency, rewarding her with a pay increase.

Through practising unconditional self-acceptance, she has also become more realistic about herself. Following a series of coin exercises, she is now able to accept the uncertainty of life. As promised, Dr Jim assists her at a later stage to deal with her perfectionism, using the skills and techniques outlined in the previous chapter. Her anxiety levels plummet, as do her physical symptoms. But, best of all, her years of constant procrastination soon become a distant memory.

Key Learning Points

1. Procrastination can cause significant damage to our mental health if not challenged.

2. Procrastination is an unhealthy behavioural pattern we frequently engage in when experiencing unhealthy emotions such as anxiety, frustration and depression.

3. These, in turn, can be caused by difficulties with uncertainty, rating, perfectionism, managing discomfort and a fear of failure. We have already explored how to deal with these in previous chapters.

4. With the assistance of some simple exercises, we can teach ourselves to challenge and change our procrastinating behaviour.

11. SKILL NINE

HOW TO PRACTISE MINDFULNESS
Living in the Present Moment

What Is Mindfulness?

Mindfulness is the awareness which develops when we pay attention to events experienced in the present moment, within the framework of one's mind/body, in a non-judgemental and accepting manner.

Mindfulness is helpful because:

1. It assists us to notice what is happening in our experience, especially when engaging in compulsive patterns of thought, such as rumination.
2. It offers a way for people to 'stay' with experiences, including whatever may be unpleasant or difficult, rather than pushing them away.
3. It produces a change in perspective on those thoughts or experiences, enabling people to see that their thoughts are just thoughts, not facts or reality, and that they need not be driven by them.
4. It allows choice, because of this new perspective. Rather than being driven by compulsive reactions to experience, mindfulness creates the mental space that enables people to respond differently.
5. It assists us in moving from the world of doing to the world of being.

Why Is this Skill Important?

As human beings, few of us live in the present moment. Instead, we fret about the past or worry unnecessarily about the future. This is usually accompanied by a lack of awareness of our immediate environment. How many of us, when walking in the forests or by the sea, remain totally oblivious to the sounds, smells and sights Mother Nature offers? If we're not thinking about past or future events, our mind is constantly wandering off into a world of its own. We miss the beauty of the moment. And that moment will never be repeated!

This is in part explained by the way our brains have evolved. This wonderfully complex organ is a large biological computer. If it were possible to enter this amazing world, one would be astonished at the incredible amount of information whizzing around at lightning speeds through the brain. We are, thankfully, only consciously aware of minute amounts of this information at any one time. Otherwise, functioning in the real world would be impossible. Much of the time, the brain is on automatic pilot in relation to the senses of sight, sound, touch and smell. We do not consciously register this continuous inward flow of information.

This allows the brain to focus on past and future events, which was useful in our ancestral past, where danger lurked at every turn. The ability to remember the emotional and contextual nature of such dangers or anticipate potential future ones was often vital for survival.

In the past, our ancestors were more aware of and interactive with their surroundings. Nowadays, senses are bombarded with non-essential information from multiple sources, especially technology. How many of us are like ghosts, floating through cities and towns with earphones in, phones in hand, eyes down, totally oblivious to the world going on around us? The skill of mindfulness has never been of greater importance.

Mindfulness has been around for over five thousand years. In the past few decades, it has increasingly become regarded in Western cultures as an antidote to many mental health conditions. Initially, it was regarded as a useful skill to assist in the management of stress and anxiety. Nowadays, it is used in the management of addiction, self-harm, borderline personality disorders and the prevention of depression. It is sometimes combined with CBT techniques (mindfulness-based CBT or MBCBT) to manage these issues.

There is an impressive body of research on the role of mindfulness in the management of many of these conditions. It has recently been proven that mindfulness is an extremely effective strategy in the management of anxiety and depression (Rodriguez et al., 2017).

I have found simple mindfulness exercises to be of great assistance in dealing with stress, anxiety and OCD, and in the prevention of depression. It can be especially useful for the management of recurrent obsessive thoughts, prevalent in anxiety and OCD. Increasingly, I believe mindfulness techniques are a skill that we all should acquire, to boost our mental health. It helps to alleviate stress, reduce anxiety and reconnect us to the real world, versus the virtual world of social media and technology.

I have long advocated that it should be introduced to children and adolescents from the earliest possible age. It is beginning to happen. I regularly recommend the three-minute breathing space exercise discussed later to students preparing for major exams. It is also useful, on occasion, during the exam itself. Mindfulness could also play a significant role in the prevention of self-harm within our adolescent population, which has reached epidemic proportions.

How to Develop this Skill

It is not the purpose of this chapter to encourage the reader to spend long periods of time learning and practising mindfulness, or the technique of meditation often seen as the vehicle required to develop this skill.

Meditation is a mental technique which involves focusing the mind on an object, sound, prayer, breath or conscious thought, to increase our awareness of the present moment, helping us to relax, reduce stress or enhance spiritual or personal growth. Meditation was being practised in India as early as 5000 BC. For most of us, this conjures up images of Buddhist monks in uncomfortable poses, spending long periods of contemplation. But this technique has been incorporated into the Western psyche through yoga and transcendental meditation. Meditation shifts activity from the right side of the brain, the source of most of our negative thoughts and emotions, to the left side, the source of positive emotions. This explains the reduction in stress and negative thinking, and the increase in positive emotions like peacefulness, calmness, forgiveness, love, compassion and joy.

For some people, the significant effort and time involved in learning and practising meditation is a price they are willing to pay for the benefits outlined above. They will spend months learning and years practising this technique – often meditating for between twenty minutes and an hour a day.

For most of us, this may be impractical, leading to the natural assumption that learning and practising mindfulness is not for us. Nothing could be further from the truth.

I would like to suggest two simple exercises, well within the capability of all of us to learn and practise. The first is the mindful awareness exercise and the second is the three-minute breathing space exercise. They will help you to develop the skill of mindfulness without having to enter the world of serious meditation. The breathing exercise in particular might play a significant role in assisting you with stress, OCD, addiction, recurrent depression or self-harm.

The Mindful Awareness Exercise

Let's assume you are reading this book beside an open window, overlooking a garden or a green or open space. I want you to put down the book and, for the next five minutes, become quite still. Open all your senses. Focus initially on sounds emanating from your immediate environment. Somebody might be cutting the grass. There might be birds twittering away, children playing nearby. You might notice the hum of traffic, the screeching of tyres, people talking. Wherever you are, focus on the sounds around you. Now open your eyes to the immediate environment. Look out and become aware of what you see. It might be the leaves moving on the trees, the birds hopping around, picking up twigs, people moving in a hurry. Wherever you are, focus on the sights around you. Similarly, with your sense of smell. You will notice that the five minutes seem like a long time, as if time has stood still.

In practice, you have eliminated the clutter in your mind, by shifting attention to becoming mindfully aware of what is happening around you. And that is the basis of the following exercise.

Each day for a period of five minutes, focus in a mindful manner on what you are doing at that moment in time. Perhaps you are eating. Become aware of the colours, smells and the taste of what you are eating. Savour each mouthful. Even try to describe to yourself what you are sensing. You may be out walking. Again, focus for this period on the information flowing in through your senses, the colour of the sky and the landscape around you, the noise of the birds or animals, the sound of the wind, the smells emanating from the environment, the shape of the trees, and so on. You are now practising mindfulness. You will observe how the mind regularly wanders off for periods, while performing this exercise. This is quite normal, as our brain and mind are restless creatures. Don't get annoyed or frustrated when this happens. Just refocus on the sense in question.

Practise this exercise daily, for four to eight weeks. Put a reminder on your phone. When you are engaged with this exercise, switch your mobile to silent for the duration. You can pick any situation or time, whether at work, at home, at college or when out exercising. All you need to do is focus for those five minutes on the information flowing in through the senses from your immediate environment. Soon, it will become second nature to be mindfully aware of what is happening around you, at any one moment in time. The more you practise this exercise, the more you will integrate this mindfulness approach into your everyday life.

As you do so, it becomes easier to apply it during periods when you are stressed or preoccupied. Simply stop what you are doing and switch focus to becoming mindfully aware of your immediate surroundings. After five minutes, you will notice how much calmer you are and you will focus more clearly on the issues causing you distress.

This exercise has one extra bonus. It reconnects us to the world around us. A world full of sound, smells and sights, most of which we ignore, at a cost to ourselves and our mental health. We need to get back in touch with Mother Nature. The world of technology and social media is disengaging us from the real sensory experiences of life. That beautiful pastoral scene, the sound of the waves, the chirping of birds, the smells emanating from the garden, that one-off sunset, and so on. Within three months of performing this exercise you will have subtly absorbed the skill of being mindfully aware, with genuine long-term benefits for mental health.

The Three-minute Breathing Space Exercise

This is a simple mindfulness exercise requiring little time, but bearing much fruit if performed regularly. While few of us can find blocks of time to practise long periods of meditation, we can afford to lose three minutes of our valuable time once or twice daily. Just consider the time spent on social media or checking emails and messages.

The three-minute breathing space exercise can be carried out at any time of the day. It involves turning your phone to silent for the allotted time, finding a quiet space, a comfortable posture, closing your eyes and engaging with the following:

Minute One: close your eyes, focus your mind on inner experiences, whether it is your thoughts, emotions or physical sensations. Do not try to change or challenge – just become aware of them.

Minute Two: focus on the simple physical sensation of breathing, noting your abdomen rising and falling with each breath, again not trying in any way to control it. This focus on the breath helps centre us. This portion of the exercise is especially useful for anxiety.

Minute Three: increase focus or awareness on the body, including posture, facial expressions and sensations, with total acceptance and without judgement. Another option is to focus for fifteen seconds on the sensation of each of our four limbs.

This sounds like a simple exercise, and in practice it is. You will notice once again how difficult it can be, however, to keep your busy mind focused on anything for more than fifteen seconds before it shifts off at a tangent. The secret is to keep returning it to the task in hand, without becoming frustrated with yourself, as inevitably happens. It is amazing how long these three minutes will seem, and how calm you will feel following this exercise.

Like many of the skills in this book, it will feel strange to begin with. You may feel anxious, even foolish doing it. But for those who persevere, it will be an invaluable exercise to learn and practise.

If you would like to acquire this skill quickly, perform it more often – say, three or four times a day, for a month. Then revert to once or twice daily. If you perform it regularly, you will become less stressed and anxious and you will cope better with what is going on around you. A good rule of thumb should be that the busier you are, and the less time you have available to do this exercise, the more important it is to find the time to do it! I encourage students who become extremely anxious before and during exams to practise this skill for up to six months before sitting them. They will then be quite expert at applying it when the day of reckoning arrives.

If you can practise these short, effective mindfulness exercises, you will have acquired an important skill for life, buffering you against the ravages of stress. It will also significantly increase your emotional resilience.

PAUL'S STORY

Paul is referred by the university doctor to see Dr Jim while still three months away from his end-of-term exams. Paul is twenty-three, a high achiever, with a history of anxiety verging on panic. He admits to being a total perfectionist. 'But I can't cope with my anxiety coming up to exams,' he explains. 'Every time I promise I won't let it happen. But it takes over, and I find myself a quivering wreck for days leading up to them.'

Dr Jim empathises, and suggests he might assist Paul with some CBT approaches. He then explains what rational and irrational beliefs are, and how they will use the ABC concept to locate them. Dr Jim and Paul use Paul's approaching exams as the trigger, and decide that his emotion is one of anxiety until the exams are very close, at which point his anxiety becomes more acute, verging on panic.

Paul describes the typical physical symptoms of anxiety, such as a stomach in knots, tension headaches, shallow breathing, teeth-grinding and fatigue when he is anxious. These symptoms become more acute the closer he gets to exams.

'What is it about the upcoming exams, Paul, that is causing you to become so anxious?' Dr Jim asks. 'This usually means that you are assigning some danger to the trigger. In this case, what danger are you assigning to sitting the exams? What do you visualise is going to happen?'

'I know it makes no sense,' Paul replies, 'as my grades have been fine. But my danger is that I will mess up the exams and either fail or not perform to the high standards set by myself. I have always been a perfectionist.'

'And how would you feel about yourself if you didn't achieve these standards?'

'I would feel like such a failure,' Paul answers.

'So now let's examine what irrational belief is triggered by this situation and the danger you have assigned to it,' says Dr Jim. 'This usually takes the form of some absolute demand you are making about the trigger.'

Dr Jim and Paul discuss this further, and agree that Paul's demand is that he must do well in his exams, otherwise he will be a failure. They then review his behaviour on becoming anxious because of this demand. Paul admits to worrying and catastrophising about the exams themselves, and about how he will feel physically, coming up to them. He also over-prepares for every exam. 'I am usually physically and mentally exhausted after the exams as a result,' he notes. He also admits that he self-soothes with alcohol.

They then put together the following ABC:

A   Activating Event:
- Trigger: his upcoming exams
- Inference/danger: he will mess up in his exams; he might not achieve the high standards set by himself; if this happens, he would feel like a failure

B   Belief/Demands: 'I must do well in my exams. If I don't, I will be a failure.'

C   Consequences:
- Emotional reactions: anxiety
- Physical reactions: stomach in knots, shallow breathing, tension head-aches, teeth-grinding, fatigue

- Behaviour: tries to ensure he will not make an error by over-preparing; catastrophises about how awful it will be if the exams do not turn out well; uses alcohol to reduce his anxiety

'Now that we know what makes you so anxious about the upcoming exams, let's help you to reshape both your thinking and your behaviour in relation to this. Because if we're successful in this instance, we can apply the same concepts to similar situations in the future,' says Dr Jim. 'We could dispute or challenge your "A", or interpretation, and we could dispute whether there was proof that the exam results would turn out to be a disaster. But it is more effective, Paul,' continues Dr Jim, 'to challenge your irrational belief, the real driver of your anxiety, and the emotional and behavioural consequences of this belief.'

Initially, they discuss how to manage the physical symptoms of anxiety using the flooding technique discussed in Chapter 4. This is a watershed moment for Paul. He now understands what is happening when he becomes physically anxious. He is relieved there is a skill he can learn to help him to manage his symptoms. 'Later we will go through some simple mindfulness exercises,' promises Dr Jim. 'Let's now examine and challenge your "B", or your irrational belief. This took the form of an absolute demand that you must not mess up your exams. Is this demand rational or irrational?'

On reflection, Paul agrees it was probably irrational.

Dr Jim then asks, 'What would a healthier demand be?'

After some discussion, they agree that a more rational or healthier demand might be that he would prefer if the exams went well, but this was out of his control.

This leads to a discussion on the importance of control, and especially absolute certainty, in Paul's life. To teach him how to challenge this demand for certainty, Dr Jim sets Paul the coin exercise detailed in Chapter 5 to perform during the following month. He also challenges Paul's irrational belief that he would be a failure if the exams did not turn out as well as desired. Would he be a failure as a person or would he simply have failed on this occasion, at this task? This leads them to a discussion on Paul's perfectionism.

He introduces Paul to the Members Only club, where to be a member he must agree that he is not allowed to rate himself or allow others to rate him, but that he can rate his behaviour or skills. Like many others suffering from perfectionism, Paul struggles to accept that he will have to cease his high self-rating. However, he agrees that it is not helping him in his life. Dr Jim also lays out for Paul the exercises detailed in Chapter 9, to assist him in challenging his perfectionism over the following months.

They also discuss his behaviour. Is alcohol, for example, the best means to cope with the physical symptoms of anxiety? They also discuss his catastrophising and the exercises, described in Chapter 8, that can be used to challenge it.

Dr Jim then returns to mindfulness. 'All of us tend to live either in the past or the future,' he explains, 'but we struggle to live in the present moment.'

Paul can relate to this: 'I spend all of my time worrying about the future or berating myself about the past!' he exclaims. 'I feel it explains why I am constantly exhausted.'

Dr Jim suggests some mindfulness exercises. Paul immediately envisions hours of sitting like a Buddhist monk in prayer, and he expresses his reservations. Dr Jim reassures him that this won't be the case. Instead, he shares with Paul the mindful awareness and three-minute breathing space exercises.

Paul is intrigued by these exercises, as they seem simple and easy to put into practice. 'But what is their objective?' he asks. 'How will they assist me to deal with my anxiety symptoms?'

Paul and Dr Jim discuss the benefits of mindfulness, that it will help Paul by encouraging him to live in the present moment, thus reducing his tendency to worry and catastrophise, and that if he achieves this objective, his physical symptoms will also decrease. 'There is one final advantage, Paul, in relation to your upcoming exams,' adds Dr Jim. 'If you have practised the three-minute breathing space exercise regularly, your anxiety levels before your exams will drop significantly. And if you go blank or become anxious during your exams, performing this exercise for three minutes will calm down your emotional mind, allowing your rational brain to come into its own.'

Paul sets about learning and practising these exercises. In the beginning, it's difficult to prevent his mind wandering when performing them. But he keeps returning his mind to the task in hand and completes the exercise. He notes that he feels calmer, and it has become easier to let negative thoughts go, without interacting with them. He has also worked hard on challenging his perfectionism. Through regular coin and chaos exercises, and by practising unconditional self-acceptance, he has become more pragmatic about himself and about life.

He finds the mindfulness exercises especially helpful in the run-up to and during his exams. Combining them with the flooding technique has led to a significant improvement in his fatigue and the acute physical symptoms of anxiety. He has now developed a skill that will improve his emotional resilience for life.

Key Learning Points

1. Mindfulness is the awareness which develops when we pay attention to events experienced in the present moment, within the framework of our mind/body, in a non-judgemental and accepting manner.
2. Mindfulness assists us to remain in the present and to become more aware of the world around us. By doing so, it is helpful in dealing with stress, anxiety and emotional distress, and in the prevention of depression.
3. Simple exercises such as the three-minute breathing space exercise are easy to learn and apply, and can greatly improve your mental health.
4. The practice of mindfulness should be the cornerstone of any modern emotional resilience programme.

12. SKILL TEN

HOW TO PROBLEM-SOLVE
The Riddles of Life

What Is Problem-solving?

Problem-solving relates to our ability to find solutions to the many, often complex riddles thrown up by life. It is one of the most important skills for human beings to acquire. To be a successful problem-solver requires patience, adaptability, creativity and a solution-based focus. You may assume problem-solving only relates to work, academia or areas such as science, mathematics or engineering. Indeed, the greatest scientists are creative problem-solvers. Just reflect on the problem-solving genius of Einstein in unmasking the mystery of relativity. Or Watson and Crick in unmasking the structure of DNA.

But this skill has more practical applications. In real life, we are constantly problem-solving. Every time we encounter challenges, whether small or large, from fixing a broken appliance at home to managing complex family or relationship difficulties, we are applying this skill.

Problem-solving is the skill which has allowed modern human beings to advance faster in the last two hundred years than in the previous hundred thousand.

Why Is this Skill Important?

We have left problem-solving to the final chapter on personal emotional resilience skills. This is because a good problem-solver frequently requires a healthy knowledge of the skills already covered. We are often envious of those who seem to handle problems with ease. They appear to pluck solutions out of the air while the rest of us struggle. It's easy to assume that this is a gift granted to a lucky few. The reality is that this is a skill we can learn, practise and pass on to others.

In life, we are constantly faced with complex scenarios in the areas of relationships, academia, working lives and practical domestic affairs. These situations require specific skills to unpick the problem, draw out its essence and seek out potential solutions.

It is the word 'solution' that we must focus on. We often become paralysed when presented with life challenges or problems, especially if these arrive, like London and Dublin buses, in droves. The difficulties arise when we focus more on the problem than the solution. The more we focus on a specific problem, the more our emotional mind will enlarge it, until it is all we see. Instead, we need to encourage our rational mind to focus on potential solutions until they are all we see.

Over time, I have found significant links between problem-solving and mental health. Many of us struggling with anxiety and depression find our capacity to problem-solve impaired. This leads to problems piling up until all we can visualise is a mound of difficulties. The greater the mound, the more anxious and depressed we become. As we explored in Chapter 10, our behaviour is often to procrastinate. Studies into the role of social problem-solving in treatment outcomes (Becker-Weidman et al., 2010; Bell et al., 2009; Thomas et al., 2015) and prevention of depression (Wise, 2017) support these links.

Problem-solving in depression can be compounded by difficulties relating to cold cognition (Rock et al., 2013; Rosier et al., 2013). Cognition relates to our capacity to focus, pay attention, analyse and make decisions, all key ingredients of problem-solving. Cold cognitive difficulties are most often seen in depression, but they can also be a feature in general anxiety and PTSD, where it is especially important to develop problem-solving skills. You can read more about the topic of cold cognition in my book *Depression*.

Difficulties with problem-solving can become especially serious in self-harm and suicide. Suicide occurs when we take our own life because we are unable to find a 'solution' to a particular problem by any other means. This problem can relate to a mental health condition such as depression or a life crisis situation such as financial ruin, addiction or relationship breakdown, among others.

There are also clear links between problem-solving and self-harm and suicide. This has been borne out by research. A recent study (Walker et al., 2017) confirmed that individuals with poorer problem-solving techniques were at increased risk of suicidal behaviour.

It is often the inability of the person who self-harms or dies by suicide to problem-solve the situation that leads them into dark places. If we are unable to do so, the only other option may be to regard ourselves as the problem, with tragic consequences. This would suggest that teaching skills to resolve practical or psychological problems might reduce the incidence of both self-harm and suicide. If we knew how to recognise specific mental health problems, such as anxiety and depression, and problem-solve them at an earlier stage, future emotional distress might be averted.

We, as a society, must assist our children and adolescents to develop this skill from the earliest age, at home and at school. Parents need to stop solving problems for their children and, instead, to encourage them to seek out potential solutions for themselves; to tussle with the challenges of problematic situations and, from their innate emotional and cognitive reserves, problem-solve themselves.

But problem-solving is a skill all of us need to develop and practise. We all encounter difficult and, on occasion, seemingly impossible situations throughout our life journey. If we lack this skill, such problems will grow legs and mount up. The end result can be toxic stress, with its physical and psychological consequences for ourselves and for those we love. We looked at this in *Toxic Stress*.

Develop and practise this skill, and you will find your life running smoother and your stress levels significantly reduced. You will cope more efficiently with any mental health challenges which may arise. You will learn to focus quickly on finding solutions and preventing problems taking over your life. You will become truly emotionally resilient.

How to Develop this Skill

Some of us merge problems together in our emotional mind. This can lead to unhealthy emotions, such as anxiety, and negative behaviours, such as procrastination. Other difficulties arise if we are perfectionists, dislike uncertainty or worry about failure. The skills to manage these were dealt with in previous chapters. If you can relate to any of these, consider visiting those chapters before proceeding further.

If you are ready to proceed, the next step is to acquire a structured problem-solving approach. To achieve this, I recommend the following exercise.

The Problem-solving Exercise

For the next four to eight weeks, when faced with a bundle of problems, disentangle them. List them out individually in your notebook. When you have time, copy this list on to a sheet of paper. Writing them down is especially important, because the rational brain responds best to seeing information laid out visually in front of it. This also reduces the power of our emotional mind to obstruct our capacity to solve problems, by flooding the rational brain with negative emotions such as anxiety, depression or frustration. It is also easier to tease out problems on paper. Only then should you attempt to solve them.

Now, prioritise! Once you have set down your list of problems on paper, enumerate them in order of priority. Always begin with the most pressing one. Begin problem-solving each individual item on the list. If a problem seems unresolvable at that moment, proceed to the next item on the list. Again, this task should be carried out on paper. You need to analyse the problem without becoming obsessed with it. It is easy to stumble at this first hurdle. If you focus too intently on a problem, then it may become insurmountable. Let it float for a while. You need to break down the individual problem into its principal components and proceed quickly to focus on potential solutions to them.

We can summarise these steps as follows:

1. When faced with a group of problems, write them down individually on paper and list them in order of priority.
2. Start with the most pressing one and proceed down through the list one by one. If a problem seems insurmountable at that moment in time, leave it and move on to the next one on the list.
3. Then begin to problem-solve each one on paper. It can sometimes help to break each problem into separate parts and problem-solve each part individually.

Let's take an example. In Chapter 6, we met Michael, who was deeply unhappy in a job where he felt undervalued and overworked. His difficulties lie in the fact that he has a partner, children and a mortgage to be paid. He feels trapped and cannot see a way out of his dilemma. He is anxious and frustrated by the situation. Let's explore how he could have problem-solved this issue by using these techniques.

Clearly, he has issues that need to be resolved. But when he attempts to solve them in his emotional mind, a mixture of anxiety, frustration and procrastination prevent him from coming up with a solution. This is a typical life situation many readers can relate to.

If he had broken down his problem on paper into smaller units, it would have looked like this:

Michael:

- is unhappy in his job, undervalued and overworked
- has financial commitments, especially his mortgage
- has a partner and children
- feels trapped between unhappiness at work and his duty to look after his family

Now Michael has a clear picture on paper of the situation he faces.

The next step in problem-solving is to focus on possible alternative options to deal with the issues identified on paper. This is where your creative mind comes into its own. Freed from paralysis by analysis, and more importantly free of the interference from your emotional brain, your creative mind can focus on a range of potential solutions.

List on paper any reasonable solutions that enter your mind, however bizarre. Just allow your brain to float freely for a period. Be open to seeking out somebody close to you to develop a range of options, too – two heads are indeed better than one.

Once you have unearthed a menu of options, your next task is to ruthlessly analyse each one on paper, and either accept or reject it as a possibility. This may involve doing further research on the viability of a specific option before deciding. At the end of it all, most solutions involve some form of decision-making. Sometimes this may involve a change, other times this might mean leaving things as they are.

You will emerge with a small number of realistic solutions which you can now list in order of priority. Finally, decide which solution seems to be the most viable. Then attempt to put this solution into practice and monitor whether it solves the problem. If it is unsuccessful, proceed to the next most viable option, and so on, until you arrive at a working solution. This is how you problem-solve.

We can summarise these steps as follows:

1. With each problem, focus on a range or menu of options to solve that specific difficulty. If necessary, research possible solutions or seek advice from a suitable advisor.
2. Then decide on a small number of options that appear the most realistic, and choose the one that seems to be the most viable.
3. Attempt to put this solution into practice. If it is effective, that problem has been resolved. If not, move on to the next possible option, and so on, until a solution is found.

In Michael's case, this might work out as follows:
Michael could:

- consider requesting a transfer to a different section of the company

- liaise with his manager and personnel department, detailing his current unhappiness to see if a potential solution, such as a transfer, could be considered
- seek a widening of his brief or a reduction in workload, if the second option is not viable
- review the possibility of upgrading his skills to improve his chances of a move to a different company. This might mean enrolling on a night course
- continue in his current job in the short term – even if he is unhappy, as it pays the bills – while considering other options
- seek out a new job with a different company
- consider a total change of career, and plan to retrain in a different sector

Michael would then research these options and discuss them with his partner. Finally, they could decide on two or three options. He might decide that the first viable solution is to request a move to a different section. If this doesn't resolve the issue, his next option might be to upskill and consider moving to another company. If he makes this decision, he could also decide to stay where he is until ready to make the jump to a new company. As we saw in Chapter 6, this is in fact what he decided to do.

The important point is that most of his energy has gone into coming up with potential solutions, rather than being exhausted through focusing solely on the problem itself.

So, we can summarise how to problem-solve as follows:

1. Write down the problems on paper.
2. Enumerate them in order of priority.
3. Deal with the most pressing problems first and then move on to the rest.
4. Break up each individual problem into smaller chunks of relevance to you.
5. Allow your creative brain to float free so that you can gather a wide range of potential solutions, then write down the results.
6. Narrow down this list to a smaller number of realistic options, researching some of them further if necessary.

7. Prioritise these options in order of viability.
8. Decide what you feel is the best solution.
9. Put this option into practice. If it is effective, then your problem is solved; if not, proceed to the next best option.
10. If you notice that your capacity to problem-solve is being impaired by difficulties with perfectionism, procrastination, frustration, uncertainty or fear of failure, then revisit the chapters on the skills required to deal with these issues.

To develop the skill of problem-solving, it is necessary to practise it regularly. If you do so for several months, you will notice a significant improvement in your problem-solving skills. The benefits that will accrue are incalculable.

Key Learning Points
1. Problem-solving is one of the most important skills for both mental health and emotional resilience.
2. When faced with a group of problems, it is essential to write them down individually in order of priority.
3. We must then problem-solve them one by one, by drawing up a range of realistic solutions for each problem.
4. Once we have a number of solutions, we can put them into practice. If it is effective, the problem is resolved. If not, move on to the next solution.

PART THREE

Social Resilience Skills

13. SKILL ELEVEN

HOW TO DEVELOP EMPATHY
A Meeting of Minds

What Is Empathy?

Empathy is the ability to sense where another person is 'at' emotionally. We all possess this innate ability, though we may not recognise it. I often describe empathy as the capacity to open the door into the mind and heart of another human being. There are so many treasures to be found within them, so many mysteries to be unlocked. Empathy is the key that opens the lock to this door. It is like passing by the gate of a beautiful hidden garden, and catching a tantalising glimpse of some of the flowers and shrubs within it. But to explore the garden in its fullness, you must be able to open the gate and enter. For this, you need the key. Some of us will pass by this hidden garden without even registering it. Others will be drawn to it but, without a key, must forego the pleasures within.

Of the five social skills that we will explore, empathy is the most important and least understood. You may question the wisdom of including it as a skill at all. Surely this is something we are born with, a natural capacity to relate to other human beings? Are not some people fortunate in inheriting this capacity to a greater degree than others? Are they not the healers, doctors, spiritual leaders, teachers, nurses and therapists? Indeed, some people who are attracted to such vocations do have this ability in abundance. But, while some of these observations may be true, they overlook the amazing capacity of the human mind and brain to learn and develop new skills. Empathy is a skill, something we can learn, practise and pass on to others.

The Different Types of Empathy

The modern view of empathy (Denworth, 2017), supported by many years of psychological and neuroscientific research, is that it can be subdivided into three different but interlinking types.

Emotional empathy: this is the most visceral form, where we unconsciously and automatically 'tune in' to another person's emotional state and often mirror their behaviour as a result. This is the form of empathy that is involved in 'emotional contagion'. One of the most beautiful and poignant examples of this in practice followed the death of Diana, Princess of Wales. The national and international outpouring of grief, and the subsequent manner in which so many of us responded behaviourally, can be explained by this form of empathy.

Many of us to this day, on hearing the beautiful rendition of 'Candle in the Wind' sung at the funeral service, will find our emotional empathy responses retriggered and eyes becoming moist. Although emotional empathy is normally an unconscious process, we can direct our conscious mind on it by becoming more self-aware of it in ourselves and others. This understanding is critical when we explore later in this chapter exercises to increase our awareness of empathy.

Cognitive empathy: this is where we consciously try to identify and understand another person's feelings. For this reason it is often called 'perspective-taking'. This is seen as a more deliberate, thought-out process and one therefore very much open to being learned and practised as a skill. This is the form of empathy which allows doctors and therapists to assist those in distress, while keeping their own responses in perspective.

Empathetic concern/Compassion: this is seen as empathy in action. We have picked up emotionally someone's feelings, consciously tried to identify them and as a result find ourselves moved to do something to assist them. A simple example might be where we encounter somebody who is homeless and feel an initial emotional empathy bond, try to then cognitively take perspective on where they are at, and then respond with some practical steps to assist them.

I will not be dealing further in this book with compassion but hope to return to it at a later date.

There has been an ongoing debate on whether breaking up empathy into these subtypes is either accurate or, more importantly, useful. My own view is that emotional and cognitive empathy are intimately and intricately interlinked from both a neuroscientific and, more importantly, from a pragmatic, every-day point of view. If we lack the ability to sense where someone is emotionally, then cognitive empathy is of little use. Equally if we do have good emotional empathy but lack the capacity to put things in perspective through a cognitive empathy process, then we may react inappropriately. For the rest of this chapter I will be treating them as one unit, a vital social skill we can all master.

Empathy and the Brain

The ability to sense what is going on in the emotional world of another is facilitated by the mirror neuron system in the brain, a system I explored in *Flagging the Therapy*. It allows us to 'mirror' in our emotional brain what is happening in the emotional brain of another. This is done through a combination of verbal and non-verbal cues sensed when interacting with that other person socially. You can learn to use this amazing internal system, to better effect this skill in yourself.

The mirror neuron system is important in both emotional and cognitive empathy. But further research (Nummenmaa et al., 2008) has identified other areas of the brain which are specific to both. Parts of the limbic system or emotional brain such as the insula (which is our 'control centre' for physical and emotional pain) are brought into play more in emotional empathy. Similarly areas of our prefrontal cortex or rational brain are more associated with cognitive empathy. This makes sense as this part of the brain is key to our processing of language.

While there are both similarities and differences in relation to emotional and cognitive empathy (and indeed in compassion), it is wiser to consider the brain as one unit when considering empathy. In real life, if we develop our empathy skills, all of these structures and pathways will be working in harmony.

Why do some of us struggle with empathy more than others? Clearly the brain pathways set in motion through our genes and upbringing play a part.

The most important message, however, is that the brain as discussed earlier is neuroplastic so capable of restructuring key pathways. We can therefore, through practice, significantly improve our empathy skills.

The Experience of Empathy

Empathy can be positive or negative. Our emotional brain can pick up positive or negative waves from another person and respond accordingly. Let's take a simple example. Today, you pop into your local supermarket. You meet a lovely young girl, Lisa, at the checkout. She engages with you in a friendly manner, helps you to bag up your shopping and wishes you the best for the day. You come away with a lighter step, a smile on your face. What a lovely interaction that was. You have experienced a positive empathy experience!

The following week, you pop into the same supermarket. You meet her alter ego, Louise, at the checkout. She has a scowl on her face, refuses to help you pack your groceries, fires the change at you and ignores you as you leave. You come away with a heavier step and a frown on your face. What an unpleasant encounter that was. You have just experienced a negative empathy experience. Welcome to the world of empathy!

Why Is this Skill Important?

Empathy is a critical skill that allows us to navigate our social world with greater ease. We spend our lives in the presence of others, whether at home, work or in leisure activities. Struggling to sense where people are at from an emotional point of view makes these social interactions more challenging. We may also lose out on potential life-enhancing riches garnered by positive empathy bonds. Lack of empathy skills explains why we may struggle to be sensitive to the feelings of others. Those who live in the world of frustration, due to high personal ratings, can find empathy for others challenging. It is no surprise that frustration is the most common emotion triggered in those struggling with empathy, and intolerance becomes a secondary behavioural response. The results of both are plain to see.

Empathy is intimately connected to our mental health, positively and negatively. Many with depression have, in my experience, a highly developed sense of empathy. They are especially sensitive to negative empathy. Like flowers, they will bloom if they encounter warm, positive empathy and shrivel if it is the opposite. Any negative empathy experienced by the person with depression will further damage their fragile self-confidence. People with anxiety are equally affected by positive and negative empathy encounters for similar reasons.

Empathy is also of importance in toxic stress. Those struggling with empathy whose lives are ruled by frustration are especially prone to the negative physical and psychological consequences of this condition. There is significant concern among mental health professionals that modern adolescents and young adults struggle with a lack of 'face-to-face' empathy due to the arrival of technology and social media into their lives, and the resulting self-obsession.

It is not surprising, therefore, that the rate of self-harm among our school-going adolescents as already discussed is so high. Anxiety is also endemic in this age group, and a paucity of empathy skills is playing a role in this increased emotional distress. Lack of empathy is one of the destructive components of addiction, contributing to the suffering heaped on loved ones coping with the addict wall. For more on this, see *Flagging the Problem*. As is evidenced by criminals, abusers and serial killers, it is also a serious deficit in psychopaths. There is also some concern that this empathy deficit, when combined with the anonymity of social media, is contributing to the different faces of cyberbullying.

For people living with autism, or with what was formerly known as Asperger's syndrome and is now regarded as a condition on the autism spectrum, empathy is a nightmare. They constantly struggle to sense where other people are, emotionally. Indeed, they struggle with the whole gamut of emotions.

Many high achievers in the business world, such as senior managers and CEOs, may also struggle with empathy. When you speak to groups of managers, it is usually obvious within minutes which ones have developed this skill and which haven't. There can be significant mental and physical consequences for both the manager personally and for those working with them, if empathy skills are in short supply or absent. An empathic work environment is both healthy and successful.

But, the skill of empathy is essential for us all. No matter how developed your skills are in this area, they can be improved upon. The benefits are incalculable. The capacity to open the door into the hearts and minds of those you encounter will greatly improve the quality of your personal and social life.

If you become more empathetic, you will observe yourself becoming more tolerant and sensitive to the feelings of others, less anxious, depressed or stressed, and more content and fulfilled in your everyday life. You will resolve social relationship problems more easily. Finally, you will find yourself emotionally nourished, better equipped and increasingly emotionally resilient in dealing with the difficulties of life.

How to Develop this Skill

If you are struggling with the skill of empathy, firstly eliminate problem areas contributing to your difficulties. So, if you are having difficulties with frustration, for example, visit Chapter 6. Otherwise frustration may prevent you from achieving your goal of improved empathy skills.

Now let's explore two exercises I use to assist people to improve and develop their empathy skills.

Empathy Awareness Exercise

You cannot improve your empathy skills unless you observe them in practice during everyday life. I recommend this awareness exercise for the next four weeks. Focus fully on becoming aware of positive and negative empathy experiences in yourself and others. I am asking you to open your mind to what happens at home, work, school, college and during leisure activities, when you or someone within your orbit reacts positively or negatively to whatever someone else is saying or doing.

It could be observing what happens when a child or a teenager asks their parent a question. If the parent responds empathetically, you will observe the positive response of the child; the opposite will be true if the parent's response is negative. It could be at work when a colleague, or indeed yourself, receives a positive or dismissive response to some observation or request made of a work colleague or boss. Once again, you may notice hackles rising if experiencing a negative empathy experience and vice versa if a positive one. It could occur within your relationship, or when engaging in a sporting activity, or involved in any interaction with friends or others. You may observe someone, depending on the empathy interaction experienced, responding positively or pulling back. It may occur during an interaction involving a service, whether shopping, banking, attending the dentist, doctor or nurse. Become aware of how you are responding and people's responses to you. Try to gauge whether you can pick up any associated non-verbal cues. We will be exploring these in the next chapter. It is worth carrying a notebook round with you and writing down any unusual positive or negative empathy interactions. Later, go through them and see how they made you or others feel.

Within a month, you will notice that you are becoming increasingly observant of the social interactions you had previously taken for granted, increasingly aware of the effects of your own interactions with people and more tuned in to them emotionally. You will have developed a 'radar' for positive and negative empathy, noticing how you personally and others respond behaviourally to both. You have now made your first step towards developing genuine empathy skills for the future.

Empathy in Practice Exercise

The next step is to practise empathy in social situations. For the next four to eight weeks, I suggest the following exercise. Each time you engage with somebody within your social world, focus only on the person you are communicating with. In each interaction, push yourself into the background. This is much harder to put into practice than you might think. We are all a bit self-obsessed, only interested in what pertains to our own little world. When interacting with others, how often do you focus only on what is relevant to 'you' in the conversation?

With this exercise, the whole focus should be on trying to sense emotionally where the person is at. Involve yourself emotionally in the story they are telling you, at that moment in time. Are they sad, happy, hurt, annoyed or frustrated? Feel yourself being drawn into where they are at. It requires patience and concentration when performing this exercise for the first time. Your instinct may be to rush in and move the interaction to where you would like it to go. This may finish up with you missing the emotional impact of the conversation topic on the person you are interacting with.

If you are performing this exercise fully, you will observe your emotions mirroring those of the other person. You may feel sad or joyful while interacting with their experiences. This is the first real sign that you are opening the door into their hearts and minds. This is the point where you can begin to share your own experiences and emotions about what has been discussed. For, now, you are experiencing a two-way meeting of minds. From this point on, it is like singing from the same hymn sheet emotionally. You will notice that both parties enjoy leaving the conversation with a positive empathy experience.

Over time and with practice, you will observe how you are listening with your whole body, not just your ears. Your emotional brain is tuning in to the music emanating from the other person's emotional world. You will observe yourself speaking less, listening more and responding instinctively to the other person, as they reveal something especially difficult or sad. This you may do automatically, almost without thinking, as your two worlds meet and share the experience.

When you notice yourself gentler, warmer and more careful with other people's emotions, you have truly arrived. It is now that the real treasures that empathy can unveil appear. You will discover a richness in others' emotional experiences that you might spend your life missing out on.

If you practise these two exercises for several months, the benefits will remain with you for life. This is a skill that, once developed and practised, you can automatically and unconsciously apply. You will sense people being more comfortable around you, often revealing core insights that otherwise would have remained hidden. Your life will consequently be enriched. When difficulties arise in life, you will handle them better, as empathy skills ease the journey and increase your emotional resilience.

COLM'S STORY

Colm attends an appointment with Dr Jim following final warnings from both his company and long-suffering wife, Liz, to 'change or else'! He is also on a physical health warning from their family doctor. Colm is in his mid-forties, a tough, uncompromising section manager of a large, multinational company. He has been married for fifteen years to Liz, and they have two children. Externally, all seems perfect. Behind this public façade, however, all is not what it seems.

Colm comes from a background where empathy had been brutally stamped out. 'Feelings are for wimps' was the mantra drilled into him by his father. Colm has absorbed the message fully.

He lives in a world of impossibly high rating. Frustration is his second name. He cannot tolerate anything other than perfection at work or home. His frustration boils over constantly, leading to multiple problems within his section and resulting in a high turnover of staff. His employers are losing patience. He has been given a final warning to change his ways or demotion or dismissal will result. At home, matters are also coming to a head. His constant lack of empathy has driven a wedge between himself, Liz and his teenage children. His constant eruptions, secondary to frustration when all is not perfect, are stretching Liz's patience to the limit. Much as she loves him, living with him has become impossible. Dr Jim is her last hope.

Things come to a head when his family doctor and cardiologist discover an underlying cardiac arrhythmia. They believe this to be a direct result of toxic stress, driven by frustration, elevating his acute stress hormone, noradrenaline.

Colm now accepts that something has to change, and so is open to whatever Dr Jim suggests.

Having listened with empathy to his story, Dr Jim explains why he is in such a mess in his personal relationships and working life. They explore how to manage frustration and perfectionism. They then begin to discuss the world of empathy. Colm feels like an alien who has just arrived on planet Earth. Dr Jim is discussing something beyond his comprehension, namely emotions. Colm wonders why this is such a struggle for him. Dr Jim suggests that the most likely explanation lies in his upbringing. He suggests some CBT exercises. He then explains what rational and irrational beliefs are and how they will use the ABC concept to locate them.

Dr Jim asks for a typical situation that might reveal Colm's difficulties with lack of empathy, which they could use as a trigger.

'A request from one of my team to take a week off for personal reasons,' replies Colm.

'And how did that affect you emotionally?' asks Dr Jim.

'I became extremely annoyed and frustrated.'

'And how did it make you feel physically?'

Colm admits to feeling extremely tense, muscles in knots and a pulsing behind his eyes. 'I was so wound up,' he explains, 'like a drum.'

'Now we have the trigger, the emotion and how it made you feel physically,' says Dr Jim. 'But what is it about this request for a week off for personal reasons that made you feel frustrated?'

'I could not accept that personal problems were more important than the efficient running of the section. We were negotiating an important business deal at the time, and he was an integral part of the team involved.'

'But why would this cause you to feel frustrated?'

'That he could not see the job was more important than humdrum issues involving his personal life,' Colm replies.

'And did you investigate what these personal issues were?'

'I am not interested in what is going on in my team's or indeed anybody else's lives. Targets are all that concern me. If they can't handle the heat, they should get out of the kitchen!'

It is increasingly clear to Dr Jim where Colm's problems lie. But he continues to explore why this trigger vexed him so much.

'Was there anything else about this situation that was frustrating you?' he asks.

'I felt that it was not my role to be a father figure to my staff. They are grown adults. I should not have to put up with all this hassle. They have been with me long enough to know the goals I set and the standards I demand.'

Dr Jim now realises the difficulties encountered by Colm's company and his wife. Colm has little or no understanding of the world of empathy. Clearly, they have work to do.

'Let's examine what irrational belief was triggered by this situation,' suggests Dr Jim. 'So, what demands were you making following this request from a member of your section to take time off work for personal reasons?' After discussion, they agree his demand was that he should not have to put up with this nonsense. Subsequently adding that he should not have to suffer discomfort, and his team and indeed the world should change to suit him.

'And what was your behaviour on becoming frustrated following this request for a week's break for personal reasons?' Dr Jim asks.

'I became irritable, and I let him know how unhappy I was with his request,' explains Colm. 'I informed him in no uncertain terms what was expected of him if he was to continue working in my section. I obviously refused his request. He became upset, of course. But I quickly squashed that emotional nonsense. I am much too busy for such childish behaviour!' He also admits that he was extremely irritable at home that evening.

They are now able to complete an ABC on the trigger.

A   Activating Event:
- Trigger: a section member at work seeking a week off for personal reasons
- Inference/danger: the employee was prioritising his personal life over his workplace; the employee in question was involved in key business negotiations; he should have understood the only thing that mattered were the targets set for the section; it would be better if his team did not expose him to hassle and discomfort by such behaviour; and, moreover, it would be better if his team and indeed the world in general changed to suit him

B   Belief/Demands: 'I should not have to put up with this nonsense. The team member should not have put in a request for leave to deal with personal issues. My team (and indeed the world) should change to ensure I do not suffer any discomfort. I should not have to suffer discomfort.'

C   Consequences:
- Emotional reactions: frustration
- Physical reactions: muscles tense; pulsations behind eyes; palpitations
- Behaviour: persistently irritable and moody at work and at home; lets the employee know that this was not what was expected of a member of his section; refuses permission for the employee to take the week off for personal reasons

'So now that we understand, Colm, what made you so frustrated about this situation and your resulting behaviour, let's help you to reshape your thinking and behaviour in relation to it. Because if we're successful in this instance, we can apply the same ideas to similar situations in the future,' says Dr Jim. 'We could dispute or challenge your "A", or your interpretation, but what is much more effective is to challenge your irrational belief, the real driver of your frustration, and the emotional, physical and behavioural consequences of this belief.'

First they deal with the unhealthy behaviours they have uncovered and how to challenge them. Is it helpful to dismiss his team member's personal difficulties and refuse his request? Is this going to weaken or strengthen his team in terms of bonding? How could being persistently irritable and moody at home and work, for example, advance the situation?

Colm initially argues his case, but then reluctantly agrees that his behaviour is unhelpful. They also examine the role of his aggression hormone, noradrenaline, in causing his physical symptoms and how this is triggered by frustration.

'Let's now examine and challenge your "B", or your irrational belief,' says Dr Jim. 'This took the form of the absolute demand that your team member should not have put in his request for time off, and that you should not have to put up with this nonsense. You were also demanding that you must not suffer discomfort, and that your work situation should change to accommodate you.

Finally, you were demanding that the section should achieve the high standards you expect of them at any cost. Are these demands rational or irrational?' Dr Jim asks.

After a long discussion, Colm reluctantly accepts an element of irrationality. He begins to understand how, throughout his life, he has assumed the world has a duty to change to suit him so that he doesn't have to suffer discomfort. Dr Jim and Colm also explore the world of rating and Colm's demand for perfectionism. Not surprisingly, he rates himself at ninety-five out of a hundred. He also accepts that he has been applying the same unyielding principles to his home life as well. It is one of those rare, life-changing insights. Colm becomes determined to mend his ways. Dr Jim then suggests some frustration and coin exercises, already discussed in earlier chapters, to trigger Colm and teach him how to manage frustration in everyday life. He is also given exercises to challenge his high self-rating and perfectionism.

Dr Jim then challenges Colm's demand that the world must change to suit him. Following this, Colm begins to alter his behaviour at work and home. On subsequent visits, they revisit the world of empathy. Colm freely admits that this is a skill profoundly lacking in his arsenal. They have a fruitful discussion on the usefulness of developing this skill at work and especially at home. Dr Jim then introduces him to the empathy awareness and empathy in action exercises.

Colm becomes flustered, and feels totally out of his depth. 'This is like entering a foreign country for me,' he mutters. 'I was never good on the emotions front.'

Dr Jim reassures him that it is normal to be anxious and uncertain when acquiring a new skill such as this, but he notes that the long-term benefits will make the effort worthwhile. They agree that Colm will carry around a notebook and write down his observations while attempting to apply these exercises.

For the following three months, Colm diligently performs them. In the beginning, he struggles with the world of positive and negative empathy. Over time, however, he grasps the concepts, incorporating them into his life. He notices his team seems happier, productivity has increased and there are no further difficulties with personnel. His bosses commend Colm on his turn-around. Of greater importance, his home life and relationships are transformed. He still occasionally loses his cool, but he quickly apologises when he spots the negative empathy response this creates. His physical health has also improved, as has his emotional resilience.

Key Learning Points

1. Empathy is the ability to sense where another person is 'at' emotionally.
2. It is the most important social skill of all, and essential for emotional resilience.
3. A positive empathy experience will encourage us to open like a flower to the warmth of the sun; a negative one, to shrivel like a flower exposed to harsh, cold conditions.
4. With the assistance of some empathy exercises, we can learn to develop and expand our empathy skills.

14. SKILL TWELVE

HOW TO READ AND INTERPRET NON-VERBAL CUES
Reading the Signs

What are Non-verbal Cues?

We often fail to recognise how much interpersonal communication is non-verbal. While verbally conversing, a world of subliminal processing is occurring behind the scenes. We absorb messages from a person's face, eyes, tone of voice, presence or absence of body tension, and smell. We are unconsciously registering if what they are saying is in harmony with information received through these senses. Ninety per cent of our interactions are non-verbal. Yet, frequently, we either fail to register such cues or we misinterpret them, which can lead to unforeseen consequences. Being able to recognise and interpret such cues is an important social skill which can dramatically improve the quality of your everyday life.

Why Do We Need this Skill?

It has happened to us all. We meet someone socially and experience an immediate 'gut' feeling of liking or disliking them. We make resulting snap decisions to encourage or discourage further contact. We tend to lock this information into our emotional memory and behave accordingly if we encounter them in the future. Let's take an example. Theresa meets Tom at a party and her gut feeling is that he is not her type. He seems full of himself, even cocky. She adroitly ends the conversation. Poor old Tom is now history. She made her assessment based not solely on their conversation, but also on subliminal messages picked up non-verbally.

In *Flagging the Therapy,* I explored the lightning-fast neural systems in the brain that mediate these rapid assessments. Some involve the mirror neuron system, already discussed in the previous chapter on empathy. Others involve specialised nerve cells called spindle neurons. These have the onerous task of assisting us in making such assessments and the resulting behavioural responses. Theresa was unconsciously using these systems to make her initial assessment.

But was she reading the signs correctly? More importantly, had she made an instant judgement, without taking extra care to confirm the accuracy of her initial assessment? As events unfolded, she would later discover her gut assessment was completely unfounded.

Theresa subsequently encountered Tom in a different setting, both finding themselves helping at a soup kitchen for the homeless. This time, Theresa discarded her initial assessment and sat down afterwards, to chat with Tom at a deeper level. He revealed how anxious he becomes in social situations, how his seemingly cocky demeanour in social situations camouflaged this anxiety. They ended up dating and became a couple.

There is much to be learned from this little scenario, often played out in our social world. We constantly misread non-verbal cues, and can end up behaving accordingly, stubbornly refusing to accept our first assessment may have been incorrect.

Empathy and the reading of non-verbal cues go hand in hand. If struggling with one, you will usually struggle with the other. These skills are important in relation to our mental health. One of the most common and distressing difficulties arising in depression is the misreading of non-verbal cues. This occurs in two ways. The person with depression struggles with reading the signs, focusing only on non-verbal cues that support their view that they are not worth being around. Other people who interact with the person also misread the cues, assuming they are aloof, rude, boring or lazy. This is also common in some forms of anxiety. Many people with social anxiety persistently misinterpret non-verbal social cues. They believe the physical symptoms of anxiety will be noticed by others around them, which is untrue. Others with general anxiety may also misread non-verbal cues, seeing danger where none is present. People with sociopathy and psychopathy, who struggle to feel emotions, learn to develop their non-verbal cues skills to make it seem as if they do experience them.

The misreading of non-verbal cues is one of the main signs of autism and what was previously known as Asperger's syndrome, now regarded as a condition on the autism spectrum. It explains why such conditions are so distressing for the sufferers. They struggle to pick up on non-verbal cues and thus do not know how to respond to other people's emotions.

This skill is essential for all of us. We live in a social world, where the ability to sense and interpret such cues can be of tremendous benefit. If you develop this skill, it will allow you to read people better and sense where they are at emotionally. It will prevent you making rash snap judgements which later turn out to be unhelpful or even damaging. If you can develop this skill and combine it with a healthy mix of emotional and cognitive empathy, your social and personal life will be transformed. You may also find it easier to navigate the complex world of relationships.

How to Develop this Skill

To develop the skill of reading non-verbal cues correctly, we must first explore how the brain imbibes and analyses information in social interactions, especially when meeting a person for the first time. The brain is particularly interested in first impressions. This is our emotional mind and brain rapidly coming to a snap decision as to how best to manage an interaction. All the information pouring in from our senses is integrated to create this first impression. The emotional brain combines with lower parts of the logical brain to draw these lightning-fast conclusions. Later, if further information arrives that contradicts these first impressions, the rational brain re-analyses and regularly overrules them.

To become a good reader of people and situations, we need to be skilled at engaging with the following. Firstly, we need to practise observing non-verbal cues and, secondly, we need to train ourselves to put initial assumptions to the test before accepting them as true. This is not, of course, to dismiss first impressions, which are sometimes quite accurate. It is more to seek evidence that they are indeed so. To acquire this skill, I suggest two exercises.

The Non-verbal Cues Exercise

One of the important capacities of the brain is to focus attention, if required, on functions normally carried out automatically. Generally, when chatting to someone, we are unconsciously absorbing non-verbal messages. It is a fascinating exercise, however, to *consciously* focus our rational or logical mind on non-verbal cues emanating from the other person.

For the next month, consciously focus on information coming in from your senses during every social interaction. As with empathy exercises, you need to remove your natural inclination to focus on yourself during each conversation for this to be effective. Become mindfully aware of their facial expressions, tone of voice, bodily stance, how they use their hands, the presence or absence of muscle tension, whether they look you in the eye or away, and any other relevant information. These are the non-verbal cues, which up to this point you may have taken for granted.

Now assess if the non-verbal cues seem at one, or out of character, with what the person is saying. For example, a person might be expressing sorrow about something, while non-verbal cues suggest otherwise. Or they may be laughing at some joke, while their body language indicates they are not amused. Try to analyse what the body language and cues are telling you on first impression. It might be interesting to write these impressions down in your notebook and later compare them to your final assessments. This is a powerful exercise, assisting you to become increasingly aware of non-verbal cues and how to interpret what they are implying.

Second Impressions Exercise

This is a wonderful exercise if you find that you are regularly putting your foot in it, socially! If you are constantly misreading cues and later feeling foolish, this exercise is for you. For the next month, seek out non-verbal cues in every social situation, on your initial meeting with a person. List your first impressions in your notebook when you have a moment.

Then, rationally seek out evidence proving these first impressions are accurate. This might mean seeking information from other sources as to what the person is like in real life. Or probing the person more deeply either on first or subsequent meetings. In such situations, try to uncover evidence, supportive or not, for your first impressions. Or, when reflecting on the interaction, did the non-verbal cues clash with what the person was saying? That might lead you to question why this might be.

You will be amazed how often first impressions are false. This occurs because the emotional brain has learned to make lightning-fast observations and conclusions. It then leaves it up to your rational brain to seek out evidence to the contrary. There are often reasons why a person's non-verbal cues are out of kilter. They may be anxious or depressed, or good at masking how they feel. We may not be getting a true picture of the person at all. Some of us are very deep and, like a sculptor, you may have to chisel away at the surface to discover what lies beneath.

There will be occasions where you are certain that these first impressions are correct, others where you are unsure. Write down such results of these assessments in your notebook. In time, further evidence may appear that will strengthen or weaken these conclusions. You can later compare initial assessments with concluding ones. It can be a salutary, often humbling experience to discover how inaccurate your first impressions were.

A good rule of thumb is to assume first impressions are frequently wrong, and treat them with caution until proven otherwise. This exercise will assist you in accepting that your reading of non-verbal cues, while helpful, can on occasion be completely inaccurate. Learning to be patient and taking the effort to uncover confirmatory evidence can save you from a world of trouble!

If you practise these two exercises together with the empathy exercises discussed in the previous chapter, the benefits to your social world will be substantial. You will find yourself more tuned in to non-verbal cues, giving you increased insight into the person you are communicating with. More importantly, you will be more measured in assessing and treating people you have encountered in social situations. The capacity to read such signs correctly is a key emotional resilience skill of great assistance in times of stress.

Key Learning Points

1. Ninety per cent of our communications are non-verbal in nature, where we subliminally absorb messages from a person's face, eyes, tone of voice, presence or absence of body tension, and smell.
2. These non-verbal cues, which occur at lightning speed, play an important role in how we make sense of and navigate our social world.
3. Problems can arise, however, when we misinterpret these cues and later find out that our first impressions were in fact inaccurate.
4. With the assistance of some exercises, we can improve our reading and interpretation of these cues. Combining this skill with empathy can transform our social world.

15. SKILL THIRTEEN

HOW TO BECOME COMFORTABLE IN SOCIAL SITUATIONS
'The Party I Want to Avoid'

Why Is this Skill Important?

Some readers will know the feeling. An invitation arrives to attend a party. For some of us, this is greeted with delight, an opportunity to meet up with friends or encounter interesting strangers. For others of us, it presents a greater challenge. Uncomfortable in social interactional situations, we become extremely anxious when an invitation arrives. People who struggle in these situations are suffering from social anxiety. We deal with this condition in detail in *Anxiety and Panic*, for those who would like to understand and eliminate it from their lives. We can avoid social anxiety, however, by developing the skill of how to become comfortable in social situations.

This is a skill we should all develop as early in life as possible. Many of our adolescents and young adults, who are more comfortable communicating online, struggle with this social skill, leading to significant social anxiety in their young adult lives. Some readers may want to skip this skill, assuming it is not relevant to them, but I encourage you to bear with me. There will always be social situations where we might feel slightly uncomfortable. It is useful to understand why it is happening and what to do about it. Even if you are not experiencing significant personal difficulties in this area, family members, friends or work colleagues may not be so fortunate. We need to be empathetic to their struggles and have the knowledge to assist them.

How to Develop this Skill

When exposed to a social interactional situation, the socially anxious person is concerned that some of the following may occur:

1. They will develop the classic signs of acute anxiety, in the form of a racing heart, a stomach in knots, sweating, blushing, a dry mouth and a sense of dread.
2. Everyone will notice these physical symptoms.
3. People will notice that they are awkward, fidgety, hanging around the edge of groups, and poor at conversation.
4. Lastly, if any or all of the above do happen, people will assume they are anxious and judge them accordingly as weak or socially inadequate. Because of these concerns, people with social anxiety will engage in a host of avoidant or safety behaviours, which compound the problem.

Let's take Maria. She is invited to attend a workplace event in a local hotel, and immediately becomes physically anxious and considers pulling out. However, she is prevailed upon by her boss to attend. The closer she gets to the event, the more physically anxious she becomes.

Maria is convinced her colleagues will see her experiencing these physical symptoms, and that's when her difficulties accelerate. What will happen if they view her as anxious and, as a result, judge her as weak or socially inadequate? She will be so embarrassed.

At the event, she becomes extremely self-conscious of everything she does, which makes her more anxious. She struggles to engage in conversation. She finds herself in the toilets, constantly checking her appearance before and during the event. She stays well out, at the edge of the group, hoping nobody will see how anxious she is. These behaviours ratchet up her anxiety levels. She finds the whole night an exhausting ordeal, and leaves at the earliest opportunity. If you can relate to these emotions and physical feelings, and are uncomfortable in social situations, then the following insights and exercises may be of assistance.

In Chapter 4, we explored how to manage the physical symptoms of anxiety through flooding and, in Chapter 3, how to achieve unconditional self-acceptance. It might be useful to revisit these areas, as they underlie the difficulties such social situations present. If you have developed and practised these two skills, it becomes easier to understand and carry out the exercises that follow.

What Was Maria Anxious About?

Let's now explore what Maria was anxious about. Firstly, she assumed that other people could see her sweating, blushing, and so on. But is this true in real life? The answer is no! The reality is that the physical symptoms of anxiety are impossible to see, despite what Maria feels. She was also anxious they would see her as fidgety and uncomfortable, or a poor conversationalist. What Maria believes metaphorically is that she is wearing the equivalent of a 'high-vis' jacket which will make her stand out in the crowd and be instantly recognisable.

Once again, is this true? No. We are all so obsessed with our own worlds that we rarely register such behaviours.

Her final concern was that others would judge her, due to these anxiety symptoms, as weak and socially inadequate. It is this belief that is causing her to feel embarrassed. But does this happen in real life? No. Maria does not understand that she is a long way down their list of priorities, at the top of which they put themselves. Most people will be unaware she is even in the room! Many readers can relate to Maria's discomfort. They struggle to accept that others do not see the physical symptoms of anxiety and judge them accordingly. If you fall into this group, I recommend the following exercises. They may seem whacky, but they teach us important lessons about what actually happens in real-life social situations, for social anxiety is created by false perceptions versus reality.

The Anxiety Inspector Exercise

For the next four weeks, in every social event you encounter, seek out those people who clearly suffer from the physical symptoms of anxiety. Since a significant number in every group will be anxious, this should be an easy task! When you find them, write down in your notebook what physical symptoms you observed that convinced you they were anxious. Strangely enough, you may find plenty of blank pages in your notebook. In practice, you will struggle to identify such symptoms, as it is virtually impossible to pick them out. So, what does that say about the chances of others seeing similar physical symptoms in you, when you are anxious?

The Supermarket Exercise

I use many versions of this 'embarrassment exercise' to assist people in becoming comfortable in a social situation. Underlying the exercise is the false belief, held by many of us in social situations, that people are busy watching and assessing us as anxious and, as a result, judging us. These perceptions emanate from our emotional mind but are not borne out rationally in real life. We may cognitively agree with this, but emotionally we still cling on to our false perceptions.

Here is one version of the exercise. Visit several busy supermarkets weekly for four weeks. Take a basket, and fill it with ten separate items. Then join the busiest checkout queue. Just as you get to the cashier, excuse yourself from the queue and then reverse your steps, returning to each aisle and replacing the items back on their shelves. You then leave the store empty-handed. You will feel incredibly self-conscious. Everyone in the store will be looking at you and judging you. Right? Who is this lunatic?

Or will they? The purpose of this exercise is for you to observe what happens in practice. In your emotional mind, this exercise is going to be a nightmare of embarrassment. In practice, most people will barely notice your presence in the store. They will be so busy and preoccupied with their own worlds that you will fail to register on their horizon. They will just note a shorter queue! But you must experience this in real life to appreciate this truth. You can vary the exercise by putting on bright clothes, or a wide-brimmed hat or anything that in your mind makes you stick out like a sore thumb, while carrying out the same exercise. This is the easiest of the supermarket exercises to perform. There are other, more wicked ones!

If you do these exercises repeatedly, you will begin to understand emotionally that in practice people notice almost nothing. They are completely self-obsessed, do not register the physical symptoms of anxiety never mind judge you, and are often barely aware of your actual existence. These exercises must be carried out with a sense of humour.

In the beginning, you will feel extremely self-conscious and anxious. After performing them repeatedly you may notice, wryly, that you are less important socially than you think you are. It is so disconcerting! You will also find yourself less anxious and stressed about social interactions, approaching them more with a sense of humour rather than being anxious or embarrassed. Eventually you will be comfortable not only in your own skin, but in the presence of others. Your social anxiety will be a distant memory. Later I will introduce you to a conversation exercise to assist you further in social situations.

KAREN'S STORY

Karen has come to see Dr Jim due to her constant feelings of anxiety when socialising. She is twenty-seven and envious of her friends who appear comfortable in social situations. It is making her task of meeting someone impossible.

He empathises and suggests that he might assist her with some CBT approaches to deal with her social anxiety. He then explains what rational and irrational beliefs are, and how they will use the ABC concept to locate them.

He then asks her for an example of a typical social situation that makes her feel anxious. She outlines a recent invitation to join up with some girlfriends in the local pub. She became especially anxious when she heard there would be some guys there, as part of the group.

'And how did that make you feel physically?' asks Dr Jim.

'The nearer I got to the time, the more panicky I became,' she replies. 'I found my heart beating faster, my stomach was in knots, I had a dry mouth, my muscles were tense and I felt very shaky.' She adds that when she arrived at the pub she was blushing and sweating.

'What was it about meeting your friends including these guys that made you so anxious?' Dr Jim asks. 'What danger were you applying to this upcoming meeting in the pub? What did you visualise would happen?'

'I suppose the main danger was that they would observe that I was odd or weird,' she answers.

'And what was it about you that they would consider odd or weird?'

'They would see that I was tense, quiet, sweating and blushing,' says Karen. 'It would be so embarrassing.' On further probing, she admits that her main danger was that they would assume she was an anxious person.

'And why would that bother you?' asks Dr Jim.

'They would judge me as being weak,' she admits in a subdued voice.

'Now let's examine what irrational belief was triggered by this situation,' says Dr Jim. 'This usually takes the form of some absolute demand you are making about the trigger.' After some discussion, they decide that the demands making her anxious relate to not being exposed to any situation where people might see she is anxious. They also agree that what was making her ashamed was the demand that when the guys did judge her, she must accept their judgement.

'Underlying shame or embarrassment is the belief that people will discover something secret about us,' explains Dr Jim. 'In your case, it is that you get anxious in social situations. After learning this secret, your fear is that you would be judged negatively, a pronouncement you would be forced to accept.'

Finally, they explore her behaviour. This unveiled a complex series of rituals that Karen engaged in when she went to the pub. She spent hours beforehand checking herself in the mirror and practising what she was going to talk about in conversation. On getting to the pub, she headed straight to the ladies to check if she was blushing and she always kept a jacket on to hide any sweating under her armpits. She then gulped down a glass of wine to calm herself. She also admits that she stayed at the edge of the group, not engaging in conversation, but constantly monitoring the faces of the guys to see how she was coming across. She avoided initiating any conversations in case she made a fool of herself, and ended up coming home early, to the dreaded post-mortem.

'It just exhausted me, the whole thing,' Karen says despairingly.

Dr Jim empathises, and they then put together an ABC on the event.

A   Activating Event:
- Trigger: meeting some friends in a pub, including some guys she did not know
- Inference/danger: people will see she is tense, quiet, sweating, blushing and not interacting with the group; they will then assume she is an anxious person; as a result, they will assume she is a weak, odd, weird person, as only weak people get anxious; she will have to agree with their judgement

B   Belief/Demands: 'I must not be exposed to any social situation where people will see I am anxious. People will judge me, and I must accept their judgement.'

C   Consequences:
- Emotional reactions: anxiety; shame/embarrassment
- Physical reactions: stomach in knots, heart beating a little faster, shaking, muscle tension, sweating and blushing
- Behaviour: rehearses what she will say before arriving at the pub; checks herself constantly in the mirror before leaving her flat; goes straight to the toilets to check if she is blushing or sweating; then straight to the bar for a drink to reduce her anxiety; keeps her jacket on to make sure nobody will notice that she might be sweating; stays at the edge of the group and avoids starting a conversation; rehearses what she might say before contributing to any conversation; leaves the pub early and alone; carries out a post-mortem on how badly she has come across, especially to the guys

Dr Jim then challenges Karen's thinking and behaviour. He begins by exploring her behaviours. They agree her complex rituals are not only unhelpful but exhausting. He then challenges her irrational beliefs. Does she really have to accept any one's opinion of her? Dr Jim helps her develop the skill of unconditional self-acceptance, encouraging her to join the Members Only club. This is a major insight for Karen, who has spent years rating herself as weak and a failure. They also agree that it is impossible to avoid situations where she might become anxious.

'But do people really see the physical symptoms of anxiety?' Dr Jim asks her.

'I have always believed they could,' replies Karen, 'especially the blushing and sweating. They must be so obvious to everyone.'

'I think it is time to introduce you to some exercises,' says Dr Jim with a mischievous smile. He then introduces her to the anxiety inspector exercise, which she finds intriguing. She promises to put it into practice.

Dr Jim then asks her: 'How much do people really notice in social situations?'

Karen had never really explored this rationally, always assuming they noticed every small detail. 'I assume they see everything,' she answers.

'In practice, they see almost nothing,' Dr Jim explains. 'People are very self-obsessed and really are only interested in their own worlds.' For Karen, this was a lightbulb moment. But even though she could accept Dr Jim's words rationally, she found it difficult to do so emotionally.

On listening to her doubts, Dr Jim smiles. 'I am going to give you a further exercise,' he says, 'which will help you develop some emotional insight.' He proceeds to give her the supermarket exercise. She is terrified at the prospect of what seems like an extremely intimidating exercise. He reassures her that it has assisted countless others to get over their social anxiety, so she agrees reluctantly.

Three months later, Karen is a new person. Through performing these exercises, she has come to realise she is not as important as she thought she was! Since she could not see symptoms of anxiety in others, she has realised the same applies to herself. She has also developed unconditional self-acceptance skills. With the assistance of a conversation exercise Dr Jim gave her, a skill we will be exploring later, Karen has become increasingly at ease in social situations. Most importantly, she has met up with Mark, whom she has fancied for some time, but has previously been too anxious and embarrassed to approach. Romance is now firmly in the air, with her social anxiety consigned to the past!

Key Learning Points

1. Learning how to be comfortable in social situations is one of the most important emotional resilience skills to assist us in navigating our social world.
2. Those who struggle with this skill often believe that others can see signs they are physically anxious and that they will be judged as weak if this happens.
3. They engage in a host of safety and avoidant behaviours which can paralyse their social lives.
4. With the assistance of some simple exercises, we can challenge some of these misperceptions and behaviours and learn to embrace rather than dread social situations.

16. SKILL FOURTEEN

HOW TO DEAL WITH PERFORMANCE ANXIETY
'My Mind Will Just Go Blank'

It's the task so many of us dread! The request to speak or perform in public, whether it's giving a presentation at a work meeting or that best man or father-of-the-bride speech. It may be a reading in church, a request to speak to a group of parents, a performance on stage or an oral presentation to fellow students. Life is full of potential social performance situations, exposing us to the harsh light of public scrutiny.

The origins of why some of us struggle with this social skill may lie in our past. It may have been a teacher making a fool of us publicly at a sensitive stage in adolescence, or overtly critical parents making comments about our performance in public situations. It behoves all of us, whether parents, teachers or anyone involved in the rearing or education of children, to be careful not to embarrass a child when speaking or performing in public.

Another cause, especially of relevance in adolescents, may be 'friends' mocking us in public. Whatever the reasons, many of us end up dreading these social situations. We deal with this form of social performance anxiety in detail in *Anxiety and Panic*, for those who are interested.

Why Is this Skill Important?

We will all frequently be challenged to apply this skill in the many and varied situations in which we find ourselves in life. For those working in business, for example, this skill is essential. Meetings, internal and external, are the norm in a modern progressive business. If you struggle to present, your life can become a quiet hell!

From a mental health perspective, some people may suffer from significant performance anxiety as part of an overall social anxiety. Other people with depression may also dread performance situations, as they may also assume that everyone present will judge them harshly.

I feel this skill should be taught to all children and adolescents as early as possible in life. The knowledge of how to handle performance anxiety will then carry over into their adult lives. I also feel that we should be teaching them that we all get physically anxious when presenting to others in public. In this way, we normalise such physical symptoms. We must teach them how to harness these physical symptoms rather than fear them.

It is useful for all of us to understand why we, and others, become so anxious and embarrassed in performance situations. There is a little bit of social performance anxiety in all of us, unless we are genuine extroverts who revel in public performances.

What Underlies Performance Anxiety?

In performance anxiety, our major concern is that we will become so physically anxious that we will freeze in front of what we perceive as an extremely critical audience who will, inevitably, judge us harshly as failures. In the previous chapter, we explored how those of us who become anxious in social interactional situations have similar concerns. The difference in performance anxiety is the feeling that we are 'hanging out there' publicly, and that we will be unable to escape the searing light of public humiliation if something goes wrong.

The most common nightmare danger for the person with performance anxiety is that if they do freeze, because of the physical symptoms of anxiety, their minds will go blank or else they will clam up. This will result in them looking incredibly foolish and embarrassed. 'What will people think of me if this happens?' They are also preoccupied with the belief that people will observe they are physically anxious and judge them as weak for demonstrating such physical signs. The more they catastrophise about how awful it will be, the more anxious they become. To counteract the possibility that this social humiliation might arise, they will over-prepare for the event to the level, on occasion, of trying to memorise the presentation, in order to lessen the chances of going blank or clamming up. This leads to increased anxiety.

How to Manage Performance Anxiety

If we delve into performance anxiety at a deeper level, we find ourselves immersed in the realms of fear of failure, the physical symptoms of anxiety and especially the world of rating. We have already explored the skills required to deal with these issues in previous chapters. It would be useful to revisit them, as they underlie the difficulties such social situations present. If you have developed and practised these three skills, it will be easier to understand and carry out the following exercises. These exercises will challenge the misconceptions underlying performance anxiety. Their objective is to assist you in understanding the difference between your perceptions in performance anxiety versus what is really happening.

The Performance Anxiety Inspector Exercise

In the previous chapter, we discussed the anxiety inspector exercise, where you explored social situations for evidence of the physical symptoms of anxiety in others. It revealed how difficult the task is in real life. This exercise has a similar purpose. For the next four to eight weeks, check out anyone giving a talk, presenting at a meeting, making a speech or performing in public. Your task is to identify which presenters are anxious by picking out obvious physical symptoms suggesting this. Write your observations into your notebook. Was it easy to identify such symptoms?

If you are experiencing performance anxiety, you will automatically assume those listening will observe physical signs suggestive of anxiety. In your emotional mind, people will see you blushing, sweating, tense, fidgety and generally uncomfortable. Since many presenters suffer from performance anxiety, these physical symptoms should be blatantly obvious. Or are they? In practice, it is surprisingly difficult to spot such symptoms, despite our belief to the contrary.

If you are struggling to observe these physical symptoms in other presenters, then how can others observe them in you? This is an excellent exercise to banish the idea that people can see the physical symptoms of anxiety in performance situations. Try it and see!

The Audience Awareness Exercise

This is another exercise to back up this concept. Have you ever asked yourself how aware the audience is of the person giving the talk or presentation? We tend to assume that they are aware of every detail. But are they?

For the next four to eight weeks, I want you to observe how aware you are during social performance situations you attend. It may be a meeting, public talk or even a group in the canteen. It might be someone doing a reading at a service, or speaking at a reception. Use any opportunity that arises.

When the performance is over, wait one hour, take out your notebook and answer the following questions. What was the person wearing? What colour was their attire? Did they have a tie on? Did they wear a suit or a dress? What was their hair like, long, short, blonde or brunette? Remember, you are being asked to specifically look out for such trivial data, so it should be easy to observe and record it in your memory. You will discover that this task is not as easy as you might think. You will find it difficult to recall specific information, despite actively observing and recording it in your mind. Now reflect on how difficult it would be to answer these questions if you were not being attentive to such details!

Reflect on the past five public presentations or performance situations that you have attended and answer the same list of questions. You will be amazed by how little you observed. If we are honest, we scarcely remember anything of these simple, observable pieces of information.

The reasons for this are simple. As human beings, we are rather self-obsessed. Our external focus on such minutiae is extremely limited. If you are struggling to remember what a person was wearing, their hairstyle or the colour of their outfit, even when asked to observe it, what chance do you have of spotting the physical symptoms of anxiety? The reality is that human beings make terrible witnesses, as any detective will attest to! Our minds are too busy with other matters, mainly related to our own little world, to pay attention to such trivia.

This is a wonderful awareness exercise demonstrating how little human beings really observe in social situations. Our perception is that we see and recall every little detail. The reality is that we see little and recall even less.

The Performance Awareness Exercise

The exercises above challenged your visual observations and recall in social performance situations. Let's now explore your attention span and recall of specific information garnered during meetings and talks.

If you are bothered by performance anxiety, you are hyperaware that every word will be parsed, every idea scrutinised, and that any delays in delivery or seeming mistakes will be spotted and amplified. Is this true?

This is our perception. In real life, we, in the audience, are more likely to be totally focused on the most important thing in our lives, namely ourselves. This is especially true when listening to someone giving a speech or presenting at a meeting. Our attention span is limited. Our mind simply goes walkabout! It might be worth revisiting the section on mindfulness to explore how true this is.

For the next four to eight weeks, when you are at a talk, lecture or speech, become mindfully aware of how often your mind switches off as the person is talking. You begin with the best of intentions, and focus on the opening lines. Gradually you will observe how you gloss over sections of the talk or presentation, as your mind wanders off to reflect on an upcoming sporting event, the menu for lunch, or some issue bothering you at work or at home. If you were asked how many times your mind wandered, it might be a bit embarrassing. If you were requested, after the presentation, to write down the key elements of the speech or talk, you would also struggle. You will have been intermittently distracted by your mind wandering off.

This is a wonderful exercise to explore what is really going on in any audience. You are freaking out either that they will see you are physically anxious, or that you will become so anxious that you will make errors or have a mind blank. In your mind, the audience will notice every detail of your presentation. In reality, you will have their attention – if you are lucky – for 50 per cent of the period. You could probably hum a tune in the middle of your presentation, never mind having a blank, and nobody would notice. Their minds are much too busy.

These three exercises are aimed at assisting you to grasp emotionally how your perceptions in social performance situations are not borne out in real life. People attending your performance will not only fail to observe you are physically anxious, but will barely register simple details such as your clothes or hairstyle. They also rarely register or recall much of the information so fastidiously prepared for them in your talk, speech or presentation.

The reality is that we are all so self-absorbed that you and your presentation are a long way down our list of priorities. This is another way of saying, yet again, we are not as important as we think we are!

If you practise these exercises and understand the thinking behind them, your anxiety levels will diminish rapidly.

Performance Techniques
Here is a list of ten practical tips which, if applied with the above exercises, will make your next performance situation more successful.

1. Never over-prepare a talk or presentation. The more you do so, or if you attempt to memorise it, the more anxious you will become and the more likely you will lose track of where you were, if even the smallest interruption occurs.
2. Accept that you will be physically anxious, so harness these physical symptoms rather than trying to stop them. They are your body's stress system making you as 'ready' as possible for the event.
3. Accept that, contrary to what you might believe, few will register the full content of your talk or see the physical signs of anxiety.
4. Accept that everyone who performs or gives a talk or speech will at some stage in their lives have a mind blank, lose track of a speech or clam up. This will eliminate the demand that it must not happen, and the result of this is less anxiety and fear that it will happen in real life.

5. If it is possible or appropriate, begin your talk or presentation with a self-deprecatory joke which gets the audience on your side. Comments like, 'Has anyone seen *The King's Speech*?' gets the audience on board, as many of them will empathise, having been in similar situations themselves.

6. The greatest weapon in social performance anxiety is to introduce humour, from the beginning of the presentation or talk through to the end. We all love people who don't take themselves too seriously, who can have a laugh at themselves and the world. This approach is one I regularly use myself, finding it of great assistance. When you observe the audience laughing with you rather than at you, as so many fear may happen, the result will be a significant reduction in anxiety and stress. Spice your talk with humour.

7. It is useful to have little prompts in the form of cards with key summary pointers along with your notes, and always have a drink of water nearby. If you lose your train of thought, there are two simple solutions. The first is to excuse yourself and have a drink of water. This buys you time to get your thoughts together and then proceed. The second is to have little 'hooks' ready with your notes, which should in practice be the main points of your presentation. If you do lose track, refer to these hooks. This will quickly retrigger your thoughts, and off you go.

8. Be yourself! This may sound trite, but there is much to be learned from these two words. Many assume they must take on some new persona when asked to perform or give a speech. You will be most effective if you are being yourself while presenting a talk or performing publicly. So, develop the attitudes 'This is me, warts and all', 'I am not perfect', 'What you see is what you get'. If we are being authentic, then people will overlook minor hiccups in a presentation or performance, if they actually notice at all.

9. Practise presenting to small groups of colleagues, close friends or family, or indeed all three. This gets you comfortable presenting information socially to an audience. If you present regularly like this, before the actual event, the real-life situation will seem less stressful. Try out self-deprecatory jokes and other forms of humour with them. See what works best. They will let you know what works and what doesn't. Adjust accordingly!

10. Develop a profound sense of humour about yourself! When you realise

that you are not as important in people's lives as you think you are, performance anxiety loses its power. We need to be able to laugh at ourselves, and realise the world is not going to end if, as all of us will regularly do, we make some gaffe while performing publicly. This insight can have a profound effect on how you perceive such situations.

Key Learning Points

1. Performance anxiety is common, and developing the skills to manage it can greatly increase our self-confidence and emotional resilience.
2. In performance anxiety, we believe that in such situations we will become extremely physically anxious to a level where we will mess up the presentation or talk, and that people will judge us as weak accordingly.
3. It is created by the false perception that people can see the physical symptoms of anxiety and that the listeners will attentively note and remember every detail, especially any minor errors we make.
4. Some simple exercises can reset these false perceptions. If we combine these with some simple performance techniques, then we can quickly become comfortable in these situations.

17. SKILL FIFTEEN

THE ART OF CONVERSATION
'They Will Think I Am Boring'

Why Do We Need this Skill?

One of the most common fears expressed by those uncomfortable in social situations is 'People will think I'm boring'. This can lead to anxiety and embarrassment. People with social anxiety often assume that when they are interacting in social situations and struggling with conversation, other people will perceive them as boring. In depression, this belief can also be ingrained during active bouts and, when allied to the belief that they are worthless, it can lead to the social isolation characteristic of this condition.

Most of us, unless we are extreme extroverts, will occasionally find ourselves in social situations, struggling to converse. As we descend into the morass of technology and social media, there is an increasing risk that the importance of this skill will be overlooked and sidelined. Like all skills, it needs to be learned, nurtured, practised and worked on until it becomes automatic. Conversation is now more often being carried out online, rather than face to face, with obvious consequences.

How to Develop this Skill

To develop the art of conversation, it is necessary to challenge the irrational belief 'I am boring'. This goes back to the first skill discussed, namely how to achieve unconditional self-acceptance. This involved challenging the whole world of rating. A reminder of the rules of the Members Only club: we are not allowed to rate ourselves or accept others' rating of us, but we can rate our behaviour or skills.

So, can a human being be rated as boring? Let's explore the following conversation. Mark spends five minutes discussing his interest in ancient languages with Linda, who has little interest in the subject. She follows up by discussing her interest in quantum mechanics with Mark, who has even less interest in the topic. So, if Linda and Mark were bored respectively, are they two boring people? Hardly! It was the topic of conversation in each case that was boring, to the other person. If we believe we are boring, are we not back playing the rating game? If I or someone else wishes to rate my conversation skills, this is completely acceptable. Whereas rating myself or accepting another's rating of me as a boring person is not.

What this discussion highlights is how many of us struggle to come up with a topic that others might find interesting. This is the dilemma facing those with social anxiety. They will regularly rehearse in their heads what they are going to say before saying it. What they are doing is trying to decide if it will seem interesting or boring. It is their fear that others will find what they say boring, of no interest, that confines them to the edge of groups socially, where they can avoid initiating conversations.

To assist those with social anxiety and indeed anyone who has conversation difficulties, I recommend the following exercise.

The Conversation Exercise

Ask someone what they consider is an interesting topic of conversation. The answer can be revealing. Topics such as the weather, sport, politics or family life are assumed to be of interest to all. The reality, of course, is that we all have different interests/obsessions.

However, there is one subject that receives universal approval! We all like to talk about ourselves. We find ourselves a subject of immense interest. The key to the conversation exercise is to become skilled in encouraging others to talk about themselves. How do we manage this in practice?

There are two common social situations we may find ourselves in. The first is meeting and conversing with people we know. The second is conversing with strangers. We may also find ourselves in social situations with a mixture of both, a nightmare scenario for anyone struggling with social anxiety.

Scenario One (People We Know)

This exercise relates to social interactional situations where we know the person and are generally familiar with their lives. So, we are aware of their interests. They may love discussing their children, proudly whipping out their smartphone to show you the latest pictures. It could be some sport they play or follow, such as football, rugby, cricket, hurling, athletics, golf or tennis, or some hobby such as painting, cooking, photography or gardening. They may love social media, fashion or shopping. They may be into reading, films or theatre, or love discussing their work. The possibilities are endless. The subject needs to be one you know, from prior experience, is interesting and relevant to the person you are talking to.

The secret to this exercise is, armed with this knowledge, to immediately ask a relevant question and keep asking further questions to engage with the other person. Let's assume you meet Tom, who loves the theatre, and ask, 'Seen any good plays recently?' If he has, then there is lots to discuss – lead actors, plot, etc. Tom will be more than happy to share his experiences – all you have to do is keep the questions flowing. Or you might meet Jane who is into athletics. You might start by asking her, 'How did you do in your most recent race?' Her eyes will light up, and she will probably launch into a full-blown commentary on the race, once again prompted by further questions from yourself. If running out of steam in one area, move on to other known areas of interest.

There is one important caveat. You must be interested in what the other person is saying. Your body language should have lots of eye contact and verbal affirmation. We all love to feel that we are at the centre of somebody's attention and it encourages us to chat away and engage with each other. We are also equally adept at sensing if somebody's body language or eye contact suggests a lack of interest. This requires intense practice, but it is central to the success of the exercise.

So, if you meet Jenifer, who just loves photography, and are asking her about her latest exhibition, she needs to feel that you are genuinely interested in her work. This requires getting out of your own comfort zone, and learning to become interested in other people's worlds. It doesn't matter if you have no great knowledge of photography. What matters is that the other person feels that you are interested in their world, which just happens to include photography. You are learning how to make someone comfortable in your presence. And in so doing, you are removing the necessity to find suitable topics for conversation. This, of course, leads to significant reduction in social anxiety, as you are no longer involved in the 'heavy lifting' of social conversational situations. You allow the other person to do this for you, by encouraging them to focus on their world and share it with you. They may leave with extremely positive feelings about you, reflecting that you were the most interesting person they had talked to that day.

If you are really open to this exercise, you may also discover interesting information about many areas of life which you had previously been unaware of. It will open other worlds to you. This richness of interaction will help you in becoming a more rounded, informed and resilient human being.

Scenario Two (Strangers)

The exercise above is wonderful when you know the person and their interests and hobbies. But what do you do when the person in question is a stranger? There are no hooks to hang the conversation on. In these situations, I suggest the following exercise.

It involves asking three open-ended questions. I encourage those I work with to apply them on a regular basis. You may come up with your own variations, but for the present, you might begin with these.

1. Where are you from?
2. What do you do?
3. What do you do in your spare time, what are your hobbies/activities?

Let's start with the first question. Peter meets Margaret at a social gathering in a pub in London. He asks her where she is from. She replies that she comes from Galway in the west of Ireland. He immediately follows up with subsequent questions about Galway: Was she born there? Did she grow up there? How did she end up in London? Does she find London very different from Galway? As she answers one question, he quickly follows up with another. After a few minutes, Margaret is busily chatting away about her home town, what she likes and dislikes, what she misses, her family in Galway, and so on. Peter's only task is to hang on to her every word, showing with nods and intense eye contact that he is genuinely interested in her replies. The rest flows from there.

If the conversation is waning, then Peter might move on to the next question, namely what she does for a living. This opens another world of possibilities. Suppose Margaret replies that she is at college. Next he might ask her what she is studying. When she replies that she is doing psychology, he can ask her how she became interested in that area. Or why did she pick that subject? Or how does she find college life? And so on. Once again, after a few minutes Margaret is busily filling in information on her areas of interest, college life and so on.

Or suppose Margaret's answer to the question is, 'I am studying nursing.' Peter immediately asks her how she got into nursing. Or where does she nurse? Or what branch of nursing does she see herself ending up in? Whatever the reply to these questions, Peter can keep the conversation flowing with follow-on queries. Once again, the critical importance of Peter showing genuine interest in her replies cannot be overemphasised.

The last question – 'What do you do in your spare time?' – creates endless possibilities. Once the person shares with you their hobby or leisure pursuits, follow up with questions like those discussed in the section dealing with people we know.

For example, Mary meets Simon at a function and asks him, 'What do you do in your spare time?' He answers that he is a keen sailor. She immediately expresses interest. How did he get into sailing? Where does he sail? Is he part of a club? Does he have his own boat? And so on. Whatever his reply, she follows up with a further query until Simon is soon chatting away for half an hour about his sailing exploits. She makes it clear to him through her body language that she is genuinely interested in his replies. Simon finds Mary so fascinating to talk to that he invites her on a date. Out of a simple conversational exercise, romance blooms!

How to Practise this Skill

I often use the analogy of learning to drive. Suppose you receive three lessons from an instructor. You then set a date to sit your driving test, but you now assume because you know what to do, you can breeze in and pass the test. You have it in the bag! In real life, of course, you would fail. Most of us are wise enough to realise we need to practise intensely for months before being comfortable enough to sit our driving test with any reasonable chance of success.

Learning to develop and practise the conversation skill is similar. I recommend that for the next eight weeks you practise the conversation exercise on everybody you meet, in all areas of your life, whether it be at work, with family or friends, especially with strangers or members of the opposite sex. In each case, focus intensely on the other person's response.

In the beginning, it will feel awkward and clumsy. The more you practise, however, the more comfortable it will become. When that dreaded social situation finally arrives, you can then march straight into the heart of the group, identify someone you know, or indeed a stranger, and go straight into question mode. You will be so intensely focused on their replies and showing such interest that your anxiety levels will significantly reduce. The day you are automatically comfortable in doing this, you have passed your test! Just as learning to drive is a lifelong skill, so is this conversational skill. Never again need you worry about social situations, or whether people will think you are boring. From now on, they will find you intensely interesting. You are in the driving seat!

How the Conversation Exercise Changed Karen's Life

It might be worth revisiting Karen, who we read about in Chapter 15. Having previously struggled with feeling comfortable in social situations, she went on to meet Mark, the man of her dreams. She had practised the conversation exercise non-stop for two months before using it on Mark. The question that won Mark over was simply, 'What do you do in your spare time?' When he revealed that he was into hill walking, she followed up with question after question about the hobby he loved so much, listening intently to his answers. The die was cast – he had rarely come upon somebody so interesting. One thing quickly led to another, and they were together a year later. Her hard work and persistence in developing this skill transformed her life.

Key Learning Points

1. Together with empathy, the art of conversation is one of the most important skills in navigating our social world.
2. As our world becomes increasingly technologically advanced and social media takes over every facet of our lives, the art of conversation is waning and, with it, a key weapon in our arsenal to become more emotionally resilient.
3. The secret to the art of conversation lies in the ability to allow other people to become comfortable in talking about themselves, through showing genuine interest in them.
4. Some simple conversation exercises can show us how to develop this skill and transform our social life.

PART FOUR

Life Resilience Skills

18. SKILL SIXTEEN

HOW TO DEAL WITH THE UNFAIRNESS OF LIFE
'Hello, Life!'

Why Do We Need this Skill?

This is a skill particularly relevant to adolescents and young adults. Our fore-fathers were especially aware of and sensitive to the unfairness of life. This harsh reality has been dumbed down in our twenty-first-century brave new world. Increased prosperity and urbanisation, combined with a technologi-cal and social media revolution, are creating false expectations as to how life 'should be'. The consequences of this are far-reaching, posing significant chal-lenges to our mental and physical health.

You might be surprised to see this included as a skill. But learning how to challenge an absolute belief that life should be fair, with its emotional con-sequence of hurt, is essential for emotional resilience. Otherwise, we will struggle to cope with the multiple, frequently painful curveballs thrown at us. Underlying emotional resilience must be the capacity to restructure such er-roneous, often destructive views. When trouble comes, as inevitably happens, those holding this belief are ill-prepared to deal with the realities of life. Simply put, we learn to adapt, or founder.

I am acutely conscious that many people exist in circumstances where life is deeply unfair. Those parents of children with special needs carry possibly the greatest burden. Have they not the greatest right to rail against the unfair-ness and discomfort of life? Yet they are frequently the ones who accept the harsh reality of life, often in the most trying and challenging of circumstances. People who care for loved ones with Alzheimer's or other chronic debilitating health conditions could also argue that life is unfair in the extreme. However it is often when we are not struggling with such burdens that we encounter the irrational belief that life should be fair.

This belief often lurks in the background of many mental health conditions. Depression is often associated with deep-seated hurt about the unfairness of life. Some people believe it is unfair that they suffer from this condition while others don't. Learning how to deal with this irrational belief can play an important role in their long-term recovery. For other people, self-harm may be a response to the unfairness of life. Many school-going adolescents are self-harming. Hurt can make us bitter, unhappy and increasingly isolated, unaware of other routes out of our misery.

This life-coping skill is an essential human one. There are times when we must face difficult and distressing life challenges. The more developed this skill, the more emotionally resilient we become. Adults need to learn, practise and pass it on to their children. If we continue to protect and shield them from the realities of life, the mental health implications may be significant.

How to Develop this Skill

For the rest of this chapter, we will explore how to come to terms with the unfairness of life. If you can relate to the belief that life should be fair or, at a deeper level, we should always be treated fairly, then read on. For this irrational belief underlies a deep-seated hurt which is probably destroying your life and peace of mind.

Is life fair? While I was a doctor in the developing world, I held children in my arms who were dying from ailments that could be eradicated if the world was fairer. Over decades as a family doctor, I have encountered wonderful people experiencing the most distressing of conditions, having done nothing to deserve them. I have embraced parents who have lost their children to suicide, with no explanation as to why. Why were they chosen to carry this burden for the rest of their lives? Why them? Life is a mystery. None of us understands why such things happen. But life is not fair. It has never been.

Countless people I have worked with genuinely believe, however, that it is totally rational to assume they should be treated fairly, and respond by searching their environment for proof that everybody and life itself are treating them unfairly, ignoring all evidence to the contrary. This explains their hypersensitivity and prickly behaviour towards others. This irrational belief often presents itself as a demand that their childhood should have taken a different course and that they were treated unfairly as a result. This can cause a lifetime of pain and suffering for the person and those around them.

Let's explore what happens when the beliefs 'I should be treated fairly' and 'The world and life should treat me fairly' are triggered.

The first consequence is the deep-seated emotion of hurt. The second is that we hold a grudge, either against people we perceive as the cause of our hurt, or against life itself. The third is that we become hypersensitive to everyone around us, seek out perceived unfair treatment, lapse into sullen silence and brood, ruminate or lash out verbally. These behaviours are unhealthy, leading to inner emotional corrosion and future mental health difficulties. To challenge the unfairness of life, the above need to be reversed.

The Rucksack of Rocks Exercise

This is a favourite exercise of mine. Its objective is to demonstrate the futility of holding a grudge against life or others. Fill a rucksack with heavy rocks or equivalent weights. Embark on a one- to two-hour hike with the rucksack on your back. As you are walking, feel the weight on your shoulders, the ache in your back, the fatigue rapidly dragging you down. Your steps get shorter and more laboured. Finally, you arrive home and drop the rucksack. Just feel the relief. The weight is gone. You suddenly feel lighter and more energised. You will never again agree to carry such a weight on your back, for anyone or for any reason! It was pure hell. This is what it is like to carry a grudge. The only person suffering is you. You are the one holding the grudge; only you can choose to drop it. If you continue carrying this load, you are the one who chooses to do so. But like the rucksack of rocks, this burden is extremely heavy and the consequences for your mental health just as damaging.

This is a powerful exercise, if you recognise yourself as carrying such a grudge against life or others. Most people quickly see the parallels with their individual lives and decide to drop the load. The next exercise demonstrates how to achieve this.

The Drop-the-Rocks Exercise

1. For the next two months, carry a notebook around with you and try to become increasingly aware if someone or life itself is causing you hurt. (The easiest way to check this is in your behaviour. If you have suddenly become hypersensitive, prickly or lapse into a brooding silence, the chances are that hurt has been triggered, and with it the belief that you have not been treated fairly.)
2. Write in your notebook the trigger, your emotional response and your behaviour.
3. Later, on a sheet of paper, analyse what happened. It may be that something somebody said or did triggered the hurt. For example, it might be a work supervisor implying a task was incorrectly carried out, even though untrue. You now find yourself holding a grudge against them.
4. Ask yourself, 'Is carrying this grudge, like the rucksack of rocks, helping or hindering my sense of well-being?' The answer is usually that it is hurting you more than the person who triggered the hurt.
5. The final question to ask yourself is, 'Is it in my interests to drop the rocks, which represent my grudge?' Most of us will agree that it is, but do not know how to do so. Let's explore this further.

There are two situations of relevance. The first is when the grudge is against a person, and the second is when it is against life. We need to be able to drop the rocks in both situations, otherwise hurt will destroy us.

How to Drop the Rocks When the Grudge Is Against a Person

The easiest way to drop a personal grudge is to separate who we are as human beings from our behaviour. If we consider this further, perhaps it was not the person but their behaviour that was the core issue? They, too, are normal human beings like ourselves, who have messed up in their behaviour. Would this change how we interpret what happened? It would bring us back to Skill

One, where we accepted that human beings cannot be rated but that their behaviour can. It might be worth revisiting Chapter 3, which deals with unconditional self-acceptance. There we discussed the Members Only club and how to join. Membership involved accepting we cannot rate ourselves or accept others' rating of us as human beings, but we are free to rate our behaviour or skills. In this scenario, we no longer focus on the person as being the problem, but rather their behaviour.

If we accept this concept, it allows us to drop the rock, or grudge, against the person, while we remain free to challenge their behaviour. This allows us to formulate, in a non-confrontational manner, how to do just that. By dropping the grudge against the person in this manner, but shifting attention towards their behaviour, we prevent hurt growing legs. This is how we drop the rucksack of rocks.

On paper, we can challenge negative behavioural patterns if we are carrying a grudge. Is it helpful to become overly sensitive, verbally antagonistic or lapse into sullen moods? If we are honest, we will accept such behaviours as unhelpful and decide how best to change them.

Challenging Inappropriate Behaviour

Through the drop-the-rocks exercise, we can also learn to become comfortable challenging others' behaviour, where appropriate, as early as possible. How do we do this? I suggest the following approach.

Always challenge a person's behaviour in a calm, measured manner, explaining what it was about their behaviour that caused you to feel upset, how their behaviour affected you emotionally. The other person may be genuinely unaware that their behaviour is causing you difficulties. If you don't let them know, why would they change their behaviour? Often, when they are made aware, they will apologise and change.

This is a useful skill to prevent potential rocks building up. It teaches us to become comfortable standing up for ourselves if another's behaviour is impacting on our lives. If they continue to behave in such a manner, do not be afraid to proceed further. This may involve removing them from your life, informing HR at work or whatever other steps are appropriate. On some occasions, you may feel it is not worth the effort. The main point to learn is your right to challenge another person's behaviour. Whether you do so or not is your prerogative.

How to Drop the Rocks When the Grudge Is Against Life

But what if the incident triggering your hurt is not personal but involves life itself? Something goes against us at work or in sport, or you perceive a rejection in a working or personal relationship. To apply the drop-the-rocks exercise, I suggest the following:

1. Once again, write down the trigger, emotion and resultant behaviour in your notebook.
2. Later, challenge it on paper. Analyse what you found unfair. Why did you behave or react the way you did? Were you building up yet another wall or grudge, this time against life? Were you adding more rocks to your rucksack?
3. Now you must learn to drop the rock or grudge against life. Do so by asking yourself if there is any law in the universe stating that life must treat you or indeed anyone else fairly? Is this demand helping you in your life or adding further rocks to your load? If you are honest, you will realise this demand is unreasonable and unhealthy.

Examining and challenging such demands repeatedly on paper will gradually make you more realistic about life. Life is not going to change to suit you, or suddenly become fairer towards you or indeed any other human being.

Life is life! We have no choice but to accept its unfairness. Attempting to change this is pointless, and only adds to your rucksack of rocks. It is easier to reshape your thinking and drop the load.

The Importance of Humour

One final piece of advice regarding the drop-the-rocks exercise. Remember the importance of humour. Life is tough, often a relentless struggle, hard enough without adding to it. When you are challenging situations in your notebook, check where humour might fit in. I encourage people I work with to try to develop a sense of humour about themselves and life. When writing down your concerns and absolute demands, on paper, observe just how nuts all of us are.

Having the ability to laugh at ourselves and the world is sometimes the healthiest approach to disempower the challenges of life. Sometimes the most effective way to drop rocks is to use the power of humour with ourselves and in interactions with others, to banish hurt.

A favourite expression of mine, when someone believes the world should be fair or change to suit them is 'Good luck with that'. This usually ends up with both of us sharing a good laugh. The penny drops faster than all the debates in the world. Humour is a great tool. Apply it constantly, together with the above exercise, and benefits will rapidly accrue.

If you apply the drop-the-rocks exercise and repeatedly document and challenge situations as above, the results can be life-changing. Gradually, you will cease demanding that life should be fair. Or that as an individual you should be treated fairly. You will become increasingly realistic about life, change what you can, but accept the many situations where such change is not possible. Gradually, you will learn to embrace with humour the two words 'Hello, life!' They suggest a different way of being, a pragmatic acceptance of how the cards of life fall. This will lead to a dramatic improvement in emotional resilience, further safeguarding your mental health.

LARRY'S STORY

Larry, a twenty-two-year-old student, is referred by his doctor to Dr Jim. He is feeling down, but he is not clinically depressed. Dr Jim uncovers that Larry's recent bout of low mood was triggered by a phone call from his mother, extolling the academic achievements of his older brother. After some discussion, Dr Jim suggests that some CBT approaches might assist him in dealing with his low mood. He then explains what rational and irrational beliefs are, and how they will use the ABC concept to locate them.

They decide to use the phone call from his mother as the trigger.

'How did this phone call make you feel emotionally?' asks Dr Jim. When Larry struggles to answer this, Dr Jim gives him an emotional menu to choose from. On consideration, Larry admits to feeling deeply hurt, depressed and frustrated. They decide to focus initially on his emotion of hurt.

'What was it about the phone call from your mother that made you feel hurt?' asks Dr Jim.

'She never once asked me how I was doing,' replies Larry. 'Just shared with me how proud she and Dad were that my brother Sean had been appointed a lecturer.'

'And why did that make you feel hurt?'

'It wasn't that I was upset with Sean,' Larry replies. 'In fact, I was chuffed for him for doing so well. I was hurt that once again my parents' focus was on him, not me.'

'And why did that make you feel hurt?'

'It has always been that way, ever since we were small. He was the golden-haired boy who could do no wrong. I almost felt invisible. Even my sister got more attention. No matter how hard I tried to gain their approval, nothing made any difference. It was very unfair.' Larry also admits to a strong belief that life itself is unfair, and wishes it was different.

'And what was it about this phone call that made you feel depressed?' asks Dr Jim.

'I felt a failure for once again allowing them to treat me like this,' he replies.

'And why did the phone call make you feel frustrated?' asks Dr Jim.

'Because the situation never changes,' Larry replies. 'I keep expecting them to change, but no matter how distressed and disturbed I become, nothing is ever different.'

Larry also says he experienced some physical symptoms following this phone call. He noted increased fatigue, tension headaches and a constant feeling of being wired. He and Dr Jim also review his behaviour following the phone call. Larry admits to spending hours ruminating on the unfairness of it all. He also became short and prickly with his mother and his college friends. 'I even began to pick arguments with my girlfriend,' he adds. 'I became sullen and moody.' He also began drinking heavily which, by his own admission, led to his mood dropping further. He says that this behaviour is typical when he experiences even the smallest of perceived slights or hurt.

'Let's examine what irrational belief was triggered by this situation, and the danger you assigned to it,' says Dr Jim. 'So, what demand were you making of yourself after this phone call from your mother that made you feel so hurt?'

'That she should treat me better,' Larry replies, 'and that life should treat me fairly, and that I should be treated fairly at all times.'

On further probing about the demands underlying his frustration, they agree that Larry was demanding that the situation and life should change, and that he should not have to put up with the discomfort experienced when this did not happen. And, underlying his emotion of depression, that he was a failure, for allowing his parents to treat him the way they did.

They then put together the following ABC:

A   Activating Event:
  • Trigger: a phone call from his mother extolling the academic achievements of his older brother Sean
  • Inference/danger: his parents are only interested in Sean's progress in life and not his; this has been the case since he was young; they are not treating him fairly; life itself is not treating him fairly; the situation – the approach of his parents – is not changing, even though it is causing him much distress and discomfort; he feels like a failure for allowing all of this to happen

B   Belief/Demands: 'My parents should have treated me more fairly. I should be treated more fairly. Life should be treating me more fairly. The situation and indeed life itself should change to suit me. I should not have to suffer discomfort. I am a failure for allowing all of this to happen.'

C   Consequences:
  • Emotional reactions: hurt, frustration and depression
  • Physical reactions: muscle tension, fatigue, tension headaches, feeling wired
  • Behaviour: persistently irritable and moody with college friends, family

and girlfriend; becomes hypersensitive to the smallest perceived hurt; on some occasions becomes sullen and silent; ruminates constantly about the situation; drinks more alcohol

'So now we understand, Larry, what made you hurt, frustrated, even depressed about this situation, and your resulting behaviour, let's help to reshape both your thinking and behaviour in relation to it. Because if we are successful in this instance, we can apply the same concepts to similar situations in the future,' says Dr Jim. 'Let's begin by challenging your irrational beliefs,' says Dr Jim. 'The first one took the form of an absolute demand that your parents and indeed life itself should treat you fairly. Is this demand rational or irrational?' he asks.

Larry is adamant that it is completely rational.

'And what about your demand that the situation with your parents and indeed life itself should change to suit you?'

Once again, Larry feels this is an acceptable demand.

Dr Jim smiles, observing that in practice both were not only irrational but impossible demands to satisfy. 'Life,' he continues, 'is by nature completely unfair, random and definitely not going to change to suit you or indeed any-body else, simply because you desire it to do so. If you keep demanding that it should be different, then hurt and frustration will dog your life.'

After further discussion and some good-humoured banter, Larry accepts that perhaps his thinking and behaviour have become a little irrational, and might need a bit of tweaking.

They begin by Dr Jim suggesting that Larry is carrying a grudge against his parents, and that this is weighing him down. Larry agrees that he is carrying the same grudge into other parts of his life. Dr Jim gives him the rucksack of rocks exercise, which he agrees to carry out. They then discuss how he might learn to drop the grudge against his parents.

This involves Larry joining the Members Only club. To do so, he must accept that he cannot rate himself or accept others' rating of him as a person, but he is free to rate his behaviour. 'I need you to develop the skill of unconditional self-acceptance,' Dr Jim explains, 'to assist you in dropping the grudge against your parents and life.' He continues to say that to develop this skill, Larry will require an acceptance that, as human beings, we are all going to mess up in terms of our behaviour and that our only task is to do our best. 'If you are a member of the club, like myself, you can rate your behaviour but never yourself as a person.'

Larry willingly embraces this concept. He accepts that it is his rating of himself as a failure that is leading him to feel depressed. He wants to embrace the skill and practise it in his life.

They then discuss some healthier approaches to deal with his parents. This involves regarding them as normal human beings, who are messing up in their behaviour by focusing on one sibling versus another. Larry can love and forgive them, but remain free to challenge their behaviour. He agrees to sit down with his parents for a frank discussion on how their behaviour has been impacting on his life.

They also agree that Larry will put the drop-the-rocks exercise into practice over the following three months. This is to help him deal with his absolute demands that life should be fair and that he should be treated fairly. He sees that this perspective might be irrational and unhelpful. The exercise will also involve challenging the negative, repetitive behaviours which have become so embedded in his life.

Finally, they deal with his demand that life should change to ensure that he should not suffer discomfort. When Dr Jim wishes him 'Good luck with that!', Larry laughs and begins to see that he is constantly demanding that situations and the world change, but refuses to make the necessary changes himself. The situation with his parents is a classic example. Larry has remained frustrated about this situation for years, constantly demanding it should change. He has never considered it is up to him to accept the discomfort of an awkward conversation with his parents, if he wants matters to change. Dr Jim also gives him the coin exercise described in Chapter 5 to trigger his frustration in everyday life and help understand how to live with discomfort.

The following months are life-changing for Larry. He works hard on his exercises, with dramatic results. He learns to accept himself unconditionally. He also has an emotional conversation with his parents, who are genuinely oblivious to his distress and their role in it. With a warm embrace, they promise to work on their relationship with him. This leads to the whole family becoming closer and the creation of a new, more nourishing, environment for Larry. He also learns to identify early any underlying hurt and frustration in his life and how to challenge it on a regular basis. His personal relationships blossom and his mood difficulties clear. His inner emotional resilience has soared as he can now cope with life's challenges more easily.

Most of all he has developed a sense of humour about himself, life and the world in general. He has stopped taking himself and life so seriously. He now sees life for what it is – a mysterious, uncomfortable and often unfair roller-coaster ride, where often the best we can hope for is to hang on for dear life and see where it leads. He finally understands at a deeper, emotional level the true meaning of 'Hello, life!'

Key Learning Points

1. Learning to deal with the unfairness of life is one of the most important skills to develop to navigate the often harsh landscape of our existence.
2. If we struggle to deal with this reality, then the spectre of lifelong hurt will haunt our lives, doing significant damage to our well-being, mental health and emotional resilience.
3. Learning to cope with this reality means understanding that holding grudges against people or life is only going to destroy one person – yourself.
4. By learning and practising the drop-the-rocks exercise, we can once and for all develop the skill of coping with the unfairness of life.

19. SKILL SEVENTEEN

HOW TO ACHIEVE A HEALTHY WORK/LIFE BALANCE
'Do I Live to Work or Work to Live?'

Why Do We Need this Skill?

Achieving a balance between personal, working, family and social lives is a fundamental part of positive mental health. We rarely reflect on this balance, never mind ensure it is healthy. In some parts of the world, such as the USA, China and Japan, the balance can tip too far towards living to work. In other parts, especially Mediterranean countries such as France, Spain and Italy, the balance is tipped more towards work providing a platform from which to live our lives to the full. Of the two, there is little doubt that the second is healthier. The ideal involves a healthy tension between both. It is like stress – a reasonable amount of stress in our lives is healthy. Too much or too little can be toxic to mental and physical health.

This balance is not just a simple choice between work versus home life. A true work/life balance is present when all aspects of our life are in harmony, of which work just happens to be one. But why is work/life balance so important to mental health? The answer lies in the interactions between stress and mental health. We will explore those links in more detail in a later chapter.

For now, let's explore the links between the stress created by poor work/life balance and common mental health conditions. One of the most important stressors that can trigger a bout of depression is poor work/life balance, especially when this balance is tipped towards excessive focus on work or some other area, and too little focus on key areas of life. This sets in motion a vicious circle. Poor work/life balance can trigger a bout of depression. This, in turn, further destabilises this balance, which in turn worsens the depressive symptoms. So restoring this balance is essential for recovery.

A poor work/life balance can also underlie general anxiety. Once again, the common denominator is the stress generated when this balance is out of sync. The stress worsens the symptoms of anxiety. Once again, a vicious circle ensues. We may also misuse or abuse alcohol or substances, or even self-harm on occasion, if we are swamped by toxic stress created by this imbalance.

Failure to deal with this imbalance also makes us less resilient. We may find ourselves lacking any peace or inner contentment. It can lead to feeling fatigued, constantly wired, dissatisfied, and means we may struggle to maintain relationships with those we love. There may be a constant seeking-out of material things, an overemphasis on financial security, a sense that we are missing out on something important in our lives. All of this diminishes our real enjoyment of life.

A lack of work/life balance can become a common source of difficulty between couples, especially if one or the other partner is obsessed with some area of their lives – work or leisure. This may lead to significant stress on their relationship, with potential mental health difficulties as both struggle to cope.

We sometimes feel that we have little choice in decisions that we are forced to make. Clearly, the struggle for survival sometimes can make achieving this balance extremely challenging. However, having some insight into the importance of this balance and how to achieve it may be the key to surviving a crisis in your mental health.

Finding a healthy work/life balance is essential. While many discuss its importance, there is a dearth of information on how to attain it. In this chapter, we explore how to achieve this skill.

How to Develop this Skill

Those who struggle to achieve a healthy work/life balance have often never explored their priorities in life. They are surprised at what such a list of priorities might look like, although each individual's list might look different. For good mental health, the ideal list might look like this:

- Self: this relates to your personal well-being, both physical and mental health
- Partner: this relates to the well-being of your partner (if relevant) and your relationship
- Children: this relates to the well-being of your children (if relevant)
- Immediate family: this relates to the well-being of parents and siblings (if relevant)
- Work: this relates to responsibilities in the workplace, including employers and work colleagues
- The rest: this relates to the well-being of friends and the involvement in community, leisure or sports activities

An example of a potentially unhealthy list of priorities would look like the following:

- Work
- Children
- Relationship
- Immediate family
- Self
- The rest

Or:

- Children
- Immediate family
- Relationship
- Work
- The rest
- Self

Healthy Priority Levels

It is useful to explore the reasoning behind establishing a healthy priority level list.

Self

It might surprise you that 'self' should be considered the first priority on a healthy list. You might assume it is selfish to place oneself ahead of children, relationship or immediate family. There are, however, significant risks to not valuing or safeguarding your personal physical and mental health. You run the risk of becoming increasingly stressed, anxious, even depressed. It is vital to nourish your body, mind and soul first, before sharing yourself with everybody else. Otherwise burnout may rapidly ensue.

Relationship

If you are in a relationship, your next priority should be to nourish and protect this space. If you are in a healthy space, then prioritising and safeguarding your primary relationship must take precedence over all other matters, other than self.

Children

Placing children first, as many parents – especially mothers – do, pushes self and personal relationships down the priority scale, with resulting significant pressures being exerted on your mental health. If your list of priorities is healthy, the welfare of your children must come after the health and well-being of self and relationship. Only then will you be best placed, mentally, to care for them.

Work

Some of us place work before all other priorities, including self and relationship. This is a common pattern in men wedded to their jobs, to the exclusion of all else. This, of course, can create multiple mental health difficulties and significant pressures on relationships with partners and children.

Immediate Family

Others may put the well-being of immediate family such as parents or siblings ahead of self and relationship. Once again, this can create significant stress on both. It can often create deep rifts within our primary relationships, aside from being inadvisable for our mental health.

The Rest

Finally, some put 'the rest' at the top of the priority list, ahead of self, relationship and children. This may involve prioritising commitments to hobbies, sport, social media or other activities, to the detriment of everything else.

A Note of Caution

There will also be those who disregard the importance of relationships or children as not being relevant to them at a certain phase of life. I regularly encounter people who have put both on the long finger, often assigning a greater importance to career. This can be a significant issue in the mid- to late thirties. The rush to find a partner and have a child during this period, often involving IVF, can be a consequence of an unhealthy work/life balance, where priority is given to other areas. Ideally, we must include potential relationships/children as part of a healthy work/life balance from the mid-twenties onwards, if it is possible or desirable. Much heartache could be avoided. Failure to do so can often result in significant pressure being exerted on your mental health at a later stage.

The Importance of Flexibility

Your priority list must, of course, be flexible, as life throws up a constant supply of slings and arrows. If, for example, a child is ill, for that period they must clearly receive top priority. But when the child recovers, return to your original priority list. Similarly, with family. If a parent is acutely ill or requires immediate short-term support, they must also receive priority at that moment. Again, there may be times when work may rise to the top of the list, for short-term reasons. The key is to return to your healthy priority list as soon as the crisis ends. So, our list must be fluid and flexible to match with the realities of life.

The Priority Pyramid Exercise

I have found the following exercise immensely helpful in assisting those whose work/life balance is out of sync. Many people have commented to me that this has completely changed their whole approach to life, with immense benefits. To carry it out, we take our priority list and turn it into a pyramid shape, which we will call a priority pyramid. We will then use this concept to challenge our work/life balance over a two-month period.

Creating Your Personal Priority Pyramid

Learning how to create your own priority pyramid is a simple exercise.

1. On paper, draw up your current priority list. Be brutally honest when doing this, as it will allow you to get a real insight into where your work/life balance is at this moment in time.
2. Now draw a pyramid shape and divide it as follows. At the base, place number one on your priority list. Follow it up with number two, and so on, until you get to the last item, which will form the tip of the pyramid.
3. Let's suppose you have a healthy priority pyramid. It should look like this:

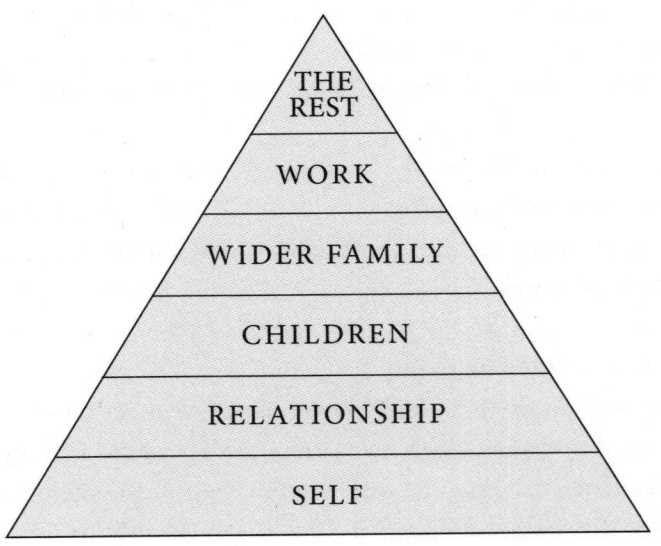

At the base should be self, followed by relationship, children, immediate family, work and the rest. You will notice that the tip of the pyramid is a lot smaller than the base. Self should dominate, while priorities such as work or social media should form the tip.

4. If you have an unhealthy priority pyramid, you may find that work is at the base, then children, immediate family, the rest, with self and relationship at the tip.

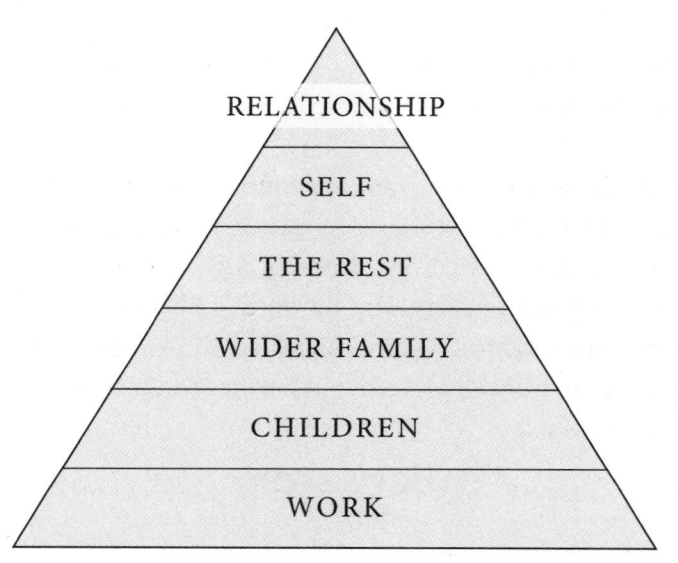

You can learn much from studying your personal priority pyramid. We are often extremely stressed or struggling to cope with conflicting areas of our lives, without grasping that the cause and potential solution may lie in a careful analysis of our pyramid.

Applying the Priority Pyramid

1. For the next two months, ask yourself every weekend, 'How healthy was my priority pyramid this week?' Usually, the pyramid will regularly look less than ideal. The base may be children or work, and the tip may be self.
2. Compare this unhealthy priority pyramid to the ideal healthy one. Then

plan how best to improve it for the upcoming week. Write down suggested changes in your notebook. Then do your utmost to put them into practice.
3. The following weekend, repeat the exercise. How many changes did you put into practice? Is your priority pyramid starting to look healthier?

The priority pyramid exercise focuses your mind on the importance of balance in your life. Where are you spending your time and energies? Where are the deficits? What does it feel like when the balance is correct? Do you feel less stressed and anxious when the balance is right, and more stressed and anxious when it is not?

At the end of eight weeks performing this exercise, you will have retrained your mind and brain into healthier habits. This will bring significant benefits to yourself and especially to your relationship. Others find their working lives more rewarding and productive, due primarily to improvements in these other, essential areas of their lives. You may also enjoy and appreciate your children more, as they are now 'part of the house' rather than the 'house itself'.

You will be increasingly resilient emotionally, and cope better with stress and life's difficulties. You will also be more immune to mental health difficulties.

LUCY'S STORY

Lucy is twenty-seven, and has been married to Peter for five years. She has two children and works as a buyer for a large firm. She attends Dr Jim in a distressed state. Persistently fatigued and anxious, she is now experiencing panic episodes. She feels constantly frustrated and is also fending off cold sores, mouth ulcers and persistent low-grade infections. 'My life is just a mess,' she admits.

Her relationship is also in trouble. 'We are not on the same page anymore, and I don't know why.' She also acknowledges that she has too many balls in the air. Lucy is convinced she is depressed. It seems like the only explanation for how she feels.

Dr Jim reassures her she is not depressed but exhibiting the physical and psychological symptoms of toxic stress. They discuss how to manage her panic attacks using the skill of flooding detailed in Chapter 4, and then they explore the world of toxic stress. This uncovers the source of Lucy's stress, namely her work/life balance.

Dr Jim outlines the concept of a priority pyramid list. When she lists her priorities in order of importance, it read as follows:

- Children
- Work
- Immediate family
- Relationship
- The rest
- Self

Together, they create a priority pyramid to reflect this list. In it, her children form the base, followed by work, her immediate family, her relationship, the rest and, finally, self. After further probing, Lucy reveals to Dr Jim the reasoning behind her priority pyramid.

'My children always come first,' she says, proudly. 'I learned that from my mother. I always ensure their needs are met first. My next priority, of course, is work, which uses up most of my remaining energy.'

'And why would immediate family come next?' asks Dr Jim.

'I have always felt blood is thicker than water,' Lucy replies, 'so when my parents need something, I rush to help them.'

'And your relationship,' asks Dr Jim, 'would you place your parents ahead of it?'

'I always assume that Peter is able to look after himself,' she answers.

'And the rest?'

'I am a great fan of social media,' she explains, 'so if I do have any spare time, I try to keep up to date with all my friends.'

Dr Jim can see why Lucy's life is in turmoil. 'I note you just about got self in there,' he observes wryly. 'Do you not feel your mental and physical health should have greater relevance than, say, social media?'

Lucy admits that she has never considered the importance of focusing on herself. This leads them into a long discussion on the importance of realigning priorities. Lucy increasingly realises that her stress is being caused primarily by placing herself at the back of the queue! They agree that she will examine lifestyle areas such as diet, exercise, yoga and mindfulness, to carve out time for herself. She is also beginning to feel that her current difficulties with her partner have been worsened by banishing him to a lower level on her priority list. Lucy needs to rebalance this equation and prioritise her relationship.

She can also see that putting her children first, while seemingly the best course of action, is in practice affecting her well-being and that of her relationship. They will now become 'part of the house' rather than the 'house itself'. So, too, with her parents who, she now sees, are taking priority over her own mental and physical health.

Lucy knows that she has to push the workplace down her priority list. She agrees it is healthier to 'work to live', rather than to 'live to work'. She and Dr Jim also discuss the importance of social media in her life, and the need to limit the time she spends on it.

Lucy's new priority list will be:

- Self
- Relationship
- Children
- Immediate family
- Work
- The rest

Her healthy priority pyramid will now reflect this change.

Dr Jim then suggests that Lucy applies the priority pyramid exercise to her life over the following two months. She diligently performs it on a weekly basis and finds it transformative.

Six months later, Lucy is in a different space – less fatigued, no more mouth ulcers or cold sores. Her panic attacks have gone, courtesy of the flooding technique. She is less anxious and frustrated. Her relationship is back on an even keel. Her children are equally content, seemingly unaware of any real change in their lives, other than perhaps subconsciously noting that their parents seem to be happier. Her work efficiency has improved, with colleagues observing that she is 'more herself'. Her parents seem unaware of any appreciable reduction in time spent with them, and remark that she is on better form. The only area suffering now is her social media interactions, which have been reduced to a minimum. This turns out to be a pleasant relief. She no longer feels like a 'slave' to her Facebook and Twitter sites. She has freed up extra time to spend on more interesting activities with Peter. She is now more resilient and can cope better with stress. As she happily reveals later to Dr Jim, 'I have my life back!'

Key Learning Points

1. One of the simplest and most effective ways to become more emotionally resilient is to develop a healthy work/life balance.
2. An unhealthy balance is a significant cause of much of the emotional distress and mental health difficulties experienced by many of us.
3. We can learn to reshape our work/life balance, which will bring peace and calm into our stressful lives.
4. Creating and applying a simple priority pyramid exercise in our lives can teach us the skills to achieve this objective.

20. SKILL EIGHTEEN

HOW TO RESOLVE CONFLICT
Peace versus War

Why Do We Need this Skill?

Resolving conflict is a key emotional resilience skill. Interpersonal conflicts can inflict significant damage on our mental health. Resulting wounds can leave deep-seated psychological scars. I named this section 'peace versus war' to emphasise that it is our choice which road we wish to travel.

Everyday life is replete with situations where this skill could prevent potential conflict. For example, all couples experience normal, healthy disagreements. Sometimes attitudes harden, ending up in destructive separations or divorces. When break-ups do occur, separated couples and offspring must deal with the arrival of new partners on the scene. This can also become nasty and combative.

Sibling rivalry triggered by issues such as ageing parents, disputed wills, the belief that one's siblings have been treated more fairly, and jealousy also create conflict, leading at times to poisonous long-term relationships. Conflicts between parents and offspring at all stages of life are also common, often over seemingly petty issues. Other potential areas of 'war' include the workplace, friendships and neighbours. Most situations could be resolved earlier if those involved had the appropriate conflict management skills.

The consequences of choosing 'war' over 'peace' in such situations can be devastating. Emotions such as hurt, anger, frustration, jealousy, anxiety and depression are frequently triggered. Resulting unhealthy behaviours will often follow.

Depression can be triggered by the stress created by such conflict. It can also lead to self-harm and, on occasion, suicide. Others may turn to alcohol or substance misuse to manage their emotions.

One important but rarely discussed consequence of interpersonal conflict is lack of sleep. When such situations begin to fester in our minds sleep can quickly become a casualty as we struggle to switch off the washing machine of ruminatory thoughts in our mind. This in turn can make us more distressed and more likely to stay in 'war mode', perpetuating the conflict situation. Research (Gordon et al., 2013) into this hidden link demonstrated that couples in conflict were more likely to fight more if sleep became disturbed and vice versa.

There are important benefits to managing conflict. Life is difficult enough without wasting time and emotional energy avoiding the firefighting of issues which should have been resolved at the outset. Interpersonal relationships will also benefit from preventing wounds festering. Conflict is inevitable for all of us at some stage during life. Managing it can be a real test of our emotional resilience. Those possessing this skill will navigate more easily through such turbulent periods.

How to Develop this Skill

The aim here is simple. It is the peaceful resolution of a problem that is causing difficulties or conflict to the various parties involved. We previously explored the skill of problem-solving in Chapter 12, and it might be worth revisiting that section. In principle, it should be easy enough to tease out the parameters of an interpersonal problem and find a solution by working together with those involved. In practice, as with many areas of life, it is not so simple. There are ten common hurdles which can get in the way:

1. Emotions.
2. Fixed positions.
3. Delays or procrastination in dealing with conflict issues.
4. An inability to put ourselves in the place of other parties.
5. Looking only at the problem, rather than at possible solutions.

6. An inability to think outside the box.
7. A tendency to make situations personal, rather than focusing on both our own and the other party's behaviour.
8. Taking ourselves too seriously. This can remove the potential of humour to de-escalate such situations.
9. A tendency to turn everything into a competitive situation, where winning is everything.
10. Refusing, on occasion, to involve a sensible mediator to resolve differences where positions have become entrenched.

Let's explore these obstacles.

Emotions such as hurt, anger, anxiety, frustration and jealousy have lain at the feet of human disputes since the dawn of time. These emotions are powerful, often emanating from fixed positions which sometimes have little to do with the issue in question.

Suppose, for example, you are a sibling who feels hurt or jealous because, in your mind, another sibling was treated more fairly during childhood and adolescence. Issues relating to, say, a family get-together can assume more importance than they truly deserve. Because delays in dealing with such issues arise, positions can quickly harden.

The situation can deteriorate quickly if matters become personal, rather than the parties focusing on their individual behaviours. It can turn into a power struggle, with both sides determined to win at all costs. If neither is prepared to look at matters from the other's point of view or explore alternative solutions, emotions harden even further. If both parties are taking themselves too seriously or refuse to seek out a third-party mediator, we can be looking at a long, protracted, often bitter dispute, where nobody wins.

So, what should we do if we wish to de-escalate potential conflict situations? We might consider the following ten principles:

1. Deal with the issues at the beginning of a potential conflict.
2. Identify the emotions the conflict is engendering in yourself and the other party involved.

3. Explore the reasons underlying such emotions, especially putting yourself in the place and mind of the other party. Are they coming from fixed positions and what might the origins of these be?

4. From the outset, refuse to focus on the personal. Focus on the behaviour of yourself and the protagonist.

5. When meeting up with the other party to resolve the issues in question for the first time, listen carefully to their views. And as discussed in earlier chapters, focus on their body language and emotional state. This will give you essential information, allowing you to sense where they are at in relation to this dispute.

6. Focus on potential solutions from the beginning. Be prepared to think outside the box if required.

7. Do not regard ceding on certain issues as an indication that you are 'giving in' or 'showing weakness'. Regard it rather as a sign of emotional maturity, where you are prepared to make appropriate changes to resolve a dispute. Think of it as a game of chess, where you might cede a key piece with the aim of placing yourself in a stronger position on the board.

8. Adopt a sense of humour about the situation. Too often, issues of relatively minor importance can be given life-or-death significance. This usually happens because we are taking ourselves too seriously.

9. It is important for the other party to feel that they have been listened to, validated and taken seriously. Whatever the final solution, they must be allowed to save face.

10. If, from an early stage in the dispute, positions seem to be fixed, then it should be a priority to introduce a mediator acceptable to both at the earliest opportunity.

With a clear understanding of the hurdles obstructing and the principles underlying conflict resolution, let's explore how to put them into practice. We will take two scenarios. The first is where a potential area of conflict suddenly manifests itself. The second is where there is an ongoing, long-term dispute you would like to resolve.

Once again, we will apply the technique of writing down the issues involved while coming up with potential solutions. This is often underestimated. We have discussed the power of the emotional brain to sideline our more rational or logical brain. Never is this concept more relevant than in the often emotionally charged and fraught environment of interpersonal conflict. If we attempt to solve the problem in our mind, emotions may obstruct any progress towards a solution. If we write things down, our rational mind can now problem-solve the issue involved.

The techniques involved can be applied to many problem areas of life, whether related to family, social or working life, friendships or community. The common denominator in such conflicts is human beings. We all think irrationally at times, developing fixed positions and allowing emotions to run riot. If you can learn how to apply these conflict-resolution techniques in one area, you can apply them to all.

Technique One: How to De-escalate a Potential Conflict Situation

In this scenario, you are suddenly presented with a potential conflict situation appearing on your doorstep. It might be that you, as a younger sibling, receive a telephone call out of the blue. It is your older brother Vincent, remonstrating with you for not visiting your mother regularly enough. In reality, you do visit her regularly, so you immediately feel quite hurt at this accusation, which you consider as unfair. This would commonly lead to an acrimonious conversation. This, in turn, could lead to subsequent hardening of attitudes and a family rift. You want to avoid this occurring. So how should you handle this situation? I suggest that you handle it in the following series of steps.

Step One

Our first and quite natural behaviour in such situations is to lash out, vehemently denying the accusation. This is often accompanied by some personal comments about the person making the accusations. To counteract this, I recommend the turtle exercise. This is a technique I use to assist adults and children in managing anger outbursts. They are encouraged to retreat, like the turtle, into their shells. Once the waves of anger have subsided, they may re-emerge and deal with the issue in question.

To do this, you might listen quietly to the accusations and then excuse yourself for a short period. You might say to your brother Vincent that these are important issues and you would like an hour or so to consider them. By that point, you will be in a calmer frame of mind, having had more time to reflect on the issues brought up.

Step Two

The next step is to take out a sheet of paper and analyse the issue. Why did Vincent make this phone call at all? Why now? You note that he has two small children and a very busy job. Is he feeling under pressure? Possibly guilty he cannot visit your mum, a widow, as often as he would like? Or does he genuinely believe that you do not visit often enough, even if your honest assessment disagrees with this viewpoint? Has anything changed in Vincent's life that is putting him under pressure? Or has he got some unspoken concerns about your mother, who has become slightly more forgetful? Laying out this information on paper often clarifies where the areas of possible conflict might lie, and helps to identify issues you need to explore further. You are now ready to proceed to the next step.

Step Three

You ring Vincent back, arranging to meet him as soon as possible. This turns out to be for lunch the following day. At lunch, you thank him for making his concerns known and say that you would like to use this meeting to tease out the issues bothering him. You then listen calmly and intently to his concerns, reassuring him through your words and body language that you are not treating this as a personal attack. Rather, it is an information-gathering exercise. As a result, he reveals his concern that your mum has indeed become more forgetful. It emerges that a visit from one of her close friends triggered his irate phone call.

He admits to being frustrated and guilty, as he is struggling to visit her as often as he would like. He also reveals your mum's friend's comment that perhaps her family were not visiting as regularly as they should. It was this statement that triggered the phone call. He admits to feeling upset after making the call. Maybe he had overreacted, but he felt trapped by the situation he found himself in.

You, at this stage, empathise with his situation, acknowledging how busy his life is, no more than your own. You agree that this is indeed a joint problem for you both, as her only children. This new situation is going to require a multi-faceted approach involving yourselves and other agencies.

Step Four

Then you explore how this might work in practice, agreeing a new timetable of visits, ensuring that she will be monitored more closely. You discuss and split the task of involving relevant health and community services, while both wryly acknowledge that dealing with your mum was going to require patience and a healthy sense of humour. She is known on occasion to be 'difficult'. But you agree to support one another when things become difficult. You also arrange follow-up meetings to ensure both of you are now singing from the same hymn sheet.

What has subtly occurred is the shifting of the issue from a potential interpersonal source of conflict into the practical world of problem-solving. Because of this meeting, you have dealt with a potential area of dispute immediately, before a further hardening of attitudes occurs. You have attempted to understand the problem from Vincent's point of view. More importantly, you have initiated a discussion about how best to jointly reach a viable solution. In this case, a third-party mediator is not necessary.

What Can We Learn?

1. Never react immediately or emotionally to a sudden potential conflict situation. Rather, using the turtle exercise, buy yourself some time to calm down before proceeding further.
2. Try to tease out on paper what the main issues might relate to, how the other party is feeling emotionally, what is bothering them most and why. Try to put yourself into their shoes.
3. Arrange a meeting as soon as possible.

4. At the meeting, listen carefully to concerns expressed by the other party. Validate and empathise with their position.
5. Make it clear with your words and body language that you are not making this issue a personal one.
6. Summarise the main issues with them and begin the task of formulating a solution to the problems identified.
7. Before the meeting ends, ensure that you have come up with a joint approach to solving the problems outlined and arrange follow-up meetings to ensure the agreed solutions are put in place.

Technique Two: How to Resolve an Ongoing Conflict

In this scenario, we explore the techniques required to resolve ongoing, often long-running conflict situations. Here, the original cause of the dispute has regularly been lost sight of as emotions harden, positions become entrenched and the conflict becomes personal and a power struggle. Both parties are determined to be vindicated, irrespective of the cost to personal physical and mental health. This is a common scenario affecting most of us, at some stage in our lives.

The Bust-up

Caroline, a sixty-three-year-old grandmother, received a phone call from her daughter Miriam a few months ago, asking, yet again, if she would look after the grandchildren over an upcoming weekend. Caroline, as it happened, had arranged an eagerly awaited break with her husband Michael for the weekend in question. She was used to receiving such phone calls, as Miriam regularly asks Caroline to mind the two grandchildren, allowing her to engage in a hectic social life with her partner and friends. It has become an almost fortnightly exercise.

Caroline has increasingly felt used, often gently suggesting she and Michael were not as young as they used to be, and that they were finding the grandchildren, whom they loved dearly, exhausting to manage for so many weekends. Her comments had fallen on deaf ears. The situation is made more complex by the fact that Miriam is an only child. She has always resented this fact, holding a grudge against her parents. She also assumes that it is her mum's role to make sure she can live in the style to which she has become accustomed.

For Caroline, this last phone call was one request too many. She refused to take the grandchildren on this occasion, citing the break she had already organised. She was not prepared for what occurred next. Miriam exploded on the phone, calling her selfish, looking after her own self-interests, unconcerned about the welfare of her daughter or grandchildren. Did she not realise that it was her duty to take pressure off her daughter? Was it not the least she could do, considering she had been left, as an only child, to fend for herself at school? While her friends had siblings to relate to, she was always the odd one out. She could never forgive her mother for placing her in this situation. And just when a close friend, who is returning from Australia, wanted 'the girls' to come out for a weekend of socialising, Caroline was yet again letting her down.

For once, Caroline saw red. This was just a step too far. She allowed her frustration, built up over the previous two years, to boil over. A long, heated conversation ensued, where she said things she later regretted. Miriam was particularly incensed when Caroline called her a spoilt brat who had never appreciated all she had been given. She screamed at Caroline over the phone, called her every name in the book, vowed she would never see her grandchildren again and slammed down the phone.

For the next three months, emotions harden on both sides. Caroline feels hurt, frustrated and angry about the way she was treated. Miriam feels equally angry and hurt, determined to shut Caroline out of her life. Both, however, deep down, are distressed and saddened by the loss of this relationship. Miriam also misses her father, with whom she has a close relationship. Her partner comments on how sad it is that their children are losing out by not interacting with their grandparents, and he is concerned that they will miss out on this key relationship in the future. But stalemate has ensued. Neither party wants to be seen to give in. It has become deeply personal for both.

A Seemingly Intractable Conflict

At first glance, this conflict seems intractable, as neither party is prepared to make the first move to resolve it. Despite this, deep down, both still long for some way to bring matters to a resolution. However, if this situation is permitted to continue for another year or so, positions will become so fixed and hardened that resolution may become impossible to achieve.

So, the first message here is to break such impasses as early as possible, before they become entrenched. You may also need a mediator or mentor to advise how best to resolve them. Let's explore what happens when Michael becomes the mediator in question.

The Mediator

Caroline, increasingly distressed and missing her grandchildren, eventually sits down with Michael for a long chat about what to do. He wisely observes that life is too short for both parties to waste precious time and emotional energy on holding grudges. He offers to mediate an agreement and she agrees to assist any way she can. He then visits Miriam and, in an emotional discussion, she breaks down, admitting how miserable she has been since the dispute began. He offers once again to mediate, and she too agrees.

He then suggests that both Caroline and Miriam write down all the issues bothering them, how they feel emotionally and what possible solutions there are. He also suggests they write down possible reasons why the other person behaved in the manner they had. They both find this to be a cathartic experience. It allows them to rationally explore what has occurred, and to understand why each behaved the way they did. Both admit, on paper, that they would have preferred to have behaved in a different manner. They find it especially helpful to explore potential solutions, rather than focusing only on the problems uncovered.

The Meeting

Michael now arranges for both to meet, with him acting as mediator. Caroline is first to apologise for her behaviour and the language she used in that fateful phone call. Miriam follows up by admitting she too had been guilty of losing her rag and saying some terrible things. She apologises for her behaviour. This ends up with a hug and some tears.

With Michael's subtle nudging, the whole tenor of the meeting shifts to problem-solving the various issues and difficulties which both had written down on paper. Having done some soul-searching, Miriam admits she had been taking Caroline's assistance for granted and agrees to change her attitude. Caroline, in turn, is open to assisting her, by agreeing to mind the grand-children once a month, if she has plenty of notice. They also have a deeper conversation as to why Caroline and Michael had not conceived a second child. Caroline reveals that Miriam's birth had been a difficult delivery, with significant internal damage, and that she was advised against further pregnancies. This was an eye-opener for Miriam, who now views her childhood in a completely different light. And as Michael wisely adds, 'There is no such thing as a perfect upbringing!'

Caroline and Miriam also agree that by making things so personal, and refusing to see the other person's point of view, they had risked long-term alienation. They promise this will never happen again. Following this meeting, which finishes with more tears and hugging, Caroline and Miriam have resolved their conflict. They have also learned some key lessons about life, and how damaging and futile such conflicts can become.

What Can We Learn?

1. It is better to deal with potential conflict situations earlier rather than later. If Caroline had made her feelings of frustration at taking the children so often known, things might have come to a head sooner. Equally, if Miriam had vented her issues about being an only child sooner.
2. If Caroline had not lost her rag at the beginning of the phone call, but had performed the turtle exercise, it would have allowed her time to discuss the situation with her husband and come up with potential solutions.
3. Allowing the conflict situation to grow legs and not intervening at an earlier stage, before emotions and positions harden, had increased the risk of matters becoming entrenched.
4. By making things personal, rather than focusing on what behavioural changes both parties needed to make, they risked long-term conflict ensuing.
5. A mediator should always be sought as soon as possible if attitudes are

becoming entrenched. Both parties must respect the mediator.

6. Writing down the issues involved can be a game-changer for both parties. It removes the conflict from the emotional brain, allowing the rational brain to explore both the problems uncovered and, more importantly, potential solutions. It is also helpful to write down why the other party behaved the way they did.

7. Never be afraid to apologise for something you have done behaviourally which was inappropriate. This is not weakness, but a sign of maturity. If you put out the hand first, then you have done all you can do. It is then up to the other person to reciprocate or not.

8. Be open to accepting, with an open heart and mind, a genuine apology from the other person involved.

9. Most of the underlying causes of conflict, when approached in a problem-solving manner, are dealt with easily enough if both parties are open to making some changes in their thinking and behaviour.

10. Life is indeed too short to carry grudges, especially over matters that have been given life-or-death significance, but which are of little import in the overall scheme of things.

Before leaving this section, it is important to accept that in real life there will always be unresolvable conflict situations. These most often occur when too much time has elapsed, or when positions have become too firmly entrenched. We all know of such scenarios. These are often sad, distressing and destructive for those involved. How best to deal with such situations?

The answer lies in Chapter 18 where we dealt with the reality that life is not fair. Sometimes we must just accept that this is the way things are, and move on. Whoever said that life should be fair or end up the way we wish it to be? In such situations, I recommend letting go of any hurt and forgiving the person, while remaining constantly open to the possibility of resolution if circumstances change to bring this about.

But, clearly, the more desirable approach is to learn and practise the skill of conflict resolution, and apply resolution techniques as early as possible in any conflict situations. We all need to develop and practise these techniques. We will notice obvious benefits to our emotional resilience and mental health if we do.

Key Learning Points

1. Interpersonal conflicts can be immensely distressing and extremely damaging to our mental health if we lack the appropriate emotional resilience skills to deal with them.
2. Most are deeply rooted in simple misunderstandings and a tendency to make matters personal, rather than trying to uncover the core issues involved and attempting to deal with them.
3. The ideal is to develop our own conflict-resolution skills and learn to spot the warning signs of a potential 'war', using these skills to prevent it from occurring.
4. Through some simple techniques, we can develop and use these skills in both potential conflicts and long-running disputes, to the benefit of our own and others' mental health and well-being.

21. SKILL NINETEEN

PRAGMATISM
Let's Get Real

What Is Pragmatism?

Pragmatism is a life skill where we become adept at quickly analysing problematic situations with a view to finding and putting into practice the most effective solutions. It also teaches us how to carve through fixed thinking or behavioural patterns to achieve this objective. Pragmatists become experts at finding the shortcut to the best way to deal with practical, everyday difficulties. I have always regarded pragmatism as the ultimate emotional resilience skill, in terms of managing many of life's difficulties. It involves taking the world where we find it, not where we would like it to be. Pragmatists, as a result, are the ultimate problem-solvers!

Why Do We Need this Skill?

An oft-quoted aphorism is that common sense is sometimes not that common. While many dismiss this seemingly inane observation about life, it contains an element of truth. An example is our modern obsession with positive thinking. Numerous books have been written, explaining how to achieve this hallowed objective. Negative thinking about ourselves or life is frowned upon and seen as potentially damaging to our mental health.

Think positively and all will be well. If only life was that simple! In reality, it is manifestly unrealistic to be constantly positive and upbeat about our fraught lives. And while negative thinking is often unhelpful, it is equally unrealistic to assume that we can simply block out such thoughts.

The implications of assuming that our thinking should only be positive are significant. What do we say, for example, to those who struggle to banish negative thoughts or embrace positive ones, due to depression or anxiety? It creates the illusion that life can be categorised in such a manner, when life, of course, is neither black nor white, but intensely grey.

I have argued for the past decade that such perceptions need to be disputed. Would it be more sensible, instead, to embrace the power of realistic or pragmatic thinking? Real life is not a rosy place where positive thinking inevitably ensures the desired results, where banishing negative thoughts about life will, in practice, make appreciable differences. Rather, it is a place where pragmatism rules supreme. Where the skill to pragmatically analyse challenging life situations can make all the difference.

Our ancestors were, of necessity, more pragmatic about the world they found themselves in. Those reared on, and making their living off, the land or sea, for example, learned this skill through necessity. Practical problems required practical solutions and innovative thinking.

Nowadays, all of us, and especially adolescents, find ourselves in a new world, one in which technology is king. Those who can navigate easily through this world may seem, at first glance, to be the ultimate modern pragmatists. Are they not experts in solving problems in this new sphere? But when we examine this assumption more closely, can they apply such pragmatism to real life? The evidence seems to point to the opposite. We are experiencing a maelstrom of mental health difficulties and self-harm. Does this come from the shift from the pragmatic, solution-focused thinking of our forebears to the current belief that all problems can be solved online? Does this account, in part, for the tidal wave of mental health issues our society is currently drowning in?

I believe that pragmatism is a central pillar of emotional resilience. Those with this skill cope better with the difficulties of life, as they are clearer and more realistic in their thinking. They are also more adaptable. The pragmatist is, above all, a survivor.

The Power of Pragmatism

Over the years, I have seen pragmatism transform the lives of many with mental health difficulties. Learning how to become increasingly realistic in your thinking can be a game-changer in depression and anxiety. It is a relief for the person struggling to cope with a steady stream of negative thoughts not to be faced with a demand to 'think positively'. In my experience, people with this condition are often more realistic about life.

For those suffering from anxiety, becoming realistic or pragmatic in relation to their thinking and behaviour can greatly assist in dealing with uncertainty, perfectionism, catastrophising and procrastination. It is also a buffer against stress. Rationally analysing potential stressors, together with a more pragmatic approach to decision-making, may prevent many of the negative consequences of toxic stress. Could more suicides also be prevented if pragmatic thinking was a core component of mental health education?

We can all benefit from developing this skill. I believe this type of practical, realistic thinking and consequential pragmatic behaviour should be taught to children from the earliest age. My colleague, leading CBT psychotherapist Enda Murphy, has often commented that he has never seen a child or adolescent for therapy who has been trained by a group such as the Scouts, Guides or Order of Malta. Do these organisations train young people to be extremely pragmatic in their thinking and behaviour and, as a result, do they become more emotionally resilient?

How to Develop this Skill

Pragmatism involves a healthy working knowledge of many of the resilience skills already discussed in previous chapters, which is why we have left this skill towards the end of the book. I often describe pragmatism as our reward for developing and practising these other skills. This is because without their foundation it is almost impossible to build on and develop the skill of pragmatism. Let's enumerate the relevant skills.

1. The importance of accepting ourselves unconditionally.
2. That failure will frequently be our lot. That the only failure in life is not getting back up and trying again.
3. That success in our endeavours is often built on the bones of previous failures.
4. That the world is neither fair nor free of discomfort.
5. That the world is also an uncertain place, where perfection is a myth.
6. That there is never a perfect solution to the difficulties of life, so adaptability and problem-solving are the only games in town.
7. That catastrophising and procrastination are both unhealthy and unhelpful.
8. That good conflict-resolution skills are essential.

You might like to revisit the relevant chapters on the skills necessary to deal with the realities of life before progressing further. Let's now explore how to become more pragmatic in your thinking and behaviour.

The Pragmatism Exercise

For the next eight weeks, you will likely be faced with several potentially challenging situations or specific problems requiring resolution. They may relate to your personal, social, working or recreational life. Focus especially on situations which do not produce the required result.

1. In each situation, write in your notebook the task that was involved, the desired goal and the result of your endeavours.
2. Later, on paper, analyse what in your thinking or behaviour might have prevented you from fulfilling your task.
3. Then list the relevant pragmatic lessons learned from the situation, for future application.

Let's take an example of putting this exercise into practice. Bart finds himself struggling with relationships as every time he gets close to someone, he begins to doubt himself. I must be certain that I choose the right person! Things come to a head when he meets Samantha, who is keen to further the relationship. But yet again, although there is definite 'chemistry', Bart finds himself procrastinating and pulling back from the relationship. When Samantha, sensing his reluctance to commit, breaks off the relationship, he finds himself berating himself harshly for letting her slip away.

If Bart were to then apply the above pragmatism exercise to this event it would look like this:

1. His goal was to meet the woman of his dreams. But with Samantha as with previous encounters, his procrastinating about making a decision to continue the relationship had cost him dearly. For it was only when she left that he came to terms with the fact that there was actually great potential in the relationship.

2. It was clear when he analysed the situation on paper that it was his demands for certainty and perfection in relation to Samantha that had scuppered his chances. For these led him to procrastinate and pull back from a potentially emotionally nourishing and fulfilling relationship.

3. There were some clear pragmatic lessons that he could learn for the future:
   - Every time he enters into a relationship there is a chance that it might not work out but he must learn to accept that reality and take the chance. Otherwise he will end up on his own!
   - There is no such thing as a perfect partner or relationship. If he is seeking such he is doomed to failure in this area of his life.
   - That procrastinating and sitting on the fence in relationships is a recipe for disappointment in life.
   - The next time such an opportunity presents, and if happy that the chemistry is present, he should just take the plunge. The worst that can happen is that the relationship might not work out. If this occurred, he had to remember that there were plenty more fish in the sea.

Let's now examine typical examples of pragmatic lessons one might learn from applying this exercise in your own life.

1. You might have found yourself seeking the 'perfect' solution, when this is rarely, if ever, possible. The lesson here is, in future, to seek the most realistic or pragmatic solution, even if it does not fit all the criteria.

2. You may have been trying to control an uncontrollable situation, as you felt unable to cope with uncertainty. The lesson here is that you must learn to cede control, do the best you can and pragmatically accept that you cannot control all the variables.

3. Perhaps you found yourself waiting for the situation, and the world, to change, rather than changing something yourself? The lesson here is that, on mature reflection, this is unlikely to happen. Instead, you will have to consider pragmatically what discomfort you will have to accept to sort the situation out.

4. It may have been that fear of failure was getting in the way of handling the situation. The lesson here is to realise that we can only do our best to solve issues that arise in life. Sometimes we will be successful, but quite regularly we will fail to achieve our objective. We have to accept the necessity of getting up and trying again until we finally succeed.

5. Maybe you found yourself so busy catastrophising that you struggled to make the necessary decisions. The lesson here is that we must pragmatically accept that most of what we worry about will never happen, and make our decisions accordingly.

6. You may have discovered that you have worsened the situation through procrastinating behaviour. The lesson here is that dividing tasks up and establishing clear timelines, as discussed in Chapter 10, can help break this cycle.

7. It often becomes apparent that you have travelled the long way around while attempting to solve the problem when, in retrospect, clear shortcuts were available. The pragmatic lesson here is to change this pattern and look for the simplest, most practical solution. How often do we overlook simple, practical solutions to problems? The adage 'Keep it simple' should be our motto where possible. How often do we make matters unnecessarily complex?

What Is the Purpose of this Exercise?

This exercise is powerful in carving through much of our often-muddled thinking and behaviour. By analysing on paper any errors or mistakes in our approach to solving a problem or dealing with a situation, we will discover what is preventing us achieving our objectives. We will quickly see any unhelpful patterns we are falling into and try to reshape them on paper. This helps us to become more pragmatic about similar situations arising in the future.

By performing this exercise over a period of months, you will learn to analyse situations more effectively and emerge with more realistic, effective solutions.

PATRICK'S STORY

Patrick, a married man with two children, has been with his new company for six months. He was recently faced with a difficult choice, when his company manager asked him to carry out an important assignment on the same day he had promised to take his mother-in-law to the hospital for a cancer check-up.

Patrick was already in hot water with his partner, Helen, for missing out on a school performance in which his elder daughter had a leading role. Again, this had occurred as the result of a similar last-minute request from his boss. Patrick's thinking became extremely negative. It ranged from catastrophising about what might happen if he rejected his boss's request, to what damage might be done to his relationship with his partner and his mother-in-law, to a belief that life should not be causing him such hassle. His emotions ranged from initial panic and anxiety to frustration with life.

Patrick ended up procrastinating, only informing Helen of this issue at the last minute. He found himself in the bad books for days, and became extremely stressed. He also mismanaged the assignment from his boss, due to this conflict at home. He ended up rating himself as a complete failure and felt depressed for days. It was a truly miserable week. If only he had managed the situation differently.

He attends Dr Jim for advice over his anxiety and low mood. He also discusses his tendency to catastrophise and procrastinate. Dr Jim empathises with his situation and suggests that they explore on paper the event which had occurred. They agree that his thinking and behaviour have worsened the situation.

How Patrick's Thinking Worsened the Situation

It is clear from their analysis that Patrick's overtly negative thinking had led to the situation getting out of hand. He could only see two outcomes, both catastrophic. The first would have led to his boss being disappointed in him, with the risk of perhaps losing his job or facing a subtle demotion. The second, to the mother of all rows at home and subsequent conflict with his in-laws.

Patrick, if he had reflected further, could have been more pragmatic in his thinking.

1. Did he have any real proof that he would automatically have been fired if he had spoken to his boss and explained the situation?
2. Did he have any real proof that his wife would have been angry even if he had explained the issue to her when he first realised there was a clash between the assignment and the hospital check-up? Where was his evidence for this?
3. How could the dilemma lead him to conclude that he was a failure as a person?

After some discussion, they both agree that if Patrick had thought more pragmatically, there would have been an increased chance of a positive outcome. For example, he could have challenged his assumptions that his boss or wife would be unwilling to help him find a solution, or that he would be rated as a failure.

Dr Jim then suggests some exercises to assist Patrick in dealing with his catastrophising and procrastinating, which have already been discussed in previous chapters. He introduced Patrick to the Members Only club to teach him unconditional self-acceptance.

How Patrick's Behaviour Worsened the Situation

When Patrick examines his behaviour, it becomes clear that procrastination had led to his subsequent difficulties. Paralysed by a combination of anxiety and frustration, he had removed more sensible behavioural options from the picture. So, what should these have been?

Pragmatic Option One

Patrick and Dr Jim agree that the most pragmatic approach would have been first to explain the dilemma to his boss. He could have highlighted the fact that he had been willing to carry out assignments at similarly short notice on previous occasions and explained that his current assignment, however, would interfere with taking his mother-in-law to hospital for a cancer check-up.

This could have led to a fruitful discussion on potential options. Was someone else available? Could the assignment wait for twenty-four hours? If he came into work earlier the following day, could matters be sorted out then? Would it be of assistance if Patrick rang the client himself, to explain the reasons behind the short delay?

Unless there were major time pressures on this assignment, this pragmatic approach would likely have yielded a satisfactory solution. Most bosses are amenable, if employees explain their dilemma, especially if it involves family health issues. If this option had been pursued and proved successful, the crisis would have been averted.

Pragmatic Option Two

If this first option had not yielded a positive result, the next pragmatic approach would have been to talk to his wife and for them to problem-solve the situation together. If Helen had been aware of Patrick's unsuccessful initial effort to problem-solve the dilemma with his boss, she might have found a solution herself or within the wider family unit. She might have been able to take time off work herself, or enlisted the help of other family members, neighbours or friends to take her mother to the appointment. The crisis, with this option, could also have been averted.

Dr Jim then suggests that Patrick should apply the pragmatism exercise to any problems arising over the next two months. 'It will teach you the process of quickly and efficiently finding solutions to the trials of life,' he explains.

After ten weeks of applying this exercise to challenging situations at home and work, Patrick has become increasingly pragmatic in his thinking and behaviour. He no longer catastrophises or procrastinates when dilemmas arise. He is out of the doghouse at home. He now rapidly intervenes in such situations to defuse them. Patrick can now accept that there are no perfect solutions to the problems of life and that applying common sense to situations is often the shortest and most efficient way to achieve his goals. His new hard-earned motto when problems arise is 'Get real'. Three months later, Patrick has added pragmatism to his list of life skills. The results of this will become increasingly manifest in the years to come.

Key Learning Points

1. Pragmatism is a critical emotional resilience skill, where we become adept at analysing life's difficulties and rapidly developing shortcuts to finding simple, effective solutions. It will also involve learning how to bypass fixed positions and behaviours.
2. Pragmatism involves taking situations in life as they are, rather than as we would like them to be.
3. To develop this skill, we need to learn how to be realistic in our thinking and behaviour when trying to deal with situations.
4. Applying the pragmatism exercise can teach us how to achieve this objective.

22. SKILL TWENTY

HOW TO MANAGE STRESS IN OUR LIVES
When Stress Comes Calling

Why Do We Need this Skill?

It is appropriate to culminate our journey towards emotional resilience by focusing on the skill of how to manage bouts of stress. Stress is both normal and healthy, but there are periods when stress becomes potentially damaging or toxic to our physical and mental health. We deal with this in detail in *Toxic Stress*, and I recommend it to anyone experiencing a significant bout.

In this chapter, we will explore how to prevent toxic stress by developing this resilience skill. Many of the skills already explored in this book are involved in successfully managing stress. But we require a structure to apply these skills, during such stressful periods. This last skill involves learning how to create such a structure.

Why is this skill so essential for mental and physical health? The key lies in our body's stress system, which we explored in Chapter 1. It might be useful for you to revisit this section. When we are exposed to periods of acute stress, we release our fear hormone, adrenaline, if our emotional response is anxiety, and our aggression hormone, noradrenaline, if our emotion is frustration or anger. When we are exposed to longer periods of stress, we release our chronic stress hormone, glucocortisol.

While there are no physical consequences to bursts of adrenaline, there are potential ramifications if excessive amounts of noradrenaline and glucocortisol are floating around our bloodstream. These can predispose us to suffer cardiac arrhythmias, high blood pressure, heart attacks, strokes, diabetes and cancer.

There are also significant physical consequences to unhealthy negative behavioural responses to stress. We drink and smoke more, exercise less, eat the wrong foods, put on weight, stay up late at night and spend excess time passively engaged with technology. This behaviour predisposes us further to negative physical health consequences, such as the ones detailed above.

There are significant risks to mental health, too. Firstly, there is the obvious mental health risks of total burnout, which we deal with in *Toxic Stress*. There are also strong links between stress and individual bouts of depression. Learning how to manage stress more efficiently decreases the risk of further episodes of this illness. We deal with this subject in detail in *Flagging the Therapy* and *Depression*, for those who would like to explore it further. There are also strong links between anxiety and stress, which we explore in *Anxiety and Panic*. Many of us respond to stress by becoming extremely anxious, with the onset of panic attacks and anxiety. The more resilient we are in managing stress, the less anxious we will become. There are also powerful links between self-harm, suicide and stress.

As detailed in *Flagging the Problem*, there is significant evidence of such links in suicide, where in some post-mortem studies the adrenal stress gland has doubled in size, with concomitant evidence of high levels of stress hormones in the brain. Once again, those who have a specific interest in such links can refer to this book. Suffice to say, recognising and managing significant stress can save lives.

There are also strong links between stress and all forms of alcohol and substance misuse and abuse. These often relate to our behavioural responses to significant bouts of stress.

Developing the skill to manage stress when it comes calling is critical for all of us. Apart from reducing the physical and mental health risks outlined above, inability to cope with stress can lead to long periods of fatigue, mouth ulcers, irritable bowel symptoms, tension headaches, a reduced enjoyment of life, sleep difficulties, dental neuralgia from excessive teeth-grinding at night, etc. It can also lead to sexual difficulties, infertility, concentration issues and, on occasion, apathy. These consequences impoverish our lives.

If you want to be genuinely emotionally resilient, therefore, this last skill is essential. Conquer stress and the world is at your feet!

How to Develop this Skill

When faced with the arrival of some new or unexpected stressor, some of us become anxious or depressed, while others get angry, hurt or frustrated, with resultant unhealthy behaviours. These emotions are triggered by how we 'interpret' what is happening to us.

So, if we are struggling with uncertainty, rating, a fear of failure or catastrophising, we may become anxious. If we are railing against the stressor, believing that both it and life are unfair or should not be like this, we may become hurt or frustrated. We have already discussed the skills necessary to challenge such negative thoughts and beliefs, which, along with pragmatism and problem-solving, are all helpful in assisting us to manage stress.

To analyse and manage stress requires the application of a structure that can be applied in such situations. To develop this, I suggest the following exercise.

The ABC Stress-busting Exercise
Dr Jim uses the ABC concept throughout the book to help those who come to see him to deal with different stressors. You might like to revisit Chapter 2 before proceeding further.

This tool allows us to analyse on paper the stressor in question, together with our interpretations, beliefs, emotions, physical symptoms and resulting behaviour. This is the system used in *Toxic Stress*. But it can also be used to analyse and manage routine stressful events, with a view to preventing them growing legs.

To develop this skill, follow these steps:

1. For the next three months, carry around a notebook with you. Whenever you encounter a significant stressor, write down the trigger, your emotions and the resulting behaviour.

2. Later, when you have some free time, analyse what happened using the ABC system.

To demonstrate how to use this system, let's revisit how Sara, whom we met in Chapter 2, deals with the arrival of a significant stressor into her life.

SARA'S STORY

Sara's problems began when she received a phone call, in which she found out that a work colleague had suddenly been let go. She became extremely anxious, catastrophising about what might happen and rating herself mercilessly. Her healthy diet and exercise regime vanished, and her alcohol consumption rose. She tried excessively to please her boss, and was constantly checking her finances. She had previously attended Dr Jim who had taught her how to apply the ABC system when stressors arose. She decided to write down what happened into her notebook.

Later she begins to put together her ABC. She first writes down the trigger and the emotional and physical consequences it engendered.

A   Activating Event:
- Trigger: her work colleague is let go
- Inference/danger:

B   Belief/Demands:

C   Consequences:
- Emotional reactions: anxiety
- Physical reactions: stomach in knots, heart beating a little faster, shaking, muscle tension, increased fatigue
- Behaviour:

Her next step is to explore her inference or danger. This she does by simply asking herself (as Dr Jim had taught her) the following question: 'What is it about my work colleague being let go that makes me feel anxious?' This leads to the answer that perhaps she might be next to go. She then asks herself, 'Why would that bother me, or what do I think will happen if I am let go?' This leads to an answer that implies all kinds of negative consequences, such as ending up in serious financial difficulty. She continues to ask the question each time, 'Why would this particular consequence bother me?' Each answer draws her into the world of increased catastrophising until she reaches a point of believing that her family will end up on the street, homeless.

She then asks herself, 'If this did actually happen, why would it bother me?' This leads to an answer that she would feel she had let everybody down and would feel a failure as a result. She adds this new information to her ABC:

A   Activating Event:
  • Trigger: her work colleague is let go
  • Inference/danger: she might be next to be let go; if this happens, it will be awful; they might end up in serious financial difficulties; they might be unable to pay their mortgage; they might lose their house and end up homeless; if this happens, she will be a failure

B   Belief/Demands:

C   Consequences:
  • Emotional reactions: anxiety
  • Physical reactions: stomach in knots, heart beating a little faster, shaking, muscle tension, increased fatigue
  • Behaviour:

Sara's next step is to analyse her behaviour when she became anxious that she might be let go. This leads her to explore what her responses had been, how she had stopped exercising and eating properly, how she tried excessively to please her boss and sought reassurance from a friend in personnel, and began looking up potential future jobs. She adds this information to her ABC:

A   Activating Event:
  • Trigger: her work colleague is let go

- Inference/danger: she might be next to be let go; if this happens, it will be awful; they might end up in serious financial difficulties; they might be unable to pay their mortgage; they might lose their house and end up homeless; if this happens, she will be a failure

B Belief/Demands:

C Consequences:
- Emotional reactions: anxiety
- Physical reactions: stomach in knots, heart beating a little faster, shaking, muscle tension, increased fatigue
- Behaviour: stops eating and exercising; tries excessively to please her boss; constantly catastrophises about how awful the long-term consequences of possibly losing her job will be; drinks more wine than usual; rings a friend in personnel, seeking reassurance she is not next in the firing line; begins to look up future job options; checks her finances in case she does lose her job

Sara's last step is to explore her irrational belief. This takes the form of an absolute demand about the trigger and the inferences made about it. It is this demand that has made her so anxious, with resulting unhealthy behaviours. She examines her irrational belief by asking the simple question: 'What demand am I making in relation to hearing the news that a work colleague has been let go that is making me feel so anxious?' This leads her to a demand that she must not lose her job. If it happens she will not be able to cope and will be a failure. She adds this to complete her ABC:

A Activating Event:
- Trigger: her work colleague is let go
- Inference/danger: she might be next to be let go; if this happens, it will be awful; they might end up in serious financial difficulties; they might be unable to pay their mortgage; they might lose their house and end up homeless; if this happens, she will be a failure

B   Belief/Demands: 'I must be certain I am not let go. If this happens, I will be unable to cope. If I lose my job, I am a failure.'

C   Consequences:
- Emotional reactions: anxiety
- Physical reactions: stomach in knots, heart beating a little faster, shaking, muscle tension, increased fatigue
- Behaviour: stops eating and exercising; tries excessively to please her boss; constantly catastrophises about how awful the long-term consequences of possibly losing her job will be; drinks more wine than usual; rings a friend in personnel, seeking reassurance she is not next in the firing line; begins to look up future job options; checks her finances in case she does lose her job

What Has Sara Learned?

Now that Sara has used this simple ABC stress-busting exercise to analyse why she became so stressed, she can explore how best to manage the situation.

1. Firstly, she can identify her emotion of anxiety and how this was affecting her physically.
2. Secondly, she can identify the various unhealthy behaviours resulting from her anxiety. Were any of these assisting her in dealing with her stress?
3. Lastly, she can challenge the irrational negative beliefs and demands underlying her anxiety.

What Did this Allow Her to Do?

Through completing the ABC exercise, Sara can now identify that she is catastrophising, with no actual proof that she will be made redundant. She can also identify that she is struggling to cope with uncertainty and tending to rate herself as a failure. By analysing the stressor in this way, Sara can apply many of the skills explored in this book, especially those around uncertainty, rating, managing discomfort, dealing with failure, catastrophising, pragmatism and problem-solving.

This is what Sara did: she put into practice many of the emotional resilience skills she had learned from Dr Jim. She performed the coin exercise to help her accept that uncertainty and discomfort are a part of life. She worked hard on her catastrophising, using the spilt milk exercise. She also revisited the rules of the Members Only club and challenged the irrational belief that she could be classified as a failure.

These exercises led her to calmer waters, where she could pragmatically explore what had happened and alter her behaviour accordingly. Her anxiety levels settled. Sara now accepted that no matter what happened in the future in relation to her job, she would cope. As a result, her emotional resilience strengthened further. Applying the ABC system had also assisted her in avoiding straying into the world of toxic stress.

We can summarise the ABC steps that Sara took:

1. First, she wrote down the trigger (which was the phone call) and the emotional and physical consequences it engendered (which were anxiety and the associated physical symptoms).
2. She then explored what it was about the trigger (the phone call) that was causing her to feel anxious. She did so by asking question after question about why it was bothering her. This led her to recognise the catastrophic cascade going on in her head.
3. She then examined the unhealthy behaviour patterns that her anxiety was unleashing, namely her tendency to stop eating properly or exercising, and the safety behaviours of speaking to friends in the personnel department, and looking for potential future jobs.
4. Finally, she identified her irrational beliefs and absolute demands (which related to her demand that she must not lose her job or she would be a failure).
5. Now that she had her ABC down on paper, Sara could challenge her unhealthy thinking and behaviour patterns. She could also revisit the relevant exercises to challenge her difficulties with uncertainty, failure and catastrophising. This, in turn, helped her to become less anxious and stressed about the original trigger, the phone call.

If, like Sara, you practise this ABC stress-busting exercise over several months, the long-term benefits to your mental health will be immense. Constantly analyse the various stressors arising during this period and challenge them in the manner discussed throughout this book. You will become increasingly pragmatic and find yourself coping better, feeling less anxious, depressed or frustrated, and moving faster into problem-solving mode.

Stress will always be a constant in your life, but now you have a structure to analyse it and the skills necessary to manage it.

Key Learning Points

1. In general, stress is normal and healthy. But if prolonged and chronic, it can become toxic, with significant effects on our physical and mental health.
2. Learning how to manage stress is one of the most important emotional resilience skills of all.
3. Having a structure to deal with issues which cause us significant stress allows us to manage stress more efficiently.
4. Learning how to use a simple ABC system can transform our lives and safeguard our mental health.

CONCLUSION

We began our journey by exploring the world of emotional resilience and its importance in our lives, how it is essential if we wish to cope with the storms of life and become more robust from a mental health point of view.

As I was writing about the many skills that are so fundamental to building emotional resilience, all I could see passing in front of my eyes were the countless wonderful people whom I have had the privilege of helping during periods when their mental health was being challenged. They so often found their lives transformed by applying the simple, practical skills that we have explored in this book. It allowed them to overcome their difficulties and, more importantly, to develop and strengthen their emotional resilience. This, in turn, assisted them in staying well. Many of the people who benefited from learning these skills expressed their sadness that it had taken so many years to understand and apply them.

Together, we have often discussed the possibility that some of these skills should be taught to our children as early as possible, to prevent them emerging into adulthood and struggling, often for many years, from a dearth or absence of these skills.

Writing this book has also allowed me to put down on paper, in some cases for the first time, the methods I used when working with many of those wonderful people on their mental health development. It has been a humbling – at times both challenging and exhausting, but overall totally rewarding – task. And yet even as I review what I have written, I can sense that the job is not yet complete. There is more to add to these fundamental skills and concepts.

It is my hope that I have been successful in sharing many of these fundamental and, in my opinion, essential skills and techniques with you, my readers. If you have lasted the journey, you will have observed that hard work and perseverance are required to develop emotional resilience. This is one of the realities of life. We get out of life what we choose to put into it! Many whom we met on the journey were prepared to sacrifice time and effort to achieve their goal of learning specific resilience skills, gaining immeasurably when such skills became embedded in their lives.

At the end of our journey, it is worth overviewing what we have learned on the road. There are several insights of importance.

1. Emotional resilience is not a gift, or something only granted to a chosen few. Rather, it is something we must battle to attain. This requires fortitude, perseverance, a sense of humour and a steely determination to acquire the many skills necessary to achieve it.
2. We all have strengths and weaknesses in terms of the individual skills necessary for emotional resilience. We may have already picked up some of them on our journey through life. It is still worth doing a refresher course, by reading through the relevant sections. Others, we may find more challenging. These are the skills you must really apply yourself to learning and practising. If you persevere, they will become a new weapon in your armoury for life.
3. Our ability to be emotionally resilient requires us to be honest about our strengths and weaknesses, and prepared to work on the skills required to manage them.
4. Most of the skills required to attain emotional resilience are interdependent. It is rare that perfectionism, catastrophising and procrastination are not interlinked. So, skills to deal with one assist in dealing with the others. As you have progressed through the book you will notice how the skills stack up on one another, like dominoes.
5. We must develop a sense of humour about ourselves and about life. None of us is as important as we think we are. We should consider ourselves a group of loveable, impossible rogues, stumbling our way through the mysterious world we inhabit.

6. Some skills take precedence over others. I identify unconditional self-acceptance as the most important of all. We will never achieve emotional resilience unless we become kinder and more realistic about ourselves. We all mess up. We fail regularly. Yet we are all special, unique, wonderfully individual human beings. We must accept ourselves as we are, without any conditions. What a wonderful skill to bring with you on the journey of life!

If I have succeeded in assisting you to learn and practise this most important skill, unconditional self-acceptance, then I am content. It has the greatest power to fully transform your life. If you subjugate your life to the world of self- and others' rating, unhappiness is inevitable. If you attain unconditional self-acceptance, then genuine inner peace and emotional resilience will follow.

This is the real secret to good mental health.

My gift to you, the reader.

The key to emotional resilience.

BIBLIOGRAPHY

Introduction

Giedd, J.N., Keshavan, M. and Paus, T. (2008), 'Why do many psychiatric disorders emerge during adolescence?', *Nature Reviews Neuroscience*, 9(12): 947–957.

Heck, L. (2015), 'A generation on edge: A look at millennials and mental health', *Vox Magazine*, School of Journalism, University of Missouri.

Jones, P.B. (2013), 'Adult mental health disorders and their age at onset', *The British Journal of Psychiatry*, 202(54).

McMahon, E.M., O'Regan, G., Corcoran, P., Arensman, E., Cannon, M., Williamson, E. and Keeley, H. (2017), 'Young Lives in Ireland: a school-based study of mental health and suicide prevention', National Suicide Research Foundation, Cork.

Meltzer, H., Gatward, R., Goodman, R. and Ford, T. (2000), 'The mental health of children and adolescents in Great Britain: the report of a survey carried out in 1999 by the Division of the Office for National Statistics on behalf of the Department of Health, the Scottish Health Executive and the National Assembly for Wales', London.

Rajabi, S., Assareh, M., Shiri, E., Keshvari, F., Mikaieli hoor, F., et al. (2004), 'Evaluation of Students' Mental Health and Relation to Resilience and Coping Styles', *International Journal of School Health*, 1(1).

Sifferlin, A. (2013), 'The most stressed-out generation? Young Adults', available from: http://healthland.time.com/2013/02/07/the-most-stressed-outgeneration-young-adults/

World Health Organization (2013), 'What is mental health?', available from: http://www.who.int/features/qa/62/en/

PART ONE: SETTING THE STAGE

1. What Is Emotional Resilience?

Barry, H.P. and Murphy, E. (2015), *Flagging the Screenager: Guiding your child through adolescence and young adulthood*, Liberties Press, Dublin.

Beutel, M.E., Tibubos, A.N., Klein, E.M., Schmutzer, G., Reiner, I., Kocalevent, R.-D., et al. (2017), 'Childhood adversities and distress: the role of resilience in a representative sample', *PLoS One*, 12(3).

Dray, J., Bowman, J., Wolfenden, L., Campbell, E., Freund, M., Hodder, R. and Wiggers, J. (2015), 'Systematic review of universal resilience interventions targeting child and adolescent mental health in the school setting: review protocol', *Systematic Reviews*, 4: 186.

Fields, R.D. (2008), 'White matter in learning, cognition and psychiatric disorders', *Trends in Neurosciences,* 31(7), 361–370.

Gloria, C.T. and Steinhardt, M.A. (2014), 'Relationships among Positive Emotions, Coping, Resilience and Mental Health', *Stress & Health.*

Kandel, E.R. and Squire, L.R. (2001), 'Neuroscience: breaking down scientific barriers to the study of brain and mind', *Annals of the New York Academy of Sciences*, 935(1), 118–35.

Leppin, A.L., Bora, P.R., Tilburt, J.C., Gionfriddo, M.R., Zeballos-Palacios, C., Dulohery, M.M., Sood, A., Erwin, P.E., Brito, J.P., Boehmer, K.R. and Montor, V.M. (2014), 'The Efficacy of Resiliency Training Programs: A Systematic Review and Meta-analysis of Randomized Trials', *PLoS One*, 9(10).

McKenzie, I., Ohayon, D., Li, H., Paes de Faria, J., Emery, B., Tohyama, K. and Richardson, W. (2014), 'Motor skill learning requires active central myelination', *Science*, 346: 318–322.

Ongs, A.D., Bergeman, C.S., Bisconti, T.L. and Wallace, K.A. (2006), 'Psychological Resilience, Positive Emotions, and Successful Adaptation to Stress in Later Life', *Journal of Personality and Social Psychology*, 91(4): 730–749.

Pluskota, A. (2014), 'The application of positive psychology in the practice of education', *Springerplus*, 3: 147.

Rutten, B.P.F., Hammels, C., Geschwind, G., Menne-Lothmann, C., Pishva, E., Schruers, K., van den Hove, D., Kenis, G., van Os, J. and Wichers, M. (2013), 'Resilience in mental health: linking psychological and neurobiological perspectives', *Acta Psychiatrica Scandinavica*, 128(1): 3–20.

Schultze-Lutter, F., Schimmelmann, B.G. and Schmidt, S.J. (2016), 'Resilience, risk, mental health and well-being: associations and conceptual differences', *European Child & Adolescent Psychiatry*, 25: 459–466.

Southwick, S.M., Bonanno, G.A., Masten, A.S., Panter-Brick, C. and Yehuda, R. (2014), 'Resilience definitions, theory, and challenges: interdisciplinary perspectives', *European Journal of Psychotraumatology*.

2. Cognitive Behavioural Therapy (CBT)

Beck, A.T. and Dozois, D.J. (2013), 'Cognitive Therapy: Current Status and Future Directions', *Annual Review of Medicine*, 62: 397–409.

Beck, A.T. (2005), 'The current state of cognitive therapy: a 40-year retrospective', *Archives of General Psychiatry*, 62(9): 953–959.

David, L. (2006), *Using CBT in General Practice*, Scion Publishing, Banbury.

David, L. and Freeman, G. (2006), 'Improving consultation skills using cognitive- behavioural therapy: a new "cognitive-behavioural model" for general practice', *Education for Primary Care*, 17: 443– 53.

Dryden, W. and Ellis, A. (2001), 'Rational emotive behaviour therapy', *Handbook of Cognitive-Behavioral Therapies*, 2nd edn, Guilford Press, New York.

Dryden, W. and Neenam, M. (2004), *Rational Emotive Behavioural Counselling in Action*, SAGE Publications, London.

Ellis, A. (1962), *Reason and Emotion in Psychotherapy*, Lyle Stuart, New York.

Ellis, A. (1996), *Better, Deeper, and More Enduring Brief Therapy: The Rational Emotive Behavior Therapy Approach*, Brunner/Mazel Inc., New York.

PART TWO: PERSONAL RESILIENCE SKILLS

3. Skill One: Unconditional Self-acceptance

Ellis, A. (1962), *Reason and Emotion in Psychotherapy*, Lyle Stuart, New York.
Ellis, A. (1996), *Better, Deeper, and More Enduring Brief Therapy: The Rational Emotive Behavior Therapy Approach*, Brunner/Mazel Inc., New York.
Murphy, E. (2009), 'The raggy doll club', *Forum*, Journal of the Irish College of General Practitioners.
Murphy, E. (2013), *Five Steps to Happiness*, Liberties Press, Dublin.

4. Skill Two: The Flooding Technique

Bukalo, O., Courtney, R.P., Silverstein, S., Brehm, C., Hartley, N.D., Whittle, N., et al. (2015), 'Prefrontal inputs to the amygdala instruct fear extinction memory formation', *Science Advances*, Vol. 1, No. 6, e1500251.
Charney, D. and Drevets, W.C. (2002), 'Neurobiological basis of anxiety disorders', *Neuropsychopharmacology: The Fifth Generation of Progress* (901–930), edited by Kenneth L. Davis, Dennis Charney, Joseph T. Coyle and Charles Nemeroff, American College of Neuropsychopharmacology.
Delgado, M.R., Nearing, K.I., LeDoux, J.E. and Phelps, E.A. (2008), 'Neural circuitry underlying the regulation of conditioned fear and its relation to extinction', *Neuron*, 59: 829–838.
Goossens, L., Sunaert, S., Peeters, R., Griez, E.J.L. and Schruers, K.R.J. (2007), 'Amygdala hyperfunction in phobic fear normalises after exposure', *Biological Psychiatry*, 62: 1119–25.
Graeff, F.G. and Del-Ben, C.M. (2008), 'Neurobiology of panic disorder: from animal models to brain neuroimaging', *Neuroscience and Behavioural Reviews*, 32 (7): 1326–35.
Kim, M.J., Gee, D.G., Loucks, R.A., Davis, F.C. and Whalen, P.J. (2011), 'Anxiety dissociates dorsal and ventral medial prefrontal cortex functional connectivity with the amygdala at rest', *Cerebral Cortex*, 21: 1667–1673.

Bibliography

LeDoux, J.E. (2008), 'Amygdala', *Scholarpedia*, 3(4): 2698.

LeDoux, J.E. (2003), 'The emotional brain, fear, and the amygdala', *Cellular and Molecular Neurobiology*, 23, Nos. 4–5.

Martin, E.I., Ressler, K.J., Binder, E. and Nemeroff, C.B. (2009), 'The neurobiology of anxiety disorders: brain imaging, genetics, and psychoneuroendocrinology', *Psychiatric Clinics of North America*, 32(3): 549–575.

Mathew, S.J., Price, R.B. and Charney, D.S. (2008), 'Recent advances in the neurobiology of anxiety disorders: implications for novel therapeutics', *American Journal of Medical Genetics*, 148: 89–98.

Nutt, D.J. (2001), 'Neurobiological mechanisms in generalised anxiety disorder', *Journal of Clinical Psychiatry*, 62: 22–7.

Paquette, V., Le'vesque, J., Mensour, B., Leroux, J., Beaudoin, G. and Bourgouin, P. (2003), 'Change the mind and you change the brain: effects of cognitive-behavioural therapy on the neural correlates of spider phobia', *NeuroImage*, 18: 401–9.

Phelps, E.A., Delgado, M.R., Nearing, K.I. and LeDoux, J.E. (2004), 'Extinction learning in humans: role of the amygdala and vmPFC', *Neuron*, 43: 897–905.

Pittman, C.M. and Karle, E.M. (2015), *Rewire Your Anxious Brain*, New Harbinger Publications Inc., California.

Reinecke, A., Thilo, K., Filippini, N., Croft, A. and Harmer, C.J. (2014), 'Predicting rapid response to cognitive-behavioural treatment for panic disorder: the role of hippocampus, insula, and dorsolateral prefrontal cortex', *Behaviour Research and Therapy*, 62: 120–8.

Reinecke, A., Waldenmaier, L., Cooper, M.J. and Harmer, C.J. (2014), 'Changes in automatic threat processing precede and predict clinical changes with exposure-based cognitive-behaviour therapy for panic disorder', *Biological Psychiatry*, 73 (11): 1064–70.

Roy, A.K., Fudge, J.L., Kelly, C., Perry, J.S.A., Daniele, T., Carlisi, C., Benson, B., Castellanos, F.X., Milham, M.P., Pine, D.S. and Ernst, M. (2013), 'Intrinsic functional connectivity of amygdala-based networks in adolescent general anxiety disorder', *Journal of the American Academy of Child and Adolescent Psychiatry*, 52(3): 290–299.

Rozeske, R.R., Valerio, S., Chaudun, F. and Herry, C. (2015), 'Prefrontal neuronal circuits of contextual fear conditioning', *Genes, Brain and Behavior*, 14(1): 22–36.

Shin, L.M. and Liberzon, I. (2010), 'The neurocircuitry of fear, stress, and anxiety disorders', *Neuropsychopharmacology*, 35(1): 169–191.

Straube, T., Glauer, M., Dilger, S., Mentzel, H. and Miltner, W.H.R. (2006), 'Effects of cognitive-behavioural therapy on brain activation in specific phobia', *NeuroImage*, 29: 125–35.

Sussman, N. (2007), 'Functional neuroimaging of anxiety disorders: focus on the amygdala and insula', *Psychiatry Weekly*, 2(40).

5. Skill Three: How to Deal with Uncertainty

Barry, H.P. and Murphy, E. (2015), *Flagging the Screenager: Guiding your child through adolescence and young adulthood*, Liberties Press, Dublin.

Murphy, E. (2013), *Five Steps to Happiness*, Liberties Press, Dublin.

6. Skill Four: How to Deal with Discomfort

Duckworth, A.L. and Seligman, M.E.P. (2017), 'The Science and Practice of Self-control', *Perspectives on Psychological Science*, 12(5): 715–718.

Duckworth, A.L., Tsukayama, E. and Kirby, T.A. (2013), 'Is it really self-control? Examining the predictive power of the delay of gratification task', *Personality and Social Psychology Bulletin*, 39(7): 843–855.

Duckworth, A.L., Peterson, C., Matthews, M.D. and Kelly, D.R. (2007), 'Grit: Perseverance and passion for long-term goals', *Journal of Personality and Social Psychology*, 92(6): 1087–1101.

Ellis, A. (1962), *Reason and Emotion in Psychotherapy*, Lyle Stuart, New York.

Ellis, A. (1996), *Better, Deeper, and More Enduring Brief Therapy: The Rational Emotive Behavior Therapy Approach*, Brunner/Mazel Inc., New York.

Stanković, S., Matić, M., Vukosavljević-Gvozden, T. and Opačic, G. (2015),

'Frustration Intolerance and Unconditional Self-acceptance as Mediators of the Relationship between Perfectionism and Depression', *Psihologija*, 48(2): 101–117.

Wilde, J. (2012), 'The Relationship between Frustration Intolerance and Academic Achievement in College', *International Journal of Higher Education*, 1(2).

Yu, R., Mobbs, D., Seymour, B., Rowe, J.B. and Calder, A.J. (2014), 'The neural signature of escalating frustration in humans', *Cortex: a Journal Devoted to the Study of the Nervous System and Behavior*, 54: 165–178.

7. Skill Five: How to Cope with both Failure and Success

Barke, A., Bode, S., Dechent, P., Schmidt-Samoa, C., Van Heer, C. and Stahl, J. (2017), 'To err is (perfectly) human: behavioural and neural correlates of error processing and perfectionism', *Social Cognitive and Affective Neuroscience*, 12(10): 1647–1657.

Barry, H.P. and Murphy, E. (2015), *Flagging the Screenager: Guiding your child through adolescence and young adulthood*, Liberties Press, Dublin.

Murphy, E. (2013), *Five Steps to Happiness*, Liberties Press, Dublin.

8. Skill Six: How to Challange Catastrophising

Dryden, W. and Ellis, A. (2001), 'Rational emotive behaviour therapy', *Handbook of Cognitive-Behavioral Therapies*, 2nd edn, Guilford Press, New York.

Dryden, W. and Neenam, M. (2004), *Rational Emotive Behavioural Counselling in Action*, SAGE Publications, London.

Ellis, A. (1962), *Reason and Emotion in Psychotherapy*, Lyle Stuart, New York.

Ellis, A. (1996), *Better, Deeper, and More Enduring Brief Therapy: The Rational Emotive Behavior Therapy Approach*, Brunner/Mazel Inc., New York.

Gautreau, C.M., Sherry, S.B., Sherry, D.L., Birnie, K.A., Mackinnon, S.P. and Stewart, S.H. (2015), 'Does catastrophizing of bodily sensations maintain health-related anxiety? A 14-day daily diary study with longitudinal follow-up', *Behavioural and Cognitive Psychotherapy*, 43(4): 502–512.

Murphy, E. (2013), *Five Steps to Happiness*, Liberties Press, Dublin.

Pittman, C.M. and Karle, E.M. (2015), *Rewire Your Anxious Brain*, New Harbinger Publications Inc., California.

9. Skill Seven: How to Challenge Perfectionism

Barke, A., Bode, S., Dechent, P., Schmidt-Samoa, C., Van Heer, C. and Stahl, J. (2017), 'To err is (perfectly) human: behavioural and neural correlates of error processing and perfectionism', *Social Cognitive and Affective Neuroscience*, 12(10): 1647–1657.

Flett, G.L., Hewitt, P.L. and Heisel, M.J. (2014), 'The destructiveness of perfectionism revisited: implications for the assessment of suicide risk and the prevention of suicide', *Review of General Psychology*, 18(3): 156–172.

Handley, A.K., Egan, S.J., Kane, R.T. and Rees, C.S. (2014), 'The relationships between perfectionism, pathological worry and generalised anxiety disorder', *BMC Psychiatry*, 14: 98.

Hill, A.P. and Curran, T. (2015), 'Multidimensional Perfectionism and Burnout: A Meta-Analysis', *Personality and Social Psychology Review*, 20(3): 269–288.

Reilly, E.E., Stey, P. and Lapsley, D.K. (2016), 'A new look at the links between perceived parenting, socially-prescribed perfectionism, and disordered eating', *Personality and Individual Differences*, 88: 17–20.

Smith, M.M., Sherry, S.B., Chen, S., Saklofske, D.H., Mushquash, C., Flett, G.L. and Hewitt, P.L. (2017), 'The perniciousness of perfectionism: A meta-analytic review of the perfectionism–suicide relationship', *Journal of Personality*, 00: 1–20.

Smith, M.M., Sherry, S.B., Rnic, K., Saklofske, D.H., Enns, M. and Gralnick, T. (2016), 'Are Perfectionism Dimensions Vulnerability Factors for Depressive Symptoms After Controlling for Neuroticism? A Meta-Analysis of 10 Longitudinal Studies', *European Journal of Personality*, 30: 201–212.

Stanković, S., Matić, M., Vukosavljević-Gvozden, T. and Opačic, G. (2015), 'Frustration Intolerance and Unconditional Self-acceptance as Mediators of the Relationship between Perfectionism and Depression', *Psihologija*, 48(2): 101–117.

Wei, M., Heppner, P.P., Russell, D.W. and Young, S.K. (2006), 'Maladaptive Perfectionism and Ineffective Coping as Mediators between Attachment and Future Depression: A Prospective Analysis', *Journal of Counseling Psychology*, 53(1): 67–7.

10. Skill Eight: How to Challenge Procrastination

Abbasi, I.S. and Alghamdi, N.G. (2015), 'The Prevalence, Predictors, Causes, Treatments, and Implications of Procrastination Behaviors in General, Academic, and Work Setting', *International Journal of Psychological Studies*, 7(1).

Beutel, M., Klein, E.M., Aufenanger, S., Brähler, E., Dreier, M., Müller, K.W., Quiring, O., Reinecke, R., Schmutzer, G., Stark, B. and Wölfling, K. (2016), 'Procrastination, Distress and Life Satisfaction Across the Age Range: A German Representative Community Study', *PLoS One*, 11(2).

Duckworth, A.L. and Seligman, M.E.P. (2017), 'The Science and Practice of Self-control', *Perspectives on Psychological Science*, 12(5): 715–718.

Eckert, M., Ebert, D.D., Lehr, D., Sieland, B. and Berking, M. (2016), 'Overcome procrastination: Enhancing emotion regulation skills reduce procrastination', *Learning and Individual Differences*, 52: 10–18.

Ferrari, J.R., O'Callahan, J. and Newbegin, I. (2005), 'Prevalence in procrastination in the United States, United Kingdom, and Australia: Arousal and avoidance delays among adults', *North American Journal of Psychology*, 7(1): 1–6.

Flett, A.L., Haghbin, M. and Pychyl, T.A. (2016), 'Procrastination and Depression from a Cognitive Perspective: An Exploration of the Associations among Procrastinatory Automatic Thoughts, Rumination, and

Mindfulness', *Journal of Rational-Emotive & Cognitive-Behavior Therapy*, 34: 169.

Gustavson, D.E., Miyake, A., Hewitt, J.K. and Friedman, N.P. (2015), 'Understanding the cognitive and genetic underpinnings of procrastination: Evidence for shared genetic influences with goal management and executive function abilities', *Journal of Experimental Psychology: General*, 144(6): 1063–1079.

Hammer, G.A. and Ferrari, J.R. (2002), 'Differential Incidence of Procrastination between Blue and White-collar Workers', *Current Psychology: Developmental, Learning, Personality, Social*, 21(4): 333–338.

Hill, A.P. and Curran, T. (2015), 'Multidimensional Perfectionism and Burnout: A Meta-Analysis', *Personality and Social Psychology Review*, 20(3): 269–288.

Johnson, P.E. Jr, Perrin, C.J., Salo, A., Deschaine, E. and Johnson, B. (2016), 'Use of an explicit rule decreases procrastination in university students', *Journal of Applied Behavior Analysis*, 49(2): 346–358.

Kim, K., Hong, H., Lee, J. and Hyun, M. (2017), 'Effects of time perspective and self-control on procrastination and Internet addiction', *Journal of Behavioral Addictions*, 6(2): 229–236.

Lim, J.W., Low, M.Y., Phang, J.Y. and Tan, C.S. (2017), 'Procrastination is Detrimental to Undergraduate Students' Self-rated Creativity: The Mediating Role of State Anxiety', *Creativity. Theories – Research – Applications*, 4(1).

Pychyl, T.A. and Sirois, F.M. (2016), 'Procrastination, emotion regulation, and well-being', in Pychyl, T.A. and Sirois, F.M. (eds.), *Procrastination, Health, and Well-Being*, pp. 163–188, Academic Press, London.

Sirois, F.M., Molnar, D.S. and Hirsch, J.K. (2017), 'A Meta-analytic and Conceptual Update on the Associations between Procrastination and Multidimensional Perfectionism', *European Journal of Personality*, 31: 137–159.

Sirois, F.M. (2014), 'Procrastination and stress: Exploring the role of Self-compassion', *Self and Identity*, 13(2): 128–145.

Zhang, W., Wang, X. and Feng, T. (2016), 'Identifying the Neural Substrates of Procrastination: a Resting-state fMRI Study', www.Nature.com/Scientific Reports, 6: 33203.

11. Skill Nine: How to Practise Mindfulness

Crane, R. and Elias, D. (2006), 'Being with what is – mindfulness practice for counsellors and psychotherapists', *Therapy Today*, 17(10): 31.

Farb, N.A.S., Segal, Z.V., Mayberg, H., Bean, J., McKeon, D., Fatima, Z. and Anderson, A.K. (2007), 'Attending to the present: mindfulness meditation reveals distinct neural modes of self-reference', *Social, Cognitive and Affective Neuroscience*, 2(4): 313–22.

Flett, A.L., Haghbin, M. and Pychyl, T.A. (2016), 'Procrastination and Depression from a Cognitive Perspective: An Exploration of the Associations among Procrastinatory Automatic Thoughts, Rumination, and Mindfulness', *Journal of Rational-Emotive & Cognitive-Behavior Therapy*, 34: 169.

Hagen, I. and Nayar, U.S. (2014), 'Yoga for children and young people's mental health and well-being: research review and reflections on the mental health potentials of yoga', *Frontiers in Psychiatry*, 5(35).

Harrison, E. (2003), *The 5-minute Meditator*, Piatkus Books, London.

Jha, A.P., Krompinger, J. and Baime, M.J. (2007), 'Mindfulness training modifies subsystems', *Cognitive, Affective and Behavioural Neuroscience*, 7(2): 109–19.

Kabat-Zinn, J. (2008), *Wherever You Go, There You Are*, Piatkus Books, London; (2008), *Full Catastrophe Living*, Piatkus Books, London.

Nataraja, S. (2008), *The Blissful Brain*, Octopus Publishing Group, London.

Rodrigues, M.F., Nardi, A.E. and Levitan, M. (2017), 'Mindfulness in mood and anxiety disorders: a review of the literature', *Trends in Psychiatry and Psychotherapy*, 39(3).

Zeidan, F., Martucci, K.T., Kraft, R.A., McHaffie, J.G. and Coghill, R.C. (2014), 'Neural correlates of mindfulness meditation-related anxiety relief', *Social Cognitive and Affective Neuroscience*, 9(6): 751–759.

12. Skill Ten: How to Problem-solve

Abdollahi, A., Talib, M.A., Yaacob, S.N. and Ismail, Z. (2015), 'Problem-solving Skills Appraisal Mediates Hardiness and Suicidal Ideation among Malaysian Undergraduate Students', *PLoS One*, 10(4).

Becker-Weidman, E.G., Jacobs, R.H., Reinecke, M.A., Silva, S.G. and March, J.S. (2010), 'Social Problem-solving among Adolescents Treated for Depression', *Behaviour Research and Therapy*, 48(1): 11–18.

Bell, A.C. and D'Zurilla, T.J. (2009), 'Problem-solving therapy for depression: A meta-analysis', *Clinical Psychology Review*, 29: 348–353.

McAuliffe, C., Corcoran, P., Keeley, H.S. and Perry, I.J. (2003), 'Risk of Suicide Ideation Associated with Problem-solving Ability and Attitudes Toward Suicidal Behavior in University Students', *Crisis*, 24(4): 160–167.

Ranjba, R., Bayani, A.A. and Bayani, A. (2013), 'Social Problem-solving Ability Predicts Mental Health among Undergraduate Students', *International Journal of Preventive Medicine*, 4(11): 1337–1341.

Rock, P.L., Roiser, J.P., Riedel, W.J. and Blackwell, A.D. (2013), 'Cognitive impairment in depression: a systematic review and meta-analysis', *Psychological Medicine*, 1–12.

Roiser, J.P. and Sahakian, B.J. (2013), 'Hot and cold cognition in depression', *CNS Spectrums*, 18: 139–49.

Thomas, P., Schmidt, T., Juckel, G., Norra, C. and Suchan, B. (2016), 'Nice or effective? Social problem-solving strategies in patients with major depressive disorder', *Psychiatry Research*, 228(3): 835–842.

Townsend, E., Hawton, K., Altman, D.G., Arensman, D., Gunnell, P., Hazell, P., House, A. and Van Heeringen, K. (2001), 'The efficacy of problem-solving treatments after deliberate self-harm: meta-analysis of randomized controlled trials with respect to depression, hopelessness and improvement in problems', *Psychological Medicine*, 31: 979–988.

Walker, K.L., Chang, E.C. and Hirsch, J.K. (2017), 'Neuroticism and Suicidal Behavior: Conditional Indirect Effects of Social Problem-solving and Hopelessness', *International Journal of Mental Health and Addiction*, 15(1): 80–89.

Bibliography

PART THREE: SOCIAL RESILIENCE SKILLS

13. Skill Eleven: How to Develop Empathy

Bonnette, R. (2014), 'Rethinking Technology's Impact on Empathy', Loyola University Chicago, School of Law.

Denworth, L. (2017), 'I feel your pain. New insights into the underpinning of empathy might help us harness the emotion – just when we need it', *Scientific American*, 317(5): 50–55.

De Waal, F.B.M. (2015), 'Do Animals *Feel* Empathy?', *Scientific American*.

Goleman, D. (2006), *Social Intelligence*, Arrow Books, London.

Heirman, W. and Walrave, M. (2008), 'Assessing Concerns and Issues about the Mediation of Technology in Cyberbullying', *Cyberpsychology: Journal of Psychosocial Research on Cyberspace*, 2(2), 1.

Konrath, S.H., O'Brien, E.H. and Hsing, C. (2011), 'Changes in Dispositional Empathy in American College Students Over Time: A Meta-Analysis', *Personality and Social Psychology Review*, 15(2).

Krznaric, R. (2014), *Empathy: Why It Matters and How to Get It*, Random House, London.

Lewis, T. (2003), 'The neuroscience of empathy', Google Talks.

Nummenmaa, L., Hirvonen, J., Parkkola, R. and Hietanen, J.K. (2008), 'Is emotional contagion special? An fMRI study on neural systems for affective and cognitive empathy', *NeuroImage*, 43(3): 571–580.

Obama, B. (2006), 'Obama to graduates: cultivate empathy', Northwestern University: Topics: University News, People.

14. Skill Twelve: How to Read and Interpret Non-verbal Cues

Docan-Morgan, T., Manusov, V. and Harvey, J. (2013), 'When a Small Thing Means so Much: Nonverbal Cues as Turning Points in Relationships', *Interpersona*, 7(1).

Goleman, D. (2006), *Social Intelligence*, Arrow Books, London.

Li, D., Chokka, P. and Tibbo, P. (2001), 'Towards an integrative understanding of social phobia', *Journal of Psychiatry and Neuroscience*, 26(3): 190–202.

15. Skill Thirteen: How to Become Comfortable in Social Situations

Li, D., Chokka, P. and Tibbo, P. (2001), 'Towards an integrative understanding of social phobia', *Journal of Psychiatry and Neuroscience*, 26(3): 190–202.
Valk, S.L., Bernhardt, B.C., Trautwein, F.M., Böckler, A., Kanske, P., Guizard, N., Collins, D.L. and Singer, T. (2017), 'Structural plasticity of the social brain: Differential change after socio-affective and cognitive mental training', *Science Advances*, 3(10).

16. Skill Fourteen: How to Deal with Performance Anxiety

Braden, A.M., Osborne, M.S. and Wilson, S.J. (2015), 'Psychological intervention reduces self-reported performance anxiety in high school music students', *Frontiers in Psychology*, 6: 195.

PART FOUR: LIFE RESILIENCE SKILLS

18. Skill Sixteen: How to Deal with the Unfairness of Life

Worthington, E.L. and Scherer, M. (2004), 'Forgiveness is an emotion – focused coping strategy that can reduce health risks and promote health resilience: theory, review and hypothesis', *Psychology and Health*, 19(3): 385–405.

20. Skill Eighteen: How to Resolve Conflict

Bao, Y., Zhu, F., Hu, Y. and Cui, N. (2016), 'The Research of Interpersonal

Conflict and Solution Strategies', *Psychology*, 7: 541–545.

Overton, A.R. and Lowry, A.C. (2013), 'Conflict Management: Difficult Conversations with Difficult People', *Clinics in Colon and Rectal Surgery*, 26 (4).

Sclavi, M. (2008), 'The Role of Play and Humor in Creative Conflict Management', *Negotiation Journal*, 24: 157–180.

Worthington, E.L. and Scherer, M. (2004), 'Forgiveness is an emotion – focused coping strategy that can reduce health risks and promote health resilience: theory, review and hypothesis', *Psychology and Health*, 19(3): 385–405.

21. Skill Nineteen: Pragmatism

Sifferlin, A. (2013), 'The most stressed-out generation? Young Adults', available from: http://healthland.time.com/2013/02/07/the-most-stressed-outgeneration-young-adults/

22. Skill Twenty: How to Manage Stress in Our Lives

Hale, L. and Guan, S. (2015), 'Screen Time and Sleep among School-aged Children and Adolescents: A Systematic Literature Review', *Sleep Medicine Reviews*, 21: 50–58.

Heirman, W. and Walrave, M. (2008), 'Assessing Concerns and Issues about the Mediation of Technology in Cyberbullying', *Cyberpsychology: Journal of Psychosocial Research on Cyberspace*, 2(2), 1.

Levenson, J.C., Shensa, A., Sidani, J.E., Colditz, J.B. and Primack, B.A. (2016), 'The Association between Social Media Use and Sleep Disturbance among Young Adults', *Preventive Medicine*, 85: 36–41.

Ongs, A.D., Bergeman, C.S., Bisconti, T.L. and Wallace, K.A. (2006), 'Psychological Resilience, Positive Emotions, and Successful Adaptation to Stress in Later Life', *Journal of Personality and Social Psychology*, 91(4): 730–749.

Sifferlin, A. (2013), 'The most stressed-out generation? Young Adults', available from: http://healthland.time.com/2013/02/07/the-most-stressed-outgeneration-young-adults/

INDEX

ACKNOWLEDGEMENTS

I would like to start by thanking my editorial team in Orion for all their wonderful assistance in publishing this book. I want to especially thank my editor Olivia Morris who has believed in the Flag series from the beginning and who has been so supportive, guiding me patiently along the right path in relation to *Emotional Resilience*. I am also indebted to desk editor Ru Merritt for bringing it all together, publicity manager Elaine Egan and to Amy Davies for their assistance in the PR and social media marketing areas.

I also owe a huge debt of gratitude to Vanessa Fox O'Loughlin and Dominic Perrim my two agents who have made this project possible.

I would like to especially thank my dear friend and colleague Dr Muiris Houston of *The Irish Times*, for taking the time to review the text and for his friendship and support. His reports in the excellent Health Plus supplement are respected by us all.

I send the warmest thanks to my good friend Cathy Kelly (bestselling author and UNICEF ambassador) for her constant kindness and support throughout the years.

I am, as always, indebted to my friend and colleague Enda Murphy for his invaluable assistance. A brilliant CBT therapist and former ICGP tutor who has taught me much of what I know, including some of the exercises and concepts in this book. We share a vision of where mental health should be moving toward and I am deeply grateful for his support and insightful comments. We both highly value our national radio slot on the Sean O' Rourke Show, and I would like to take this opportunity to thank Sean (a true gentleman of Irish media) and his wonderful team, particularly Hannah Parkes and series producer Tara Campbell, for allowing us the opportunity to highlight key areas of mental health.

Special thanks as always to friend and colleague Dr Justin Brophy, founding member and first President of the Irish College of Psychiatry, who shares my special interest in the world of neuroplasticity. I would also like to thank Professor Patricia Casey of University College Dublin, who has been so supportive over the years and for once again reviewing my book.

I am also incredibly appreciative of my international colleagues: Professor Ray Lam, University of British Columbia, Canada; Professor Bernard Baune, Unviersity of Adelaide, Australia; and Professor Larry Culpepper, Boston University of Medicine, USA. You have all been so supportive – thank you for taking the time to review this book.

I am extremely grateful thar one of our great hurling icons, Iggy Clarke of Galway (who does so much for the provision of therapy services in this wonderful city) took time out of his busy schedule to review this book. And I am also honoured that Senator Joan Freeman (who has done so much for suicide prevention in Ireland and the USA) took the time to review *Emotional Resilience* too.

I also send a special thanks to Maria Molloy of Mental Health Ireland for adding her comments. My visits to her home town Ennis to speak on areas of mental health have been wonderful experiences for my wife and me.

I say a special thanks to my sons Daniel and Joseph (and his wife Sue and my beautiful granddaughter Saoirse) and to my daughter Lara (and her husband Hans and my two much-loved grandsons, Ciaran and Sean) for all their love and support and for keeping me well-grounded!

As always, I reserve my biggest 'thank you' to my wife Brenda, whose love, friendship, support, encouragement and particularly patience has made this book and indeed the whole series possible. You are my light in the darkness, and truly my soulmate. 'Mo ghra, mo chroi' (my love, my heart).

ABOUT THE AUTHOR

Dr Harry Barry is a highly respected Irish author and medic, with over three decades of experience as a GP. With a keen interest in the area of mental health and suicide prevention, Dr Barry is the author of numerous books addressing various aspects of mental health including anxiety, depression and toxic stress.

A practical guide to understanding, managing and overcoming anxiety and panic attacks.

ANXIETY
AND PANIC

How to reshape your
anxious mind and brain

DR HARRY BARRY

S

A practical, four step programme to help you
understand and cope with depression.

DEPRESSION

A practical guide

DR HARRY BARRY

A practical guide to understanding and coping with anxiety, depression, addiction and suicide.

FLAGGING THE PROBLEM

A new approach to mental health

DR HARRY BARRY

S

A practical guide exploring the role of therapy in depression and anxiety.

FLAGGING THE
THERAPY

Pathways out of
depression and anxiety

DR HARRY BARRY

S

A practical guide to identifying and managing stress.

TOXIC
STRESS

A step-by-step guide
to managing stress

DR HARRY BARRY

S